Recovery – Twelve Simple Steps to Life Beyond Addiction

A contemporary recovery handbook for users and practitioners

Dr Lynden Finlay

D1424002

321 575 62 2

Published by Accent Press Ltd 2014

ISBN 9781783752973

Praise for Dr Lynden Finlay

"An accessible entrée to that all-important world: 'life beyond addiction'. *Martin Weegmann, Consultant Clinical Psychologist/Psychotherapist, Author and 'Non-Alcoholic Trustee' with General Service Board of AA (GB).*

"I am sure that many people will be able to access AA and other 12 step programmes as a result of this myth busting book. Well done!" *Paul Myles*

"Readers will find in its pages lucid, moving and inspiring real-life accounts of the transformative effects of adopting, interpreting and using the Twelve Steps as a framework for recovery. This is at once a text book for professionals and people seeking recovery, and an important intervention into an ongoing debate about the role and place of the Twelve Steps within the burgeoning Recovery Movement."
Dr Wendy Dossett
Director (Research) of the Higher Power Project, Department of Theology and Religious Studies, University of Chester.

I dedicate this book with love and gratitude to all those amazing, courageous, recovering addicts from The Rehab and the rooms who have been part of my recovery journey and allowed me to be part of theirs. You know who you are.

CONTENTS

CONTENTS

Foreword by Professor David Best

September 2014

There is a strong and supportive evidence base about mutual aid, particularly 12 Step: it is at least as effective as any professionally delivered treatment and it is effective with a wide range of populations including those with complex and multiple needs. The evidence about mutual aid (primarily drawn from research about Alcoholics Anonymous, but supplemented with smaller amounts of evidence about other mutual aid groups) can be summarised as:

- If you go to meetings you will generally reduce your substance use
- The more meetings you go to, the more your substance use will go down
- The more active a part you play in meetings, the better you will do
- Mutual aid plus specialist, professional treatment will typically lead to better outcomes than either on their own
- However, there is weaker evidence of randomised assignment to mutual aid as motivation (whether at the start or emerging through the process) is critical for mutual aid groups to be successful

The emerging evidence base has done relatively little, particularly in the UK and Australia, to change a very polarised response to 12 Step groups, with advocates largely unquestioning of the Steps and Traditions of the fellowships, while critics and opponents challenge the safety and validity of AA, NA, and the other fellowships on a number of grounds. These include the 'religious' components of the groups, the 'cult-like' status of adherents, that mutual aid groups represent a 'substitute addiction', and that the 12 Steps themselves are disempowering and damaging to groups who are already powerless.

1

What Lynden Finlay has done in *Twelve Simple Steps* ... is to use a wealth of personal and clinical experience to do something that few have attempted – and almost none have achieved – which is to re-write the 12 Steps to make them more contemporary and relevant, and to remove the references to God or a Higher Power. This runs the gauntlet of provoking the ire of all of those who live and remain sober and well through the 12 Steps and the fellowships, and also the anger of the many sceptics who would argue that this is a doomed and fundamentally flawed endeavour.

In my own work, I have interviewed over 1500 people in recovery from alcohol, drug, and process addictions and there are only two rules about recovery – people don't do it alone and each person has a unique path to recovery.

What Dr Finlay offers is an exciting and innovative addition to the range of supports and techniques available to people in addiction that offers a fundamentally spiritual but contemporary flavour.

She also provides a range of case studies that show how this model has been applied and utilised in a diverse group of individuals. There is a long way to go in building up a suitable or supportive evidence base but what is presented in this book is a passion and a commitment to helping a group of people who need every support and assistance they can get.

'Addicts alone can achieve recovery but they can't recover alone'.

This is a long-established mantra and what Dr Finlay provides is a case for shared passion and commitment on her own terms. There are too many people who die and who spend a lifetime battling with addiction for closed minds to dismiss this remarkable endeavour. This is a ray of hope for all of those who have tried and failed (including families) with our established techniques and methods.

Introduction

When I announced that I was going to produce a new version of the 12 Steps I was greeted with agreement from some people that a new version was needed, and disbelief and horror from others. The horror came mostly from addicts who were successfully following the original Steps of Alcoholics Anonymous, many of whom believed in a Christian God. For these people it was as if I had announced an intention to re-write the Ten Commandments. Who did I think I was, to put my interpretation on words which had become so hallowed over time? How arrogant was I, that I thought I could be as helpful to addicts as the founders of AA? When I said that my aim was to re-phrase the Steps by leaving out their mention of God while retaining their essentially spiritual nature, the response from some became quite hostile. I was accused of arrogance, of betraying the fundamental principles of AA, and of cynically re-writing the Steps in order to make money.

None of these accusations is true, but I can understand why they were said. I have an addictive illness myself and I am in recovery thanks to the 12 Steps. I practice them in my daily life and because of them my life has been not only saved but transformed beyond my imagining. I had to ask myself those same questions – who am I to put forward my own interpretation of the Steps, when they have served the needs of addicts so well for eighty years? It's a fair question so here is an answer.

In what now seems like another life, before my addictive illness completely took hold, I was a student of philosophy. For my doctorate I wrote my thesis on the ethics of Immanuel Kant and spent six years thinking about the fundamental principles of morality. I then trained and qualified as a teacher. Secondary schools did not teach philosophy, so I studied for a qualification in Bible Studies which would equip me to work as a Religious Education teacher. As it turned out I preferred being a student to being a teacher. I got myself qualified as an Adult Trainer and as a teacher of Literacy and Numeracy to adults with learning difficulties.

As well as an impressive set of qualifications I also had an addictive illness which was getting progressively worse. I didn't know that, of course. I knew there was something wrong with me but I didn't know what it was; neither did the doctors and psychiatrists who over the years had treated me with so many different medications I had lost count. It never occurred to me that I might have a problem with drugs or alcohol. I thought alcoholics were tramps who slept on the streets and drug addicts took heroin, and I wasn't like them at all. Of course I had used drugs recreationally while I was a student, but so did everyone, didn't they? As for prescribed drugs, they came from a doctor so didn't count. And yes, I did get drunk sometimes, but only with my friends and I didn't drink alone. No, my problem was depression, low self-esteem, lack of energy, lack of meaning, lack of joy. I didn't feel like other people – they all seemed to be able to live quite happily in their own skin and I didn't. As this sense of unease grew my life had become unbearably painful. It was only natural that I would want to go out drinking with my new partner and his friends; it took the edge off my emptiness. It was some time before I realised that I was in a relationship with an alcoholic and that going out for a drink with him was doing me no good at all.

I first realised I was crazy at three o'clock one Sunday morning. In a sudden moment of clarity I saw what I had become. A middle-aged mother of two children, I was behaving like a spiteful child looking for a fight, and I hadn't even had a drink. I was standing in my hallway in the dark, holding a bucket of cold water, waiting to pour it over the head of my partner when he finally staggered home from the pub. I was giggling at the thought of how shocked he would be when he walked through the door, how wet and humiliated, how I would laugh. I had been standing there, anticipating vengeance, for over an hour. By four o'clock the glee had worn off and I went to bed. I left the bucket of water on the floor, hoping he would stand in it even if I wasn't there to gloat. Next day nobody mentioned the bucket of water in the middle of the floor. We just walked round it. Life went on as if nothing had happened; but for me this was the small start of a long process of change.

My partner's main aim in life was to drink as much as possible. My main aim in life was to prevent him. On that Sunday morning I realised that, no matter what I did, I could not stop him drinking. All my attempts to change him had had very little effect, but had led me into becoming a person I did not want to be. I didn't want my life to be taken over by his drinking any more. I didn't want to be so busy reacting to his drunk behaviour that I didn't spend enough time listening to my children. I didn't want to be having hangovers and feeling ill because I'd been drinking too much in an attempt to socialise with him. I didn't want to keep trying new prescribed medication which made me feel worse rather than better. I didn't want to be permanently miserable because I was achieving nothing and had no aims of my own in life. It was time for me to give up trying to change him and take steps to sort out my own life. The first thing I had to do was to make him someone else's problem.

There was a rehab nearby and I arranged an assessment for my partner. I had heard they had a 'programme' and that after 'working it' many alcoholics never drank again. I was furious when my partner returned from his assessment saying he had not been offered a place because he was not ready to stop drinking. He went to the pub, and I went to the rehab to have words with the Programme Coordinator. 'What do you mean, he's "not ready"? He's drunk every day! I can't go on like this!' The Programme Coordinator was kind but firm. 'I'm not offering him a place. He doesn't want to stop drinking yet. But I'll take you in.' I was affronted. My problem was not that bad.

It was not long before I was back at the rehab begging for help. Residential treatment was not a practical option so I attended as an outpatient. Thus began my introduction to the 12 Steps. I had no religious faith, no understanding, no belief, and very little hope. I didn't think I was an addict, all I knew was that I was in pain. I was so desperate that I made the decision to do whatever my counsellor told me to do, whether it made any sense to me or not. Over the next 6 months I learned about the first five of the 12 Steps and started to attend meetings of the Fellowships Al-Anon Family Groups (Al-Anon), Narcotics Anonymous (NA) and Co-dependents Anonymous (CoDA).

Four years later, still alcohol and drug free and happily single, I was invited to return to the rehab to be trained as an addictions counsellor. As I learned 'on the job' my own understanding and practice of the 12 Steps continued to deepen. Later I gained a postgraduate Diploma in Addictions Counselling, thus getting the usual progression from qualification to profession completely back to front. In time I became the Treatment Coordinator of the rehab, using the principles of the 12 Step programme as the basis of our treatment programme. I was there for eighteen years, giving to others what had been given to me, introducing the 12 Step programme to other suffering addicts as I continued to practice those principles in my own recovery.

Six years ago The Rehab expanded its service to include second stage residential treatment and it became necessary for me to write an extension to the treatment programme we had used for first stage. This seemed to me an opportune moment to review our whole programme and update where necessary. I had been aware for a long time that many people, both service commissioners and service users, were deterred from commissioning 12 Step services and attending 12 Step meetings because they mistakenly believed that the Steps were religious. I decided to look again at the 12 Steps themselves and see if I could come up with a differently worded version which we could use for these non-religious residents in The Rehab. My aim was to provide a simple doable introduction to the Steps which would enable our residents to get some insights into the 12 Step programme before they went to AA meetings and came face to face with the 'God as you understand Him' wording.

While non-believers may be comfortable with the removal of 'God' words and associations, many long-term members of AA are likely to be most uncomfortable. For these people the original Steps describe the path which leads to a spiritual awakening, and that spiritual awakening is seen as conceptually linked with religion. For these people it is hard to conceive of spirituality being divorced from religion. I believe that spirituality can stand alone, as can morality, and neither of these depend for their existence on religion. Some people have asked "If you take away religion can there be morality?" I would answer yes there can. You don't have to believe in God (or any other deity) in order to have moral principles and do good. It is not God who makes things good or bad, right or wrong. I would argue that there are fundamental moral principles and they do not spring from the nature of God but from the inherent value of human beings[1].

Over time I became aware that this alternative version was working well in the context of The Rehab, and that when our residents started attending AA meetings they already had an understanding of a 'power greater than themselves' which worked for them. Word of the alternative version spread in recovery circles and eventually I was invited to write a book about it.

As an addict in long-term recovery and an experienced addictions counsellor I believe I am well placed to write about the 12 Steps. This is a subject dear to my heart and I embrace the opportunity to write this book about a secular version of the Steps. I do it firstly in the hope that it will appeal to all addicts and their family members, whether they believe in any god or none; and secondly that it may be a useful resource for GPs and other professionals seeking to inform their patients about addiction and recovery.

In the following chapters I shall expand on my belief that addiction is not just a matter of the abuse of chemicals. It is an obsessive-compulsive condition and can have as its focus chemicals or behaviours, consecutively or concurrently. Furthermore the 12 Step programme offers a route to recovery from all addiction – whether it be to alcohol, drugs, gambling, self-harming, spending, working, cleaning, eating disorders, or whatever – and a route to healing for people who are not addicts but who have been adversely affected by the addiction of a loved one.

This book includes the personal stories and quotes of people who are addicted to chemicals and behaviours. They have all been willing to share their stories and insights openly in the hope that

---

[1] You will notice a bit of moral philosophy creeping in here. If you are interested in Kant's ethics you can read *The Critique of Practical Reason,* Immanuel Kant, 1788. Translated by Thomas Kingsmill Abbott, available online as part of The Electronic Classics Series.

other addicts who are still suffering may identify with them and come to know for themselves the transformative experience which is recovery.

Many people, commissioners, providers, and users of services, will vehemently disagree with everything I say. They are all entitled to their beliefs. I am not an evangelist saying mine is the only way. Your path to your recovery is your choice. If you who are reading this book identify with what I am describing and want help to stop drinking or using drugs, my message to you is simple. You can change. You can live alcohol and drug free if you want to. Help is out there. You can go to AA or NA or any Fellowship you like. You can recover. The 12 Steps tell you how to do it.

Chapter One

About Addiction

Because my re-wording of the 12 Steps came about as a direct result of my working at the rehab, it may be helpful here for me to outline its philosophy, its basic beliefs about the nature of addiction, and its concept of recovery. As its principles are more relevant than its identity, I will not name it but will refer to it simply as The Rehab.

Treatment services are all different; they use different counselling models, have different ideas about the nature of addiction, and have different standards against which the success of treatment is measured. For many years there has been debate, disagreement, and occasionally some hostility regarding the comparative effectiveness of the various models of treatment. Furthermore, there is no one agreed definition of 'addiction' nor of 'recovery'. This debate is not within the remit of this book. My aim in writing this book is not to argue the merits of one model against another but simply to demystify the 12 Step programme and show it for the simple, practical way of recovering from addiction that it is. It will help if I first explain what I mean by addiction and recovery.

The Rehab's core beliefs are these:

1. Addiction is an illness.
2. It is an obsessive-compulsive condition characterised by loss of control.
3. Addiction is not curable.
4. Recovery – that is, living drug and alcohol free – is possible.

These statements are hotly disputed by many professionals. My aim here is not to justify them but to explain what they mean for addicts.

1. Addiction is an illness

Addiction is not a moral deficiency. It is not a simple weakness of will. It is not a matter of choice. It is not caused by other people, government policies, or social circumstances. It is a no-fault condition. It does not discriminate and can afflict anyone regardless of class, race, age, gender, creed, or intelligence. Like any illness it has distinguishing characteristics, follows a known pattern of progression, has various treatment options at different stages, and has predictable outcomes. If left untreated it can be fatal.

Contrary to popular opinion, the diagnosis of addiction can be a great relief to an addict. 'You mean I'm not essentially a bad person? I have an illness and I can get better? You mean I can change?' Furthermore, the diagnosis of addiction does not let the addict evade responsibility. It gives the addict a choice: either carry on like this until you lose everything you care about including ultimately your health, your sanity, and your life; or stop blaming everyone else for your condition and take responsibility for your recovery. Recovery is possible and you have no excuse not to take the necessary action.

2. Addiction is an obsessive-compulsive condition characterised by loss of control

Addicts are people for whom one is too many and a hundred not enough. Not all addicts fit the stereotype of the homeless alcoholic drunk on the streets, or the emaciated junkie overdosed with a needle in his arm. Many addicts have periods when they are not drinking or using drugs. Binge drinking alcoholics are often unaware of their addiction because they are not drinking every day. The problem arises when the addict starts to use. As the drugs trigger a change in brain chemistry, strong cravings to repeat the experience are created: the addict experiences a loss of control and becomes unable to choose when to stop.

In the later stages of addiction, periods of not using become shorter and less frequent. Addicts think obsessively about their drug of choice – where to get it, how to finance it, how to protect it, and how to evade anyone who tries to take it away. They act compulsively in order to connect with their drug of choice – they lie, steal, commit acts of violence and neglect, and abandon any moral values they have in order to satisfy their craving to use. I do not believe people act this way out of choice but because they are in the grip of something more powerful than they are, which they cannot control.

Human beings are 'programmed' to survive. The drives to seek food and shelter, reproduce, and protect their offspring are very strong. In active addiction, all these drives come secondary to the drive to use. In this sense addiction is as powerful as instinct. Of course I have no scientific evidence for this but, when I see how using addicts prefer to use rather than eat, abandon all self-care and safety, prefer to use than to have sex, and neglect their children, I cannot help but be shocked and scared at how powerful addiction is.

3. Addiction is not curable

If a homeless alcoholic gets a home he is no longer homeless, but he's still an alcoholic. If a using alcoholic gets into recovery he is no longer using, but he's still an alcoholic. Addiction is not 'curable'. As a genetically inherited condition it does not go away, any more than blue eyes go away. With help an addict is able to stop using, but the potential for relapse remains. If using recommences, the addiction becomes active and all the obsessive-compulsive thinking and behaviour returns. Addicts in early recovery should be aware that the default position for addicts is using, and non-using is an 'abnormal' state. To maintain an abnormal state over time requires self-awareness and some effort.

4. Recovery – that is, living drug and alcohol free – is possible

This does not mean, however, that an addict is doomed to a life of using. 'Recovery' is possible in the sense that it is possible for addicts to remain drug and alcohol free one day at a time – that by following the 12 step programme they can be in a state of daily remission, which they can continue for as long as they choose.

Damage and healing

Although there is fierce disagreement among professionals about the causes and nature of addiction, it is easier to agree on its effects. Whether people identify themselves as addicts, alcoholics, problem drinkers, or substance misusers, their stories of what their alcohol and drug use has cost them are remarkably similar. Professionals may refer to them as patients, clients, service users, or any other non-pejorative term currently preferred, but there is broad agreement about the devastating consequences suffered as a direct result of their using.

People in active addiction are chaotic. They find themselves in one crisis after another. They are unpredictable; the emergency they present you with today may be entirely different from the drama that was unfolding yesterday. This can be confusing and frustrating for the professionals who are trying to help them, who can often feel overwhelmed by the needs of their clients. The problems are so severe, in so many different aspects of life, and so quickly changing, that it becomes easy to conflate the specifics into one apparently irresolvable hopeless mess of chaos.

I have found it helpful when thinking about addiction and recovery, and trying to design a treatment programme to address all these issues, to separate the different kinds of problems and see what kind of recovery solution is needed for each.

Addiction damages four aspects of the self:
1. Physical
2. Emotional
3. Cognitive
4. Spiritual

Damage also extends beyond the self to family, neighbours, and the wider community.

Each of these aspects has its particular problems which need to be addressed. That is to say, addiction does damage on different levels so recovery needs to happen on different levels. It is my belief that when recovery takes place on all these levels the recovering person is not only drug and alcohol free but is 'better than well'.

1. Physical

The most obvious consequences of addiction are physical. Addicts can be malnourished or obese, suffer from septicaemia, pancreatitis, kidney failure, liver cancer, psychosis, heart attack, hepatitis, blood clots, fits, strokes, amputations, poisoning, or, as one addict said to me, 'everything in the medical book from anxiety to zits.' One physical consequence of addiction which poses a block to recovery is that addicts when they stop using experience withdrawal symptoms, which in the case of some drugs can be extremely painful and unpleasant, and in the case of alcohol can be fatal.

It is not difficult to see what recovery means in the physical aspect. Specific medical conditions caused by addiction require specific medical treatment. A supervised detoxification regime minimises the unpleasant effects of withdrawal and reduces the risk. Physical recovery also requires good nutrition, proper sleep, and exercise. After three months in The Rehab residents were detoxed, drug and alcohol free, withdrawal over, sleeping well at regular hours, gaining (or losing) weight as they ate regular healthy meals, and taking some exercise – walking in the hills, and gardening. Residents were registered with GPs and dentists who provided treatment for damage done to the body by addiction. Although physical recovery may take time to achieve depending on the severity of the damage done, it is remarkable, with the right care, how much can be achieved in a space of weeks. Unfortunately some treatment services stop at this point. The addict is no longer using, and is looking and feeling better than they have done in years. Their energy is returning as their physical fitness improves. They feel OK now, thank you. They think they can manage by themselves.

At this point the addict is perhaps at his most vulnerable. When the usual stresses of life start to affect him again, he finds himself remembering how his drug of choice helped him relax, took the edge off harsh reality, made the problems recede. Believing himself to be cured, he is not prepared for the return of cravings to use. Thinking that the return of cravings is evidence that the treatment has failed, he does not admit that he feels like using again. As he keeps this to himself, his preoccupation with using grows. Before long he rings his dealer or goes to the supermarket and gets hold again of his drug of choice. If he tries to use in the quantity he used before he was detoxed, he is likely to overdose.

Physical damage is likely to be immediate and severe. If he survives, he will find himself not back where he started but worse. If he is lucky he will be back through the revolving door of services. Many people don't make it back.

Clearly, physical recovery, while good in itself, is not enough for the person to be well. That is to say, physical recovery is a necessary but not sufficient indicator of recovery. The Rehab was well aware of this and our programme placed much emphasis on the second aspect – emotional recovery.

2. Emotional

Addiction damages the emotional aspect of the self in ways that are harder to see and harder to mend. I have heard the stories of many, many addicts and have found this to be universal: they can't handle feelings. I believe that one characteristic shared by addicts is that they are over-sensitive. People who have been hurt by addicts may find this hard to believe as addicts in full-blown addiction are utterly ruthless and will lie, cheat, and steal from their loved ones without batting an eyelid. They may have become as cold as stone while using, but they did not start life that way. A high proportion of addicts grew up experiencing deeply painful emotions, such as shame, guilt, fear and loneliness, until they discovered that alcohol or drugs temporarily took some of these feelings away.

Most people go through life having emotional ups and downs which can on occasion be intense but which on the whole are survivable. Addicts go from euphoric highs to desperate lows which over time become unbearable. Many addicts on admission to The Rehab had been medicating and suppressing their feelings for so long that they had become numb. They were disassociated from their bodily sensations and emotions, or were unable to name any feelings they did have. They might be aware of a tightness in their throat, or discomfort in their chest, but have no idea that this was an indication of grief or remorse. If I asked them what they were feeling, they said they did not know. If I asked them what they needed, they said they did not understand the question and could not answer it. A very high proportion of new residents said 'I don't know who I am'; for one who does not have an emotional response to life events cannot help but feel unreal, an outsider, lost.

Emotional recovery begins as addicts start to experience feelings which they may not have felt for many years while they were using. After detoxing, their feelings start to return and most addicts find them frightening, or overwhelming, and don't know how to manage them. They don't understand them and they certainly don't like them. The feelings which usually return first are fear and anger. Addicts who do not like to admit their fear tend to get very angry. This is a painful stage in early recovery when feelings, suppressed so long by chemicals, can flood the addict like a tidal wave.

At the same time the addict, who now most urgently needs the understanding and support of others, is pushing them away with cold or angry or intimidating behaviour. As using drugs has been the addict's only response to stress for so long, the urge to use now becomes more powerful and to avoid relapse the addict needs all the support they can get.

The return of feelings is an indication that recovery is happening. It is also painful and confusing and a high risk factor for relapse. People in AA/NA know exactly what they mean when they say 'An addict alone is in bad company.' Addicts need to re-learn how to recognise their feelings, how to name them and how to communicate them with other people. Emotional recovery starts when addicts own their feelings, share them, and find identification with other addicts. They learn that they are not the only ones who feel the way they do. They learn that no matter how much it hurts you don't die of feelings. They learn that if you hold on long enough feelings change, because that is the nature of feelings. They learn that they do have the ability to manage their feelings without using drugs. They no longer have to act impulsively on their feelings. They are starting to regain a measure of control.

3. Cognitive

The human brain is a highly sensitive, intricate, and finely balanced miracle. Addicts hammer it with drugs and alcohol and assume it will carry on functioning as normal. Even recreational alcohol and drug use takes its toll. How many drinkers meet up after a good night out and compare amusing stories about how they fell down in the street, or got arrested, or woke up in bed with someone they hardly knew, and can't remember anything after one o'clock in the morning. Having memory blackouts and having to fill in the gaps with stories from friends is often much enjoyed and cause of a good laugh – a confirmation that a good time was had by all. This is a genuine example:

Phone voice: *Hallo. Have you lost a dog?*
Lady: *No, the dog's in the garden, I think.*
  Voice: *Well I have a dog here with your name on it. It's been here since last night.*
  Lady: *Oh no! (Pause) Where are you?*
  Voice: *In the Black Lion.*
  Lady: *How on earth did he get to be in the Black Lion?*
  Voice: *You left him here last night.*

Lol indeed, but it's not so funny when you can't remember where you live or recognise your children. Blackouts are a sign of brain damage. The brain has an amazing ability to repair itself, but you can't keep on battering something and not expect it to break eventually. Taking drugs may make you feel like Superman at the time and the risk of psychosis is dismissed because that only happens to someone else, but many addicts commonly refer to themselves as paranoid and they are not all wrong.

Cognitive damage is damage done to thinking processes. Most addicts when admitted to The Rehab had some degree of impairment. Most had lost the ability to concentrate. Highly educated and intelligent people had lost the ability to engage in a logical discussion. People with some memory loss could not remember whole decades of their life, but repeated the same few stories again and again. Most people had lost the ability to make reasoned decisions and had been acting on impulse for many years. They had never considered the possible consequences of their actions and were often surprised, or resentful, when bad things happened as a result:

'The bastard! He's divorcing me! For "unreasonable behaviour"!'
'What unreasonable behaviour was that?'
Pause. 'Well I suppose I did set fire to his car ... but I only did it

because he made me angry.'

Cognitive recovery happens after detoxification as addicts' brains start to repair. Memory improves, concentration and the ability to retain information improve, and the ability to make decisions returns. In The Rehab we encouraged residents to challenge each other's denial, re-view their core beliefs, re-evaluate their moral principles. We encouraged them to take responsibility, to identify their needs, set goals, and make realistic plans.

When admitted, many new residents had not read a whole book for years (if ever) and their writing had been reduced to form filling and sending abbreviated text messages. On completion of treatment these residents had written their life story, discovered the joy of reading fiction, were writing letters and in some cases writing poetry. People who had been unable to hold a rational conversation listened attentively to peer group discussions and gave relevant and insightful feedback at appropriate times. As they emerged from the fog of confused thinking they also started to feel better. They came to see that they were changing, so change was a real possibility and not just an empty promise: and if they had changed so much in a few weeks who knew what they could achieve if they carried on after leaving treatment.

4. Spiritual

Recovery on these three levels can result in a person becoming healthy, fit, and with fresh energy; aware of their emotions yet not controlled by them; able to reason, solve problems, and make practical changes in their life. Such a person may stay free from alcohol and drugs for a long time and may make many significant improvements in his live. Yet for many people there remains a sense of 'something missing'. Many alcoholics and addicts came to The Rehab saying they 'do not know who they are', needing to 'find themselves', lacking a sense of identity or purpose. Most people in active addiction share the same fundamental state of being: isolation, disconnection, a sense of alienation, of meaninglessness. When they are able to speak of it they describe a 'hole inside' that nothing external can fill. This appears to be a common experience of people in the grip of active addiction. I see this as the spiritual damage caused to the person by addiction, and my understanding of 'spiritual recovery' is the state of being which is opposite to this.

The spiritual damage of addiction	Spiritual recovery from addiction
• Withdrawal from community • Isolation • Alienation • Sense of emptiness / meaninglessness • Erosion of moral values • Deluded sense of power / control	• Re-engagement with others • Intimacy • Sense of belonging • Sense of purpose / meaning • Restoration of moral values • Humility and self-esteem in balance

The person suffering the spiritual damage of addiction is isolated, withdrawn from communion with others. As their engagement with the world reduces, they experience an emptiness of self and an erosion of moral values. They have become lessened, undernourished, a cold and empty self, holding on to an illusion of power and control. They are unable to trust other people and tend to use them for their own ends rather than as people with feelings of their own. They are habitually dishonest, with others and themselves.

Spiritual recovery, as I understand it is, is characterised by a sense of engagement with others in the world outside of oneself. A person experiencing spiritual recovery feels full, warm, real. They have meaning and purpose. They respect others in their attitudes and behaviour. They are aware of being a part of something greater than their own small self. If this is what spiritual recovery is, then we need a programme which helps people attain it. I hope to show that the 12 Step programme does provide this. It sets out in a simple way the practical steps a person can take to achieve it. The only trouble with the 12 Steps is that, in this age and culture, the words it uses alienate as many people as it attracts.

So far I have outlined the damage done by addiction to the addict himself. Of course the damaging consequences of addiction are not confined to the addict but spread, like ripples in a pond, to family, neighbours, and the community at large. Nations have gone to war as a direct consequence of addiction.[2] Usually the first people to suffer because of someone else's addiction are the addict's family members. 'Home is where the heart is' is not true for using addicts, more like 'Home is where you go when every other door is closed'. Adult addicts who have been thrown out by their partners often bring the all chaos and pain of active addiction into the parental home and inflict it on their mother or father. Parents are the ones who, as well as having to endure the pain of seeing their loved ones descend into poor physical health, emotional instability, and irrational thinking and behaviour, are most often blamed both by their addicted son or daughter and by society. These are the ones who carry the shame when the addict's name appears in the newspapers; who don't go to the police when the addict steals their possessions or smashes up their home. These are the ones who live in fear of the knock on the door in the middle of the night and the urgent summons to the hospital, or have their home raided by police searching for drugs.

Using addicts go home because parents are the least difficult to manipulate. The most sensible, law-abiding, responsible parent may find it impossible to refuse their child's demands when that child is needing to use. I have met many parents of addicts in the course of my work and hear time and again how they have behaved in irrational ways in response to the addiction of their loved one. The middle-aged lady, who would never dream of taking a drug herself, going to crack houses at night to buy crack for her son so that he would not have to rob another post office and

---

[2] In 1839 and again in 1856 China tried to stop the British East India Company exporting opium into China from its territories in India, so the British Empire declared war on China. Ironic really, considering the opiate drugs problem in Britain now.

go back to prison. The father who took out a bank loan to pay his daughter's drug debts so she would not get beaten up by her dealers. The mother who smuggled alcohol into hospital because her son threatened to discharge himself if she didn't. It is too easy to think 'I would never do that' but until you have stood in their shoes you really cannot be sure.

Different family members suffer in different ways and need different kinds of help. Children of using addicts very often suffer damage to their physical selves, their emotional wellbeing, and their cognitive development. They may be hit, malnourished, bullied, and suffer all manner of physical abuse. They may be ignored, starved of affection, criticised and scapegoated. They may be lied to, told they are imagining it, told this is normal, sworn to secrecy. They may not attend school or, when they do attend, cannot learn because they are hungry or afraid of what they will find when they go home. These children can grow up confused, distrustful, angry and rebellious or shameful and defeated. Some of them will grow up and start using alcohol and drugs to distance themselves from their memories and numb their pain. Some of them will have inherited from a parent the genetic predisposition to become addicted. Some of them will find themselves as adults behaving how their parents behaved, and hate themselves because they always vowed never to become like them.

It is now becoming recognised by researchers in the addictions field that the addict's family members need help as well as the addict. Unfortunately not many services provide the support the family members need. I have sometimes thought that the family members suffer from addiction even more than the addicts, because addicts at least have their drugs and alcohol while the family members are bearing the consequences without any anaesthetic. Many go to their GPs complaining of depression or anxiety and are prescribed medication appropriate for those conditions. They tend not to mention the fact that they are living with a using addict. They take the tablets, which often don't do a lot to help, which is not surprising given the circumstances.

My point is that family members of using addicts suffer the damage of addiction in similar ways to the addicts, that is, physically, emotionally, cognitively, and spiritually. Physically, they can be assaulted, over or under eating, and suffering stress-related conditions. Emotionally, they have strong feelings of fear, anger, guilt, or shame and comparatively few feelings of happiness. Cognitively, they are preoccupied with their addict's drug and alcohol use and trying to figure out new strategies for dealing with it. Spiritually, they can become worn out, empty, and hopeless; and if they don't tell anyone about it, withdrawn, isolated and disengaged from friends and community. Family members as well as addicts need to recover physically, emotionally, cognitively, and spiritually. There are not many statutory services which cater for these needs.

Fortunately for addicts and their families there is a 12 Step programme which tells them how to recover and 12 Step Fellowships where they can meet other people who are just like them and benefit from their support.

Chapter Two

The 12 Steps

The 12 Step programme has been available to addicts for eighty years but nowadays is often misunderstood and rejected out of hand. I think it is a great pity that so many people suffering from addiction are not aware of how beneficial 12 Step meetings could be for them and that so few professional addiction workers suggest that they seek help there. This is such a waste of a valuable resource and it is time this changed. The 12 Step programme is proven to be effective and unlike medical treatments has no side-effects. It is absolutely free of charge. Why would anyone who wants to stop using not give it a try and see for themselves?

Surveys of service users and of professionals tell us why. Service users, that is addicts who have approached any drugs or alcohol service and asked for help, give a variety of answers which fall into two broad categories: one is regarding the Steps themselves and the other is regarding the fact that an intrinsic element of the 12 Step programme involves going to meetings.

The reasons most frequently given by service users concern the wording of the Steps: 'It's all about God, isn't it?' 'It's not for me; I don't believe in God.' 'I don't think religion is going to get me well.' 'I've been praying to God to stop me drinking for years. It doesn't make any difference.' 'I'm not going to sit in some church hall and be told Jesus will save me.' 'I'm not handing over my life to anyone.' 'That's just brainwashing.' 'It's a cult.' 'I wish I could believe in it but I don't. It won't work for me.' 'It's written by old, white, middle-class American men who believe in God. It's not relevant to me.' 'I'm not a powerless woman. I've been a victim all my life but I'm strong; I'm a survivor. No one's going to tell me I'm powerless ever again.'

Other reasons concern going to meetings: 'I don't like groups.' 'I'm a private kind of person.' 'I'm not sitting in meetings full of old alcoholics.' 'I don't see how talking about it is going to help. I rather forget about it.' 'I don't want to hear about other people's problems. I've got enough of my own.' 'I'm not like them. I don't want to be like them.' 'This is something I have to do by myself. No one else can do it for me.' 'If I go to a meeting everyone will know I'm an alcoholic. I don't want anyone to know. I'm too ashamed.'

The reasons given by professionals for not recommending 12 Step meetings as an aid to recovery include personal prejudice as well as a mistaken view of what the Steps mean and what the meetings are like. I have come across care managers who will not refer their clients to The Rehab, even when their clients ask to be referred there specifically, because its treatment programme is based on the 12 Steps and the care managers themselves 'do not believe in it'. This in spite of their never having been to a meeting. They will not advise attendance at meetings because meetings are run by unqualified amateurs, and addicts need the expert help of professionals like themselves. They ignore or dismiss research studies which prove the effectiveness of the 12 Steps and the benefits of the mutual aid provided by meetings, and continue to promote the service they favour whether this is what a particular client actually wants or not.

Another reason care managers give for not advising attendance at meetings is that the recovery goal of the 12 Steps is abstinence and 'not all addicts want abstinence'. They say they do suggest abstinence as a goal but their clients prefer to choose a harm-reduction programme which teaches the addict to use in moderation with reduced harmful consequences. Call me cynical, but if anyone asked me if I would prefer to have a private meeting with a sympathetic care worker once a week and a prescription for a replacement drug for as long as I wanted it, or, never to be able to take another drink or drug for the rest of my life, I know what my first choice would be. Like any false choice, it depends on how you load the question.

This is not to say that everyone with a drink or drug problem ought to be abstinent. I am not suggesting that drugs and alcohol are bad in themselves. I am saying that for those people who sincerely want to stop using and find that they cannot, abstinence is the preferred goal and the 12 Step programme is a way to attain it. I believe that addicts, no matter how far their addiction has progressed, can live drug and alcohol free. I have met too many care managers who underestimate their clients and believe they cannot stop using and need to be maintained on substitute medication indefinitely.

As Treatment Coordinator of The Rehab I have attended conferences about addiction and treatment models. I have heard the research findings of experts in the addiction field and read government strategies for alcohol and drugs treatment. Over the years I have found time and again that the 12 Step programme was not appreciated for what it really is. Recently, however, there is a change. The results of long-term studies are now being published which show beyond doubt that the mutual aid provided by 12 Step meetings is a highly effective aid to recovery and service providers should recommend it to their clients. The results of Randomised Control Trials (RCTs), including a sixteen-year follow up of people attending AA, are now making an impact on government thinking. Perhaps the most impressive finding is that the longer people go to meetings the more well they get, and people who have attended for five years or more are 'better than well'[3] The study[4] measured quality of life across four categories: physical, psychological, social and environmental. It found that in all four categories people with five years or more recovery had a better quality of life than members of the general public.

This may come as a shock to service providers, but is no surprise to addicts in long-term recovery who have known this for years. In the present economic climate, when government funding for addiction services is scarce and facing further cuts, this comes as music to the ears of policy makers who decide drugs and alcohol strategy. There is a huge, nationwide resource in the community which is proven to work and costs nothing whatsoever! Not surprisingly 'mutual aid' is now in the forefront of government thinking and new mutual aid services are springing up in Britain, not free but given government funding. For the last

---

[3] This is a term used by David Best.
[4] *The recovery paradigm - A model of hope and change for alcohol and drug addiction,* David Best, Dan Lubman, Australian Family Physician Volume 41, No.8, August 2012 Pages 593-597.

eighty years alcoholics in AA have been helping other alcoholics to stay well. In 1983 the Basic Text of Narcotics Anonymous[5] wrote '... the therapeutic value of one addict helping another is without parallel.' After so many years of arguing the case in favour of addicts helping each other in 12 Step recovery, I am glad to know that politicians are at last coming round to re-inventing the wheel.

The second reason for not going to meetings is more an excuse than a reason. It comes down to 'I don't feel like it'. If you are addicted, listen to this. You have an illness which is progressive and incurable. If you don't take action to prevent it, it will at some point kill you. First it will rob you of everything you have: your family, your home, your job, your money, your reputation, your dignity, your self-esteem, your values, your memory, your purpose in life, your health, or even your dog. Addiction is hell. When the drugs don't work any more you will be more depressed, more lonely, more unfulfilled, in more pain than you were before you started taking them. Your problems have not gone away and now you have the problem of addiction on top of them. You can fool yourself into thinking you are in charge and you can control your addiction, but you cannot. If you could you would have done it by now. Addiction is more powerful than love and 'Love conquers everything' is a fantasy; nobody is going to be able to stop you using no matter how much they love you. Nobody is going to save you no matter how hard they try. The only one who can do anything to stop this descent into horror is you, and it's more powerful than you are.

The good news is that other people have been where you are and they are living drug and alcohol free. If they can do it, you can do it. If you ask them, they will help you do it. The longer you do it, the better your life will become. You will always be an addict but you never have to use again. Right now you have only two options: stay the same, or change. And you don't want to go to meetings because you might have to say something? That's not even true; you don't have to say anything unless you want to.

This may sound harsh but addiction is a pernicious affliction.

---

[5] *Narcotics Anonymous*, First published 1983, USA. 5th edition 1988, page 18.

One of its distinguishing features is that it tells you that you do not have it. It is remarkable how strong an addict's denial can be. An alcoholic can be in hospital being treated for liver disease and warned by doctors that another drink will kill him, and still try to get someone to smuggle in a bottle of whisky for him. One resident at The Rehab was admitted to the local hospital suffering from her third attack of pancreatitis. She absconded from the ward and was found in a nearby off-licence, wearing her nightdress and with a drip still attached, buying vodka. It is no use being sympathetic with addicts' disinclination to go to meetings and offering them an easier option. The truth is, there is no easy way. The Steps are very simple. No one said they were easy. Like any great achievement, some effort is required. When you think of the lengths people will go to get hold of their drink and drugs and the effort that requires, there's no excuse for not getting to a meeting.

The first reason why people don't go to meetings is because the Steps talk about God, and for many people this is an immediate turn off. In this book I suggest a new understanding which I hope will be more readily accessible to all addicts whatever their beliefs. These are the 12 Steps of AA, first published in the book *Alcoholics Anonymous* (known as "The Big Book") in 1939.

---

1. We admitted we were powerless over alcohol – that our lives had become unmanageable.
2. Came to believe that a Power greater than ourselves could restore us to sanity.
3. Made a decision to turn our will and our lives over to the care of God as we understood Him.
4. Made a searching and fearless moral inventory of ourselves.
5. Admitted to God, to ourselves, and to another human being the exact nature of our wrongs.
6. Were entirely ready to have God remove all these defects of character.
7. Humbly asked Him to remove our shortcomings.
8. Made a list of all persons we had harmed, and

> became willing to make amends to them all.
>
> 9. Made direct amends to such people wherever possible, except when to do so would injure them or others.
> 10. Continued to take personal inventory and when we were wrong promptly admitted it.
> 11. Sought through prayer and meditation to improve our conscious contact with God as we understood Him, praying only for knowledge of His will for us and the power to carry that out.
> 12. Having had a spiritual awakening as the result of these steps, we tried to carry this message to alcoholics and to practice these principles in all our affairs.

The first thing to notice is that these Steps are not orders. They don't tell you what you must or ought to do. They are not a list of 'Thou shalt not's, and no one is going to punish you if you don't do them. They all start with 'We' and are written in the past tense. AA started when a few alcoholics discovered that when they met together and talked about their alcoholism they were not actually drinking. The word spread, more alcoholics came, more meetings were started, and Alcoholics Anonymous came into being. In 1939 the members of AA decided to write down how they had managed to stop drinking and stay sober. They wanted other alcoholics to know how they had done it so that, if they wanted, they could do it too. They wrote, 'These are the steps we took …' If you take the steps we took you can arrive where we are. They didn't say anyone had to.

The Steps are a sequence of actions taken. Nowhere does it tell you what you have to believe. This is a simple but important point which most critics of the 12 Steps have failed to grasp. The people who wrote the Steps in 1939 believed in God, so naturally 'God' was the word they used to name the power that was greater than the individual. People who don't believe in God are free to use whatever terminology they like. People in the Trades Union movement believe that 'The power of many is greater than the power of one'. No one says union members have to believe in God. Neither do members of AA.

Another thing to point out is that the Steps are all positive actions. None of them says stop doing something. Step 1, for example, does not say 'Stop drinking'. While it may be very hard to stop doing something it is always possible to start doing something else. The Steps are practical and doable.

What follows is my re-wording of the Steps. I offer it to you in the hope that it may be helpful. Like the original Steps they are written with hindsight and are a record of shared experience that works.

Step by Step
Step 1

We admitted we were powerless over alcohol – that our lives had become unmanageable.	We admitted our addiction was more powerful than we were, and that we had become unable to manage our own lives.

I have changed the wording slightly in Step 1, for these reasons. Most people encountering Step 1 for the first time do not understand what 'powerless over alcohol' or 'powerless over our addiction' means. They don't usually feel that they have no power. On the contrary, many addicts feel very powerful indeed. They may be living a life outside the law and be feared in their community. They may have the power to supply or withhold drugs from others. They may have the power to run rings around their family members, probation officers, and drugs workers. They may have the power to manipulate their loved ones. They may cling to the belief that they are not chemically dependent and could stop easily whenever they wanted to. Many women object to admitting they are powerless. Much of their life so far may have made them feel like victims and they think that admitting powerlessness will condemn them to staying victims. If in their first meeting they hear about admitting they are powerless some will not come back.

I have turned this sentence round so it talks about addiction being more powerful than I am. I can't see how I can be 'powerless' because I am a human being and not a battery-powered machine. But I can understand that there are some things that are more powerful than I am. I can't control the weather. Gravity is more powerful than I am. When I come to think of it most things are more powerful than I am. Step 1 suggests that one of the things more powerful than I am is addiction. I may not agree with this at the moment but I can at least understand it. It may take a while before I believe it and even longer before I admit it, but it is an idea I can consider. The only requirement at the moment is that I keep an open mind. These people probably didn't come to Step 1 ready to admit anything, but eventually they did. I will hang around a bit longer and check this out.

I have also changed the second part of Step 1. It is not that my life has become unmanageable. To me this sounds as if life is somehow to blame for me not being able to cope with it. Life goes on as it will. It is I who have become unable to manage it. While I have been using drugs and alcohol I have behaved badly. Consequently bad things have happened. Addicts are divorced, imprisoned, bankrupted, sacked, and admitted to intensive care as a direct result of their using behaviour. Life does not do these things to them. These things happen because using addicts are unable to manage their lives. Re-phrasing the second part of Step 1 as I have reinforces the point that I am responsible. It is not's life's fault I have become unable to manage. I have become unable to manage because addiction is more powerful than I am.

Although it is not specifically mentioned in Step 1 I will add here that it is not my fault I have an addictive illness (or 'addictive personality' as some people prefer). I am not personally responsible for my genetic inheritance. I can, however, be held accountable for my behaviour and I am responsible for my recovery. The first step to recovery from addiction is to admit that my life is a mess because of my addiction and addiction is more powerful than I am. So if I want to sort my life out the first thing I'm going to need to do is have a good hard look at my addiction.

In The Rehab residents spent six weeks working on Step 1. Of a twelve-week treatment programme the first half was spent on Step 1 because it is the foundation on which recovery rests. A house built on shaky foundations will fall down sooner or later. Without a sincere acceptance of Step 1 there is diminished protection against relapse. If I do not wholeheartedly accept that I cannot control my use of alcohol or drugs there is a good chance that one day I will feel like a drink or a drug and think to myself 'one won't hurt'. The fact is one will hurt, for when has one ever been enough?

In The Rehab residents were given an intensive introduction to the Steps. They had reading and written assignments, one-to-one counselling, and group therapy all directed to confront the reality of their addiction. In Step 1 they wrote down and shared with the group the things they had done while using. All the shameful secrets, all the regret, remorse, and grief, were shared with peers who gave honest feedback on how these behaviours had hurt other people but who, at the same time, did not condemn because they in active addiction had done similar things themselves. After writing hundreds of examples and six weeks of sharing and being given feedback three times a day, residents who had thought they could control their addiction started to see that they could not.

That is the difference between being told something and learning it for yourself. It is easy to tell someone 'You are an addict. You cannot control alcohol once you start. Therefore you need not to take the first one', and just as easy for the person you are telling to think 'No I'm not, and no I don't.' If, however, you ask the person to think about all the times he got drunk, and to ask himself when was the last time he managed to stop drinking after just one, when he has shared hundreds of examples of his own behaviour he will come to see that maybe you have a point.

The belief of The Rehab was that 'unmanageability' had two aspects: the first was the damaging consequences of addiction to others and the second was the damaging consequences for the addict himself. These were referred to as 'social unmanageability' and 'personal unmanageability'. As a result of my using, this is the harm I have done to everyone around me including my community. As a result of my using, this is the harm I have done to my body, my emotions, my ability to think, and my spirituality.

Addicts working on Step 1 are in a painful place from which there seems no way out. Having to confront the awful reality which is staring them in the face, they are often overcome with unbearably painful feelings of shame and regret. As their denial is eroded and reality bites, most of them at some point get cravings to use again. Of course this is irrational but that is the nature of addiction. No amount of good advice or rules is going to stop an addict using once he has lost control. When the urge to use becomes compulsive the addict does not have the power not to act on it. There is, however, one thing that can stop him, and that is the power of the group. I have seen this happen on countless occasions. Residents who say they want to discharge themselves from The Rehab are told to talk to their group before they make a final decision. I have seen the care of a peer group wrap around a distressed addict, who wants to return to the hell of addiction, like a warm blanket round a shivering child. The addict alone may not be able to withstand the demands of addiction but in the solidarity of the group there is the strength to protect one of its members from a cravings attack.

Although residents at The Rehab did have some one-to-one counselling for the most part their healing happened in the group. People who had never met before, from different backgrounds and with different drugs of choice, who had not trusted anyone for years, who had numbed their feelings and kept their secrets, lived together as a group in a restricted environment for up to six months. Within days of joining the group they were starting to talk to each other about their addiction and identifying with each other. Staff can tell residents what is expected of them but they cannot make them do it. A group, however, is self-regulating and new members adapt in order to belong. I find group dynamics fascinating. The way people change, and the speed at which they do it, when in a group is quite amazing. Grandparents who have never even seen an illegal drug in their lives find identification with young heroin addicts who have spent years in prison, because both their lives have been ruined by addiction. The damage they have done may be different in the details but the painful feelings they experience when working Step 1 are the same.

For this reason residents were sent to local AA and NA meetings in the evenings. This was not optional, they were directed to go as part of their treatment. In this way they were introduced to the support network which was going to be a vital part of their continuing recovery after they left treatment. These residents had to learn the differences between what happens in rehab and what happens in meetings. In rehab you are given written assignments to do; you don't have to do assignments in meetings, or write anything down, or share your shameful secrets with the meeting if you don't want to. In rehab it is expected that you confront your peers' denial; it is not acceptable to do this in a meeting. In rehab you are expected to participate; in meetings it is acceptable just to listen. In meetings you are not given feedback, you don't get told what to do or what not to do, and you only get advice if you ask for it, and then usually after the meeting has ended. In rehab you are expected to move through the Steps on a tight time schedule; in meetings you don't have to complete a certain Step by a particular time, you can take as long as you like and you don't have to take the next Step until you are ready. Sometimes people in meetings wondered how a resident could claim to have 'done' 5 Steps in twelve weeks. Sometimes residents wondered why people who had been going to meetings for years still had not done Step 4. One thing you need to learn in recovery is tolerance.

As we have seen, Step 1 is a painful place. It is not bearable to stay too long in despair. The time comes when hope becomes necessary, otherwise addicts would kill themselves, quickly or slowly, just to stop the pain. When the addict accepts Step 1 he is urgently in need of some hope, and he moves on in a natural progression to Step 2.

Step 2

Came to believe that a Power greater than ourselves could restore us to sanity.	Seeing other addicts in recovery we came to believe that with help we too could recover.

There are two ideas in the original version of Step 2 that people can find off-putting. The first is Power with a capital P. People who want nothing to do with religion are suspicious of any hint of Christianity. The simple sight of a capital letter can bring down the shutters. You can argue that the Steps are not religious for as long as you like, but see a capital letter and no one is going to believe you. 'If it's any power that is greater than I am, why has it got a capital? You're talking about God aren't you?' For this reason I have deliberately removed from the Steps all the words and capital letters which are triggers to mental shut down. No more 'God', 'Him', His', 'Power' or 'Higher Power'. No 'prayer' 'spiritual awakening' or 'carrying the message'. My task then was to convey the essential meaning of the Steps, which is in fact spiritual, without using any of these words which are associated so strongly with religion.

Objectors to my re-phrasing of Step 2 say that I am removing the core belief of the Steps that the addict is made well by something which transcends the personal. My reply is that I agree an addict cannot recover by his own willpower, and that he does need something more powerful than his self alone – but a group of recovering addicts can be that greater power. This does not mean, as one objector put it to me, 'that an addict has to go around in a group all the time and can't ever be on his own, or every time he wants to do something he's got to ask his group.' This entirely overlooks the extraordinary change that happens to individuals when they come together as a group with a vital common purpose. It is true that a group is more than the sum of its parts. I have been present in groups when a sense of unity and mutual identification fills the room and every person present is part of and elevated by it. That is transcendence of the personal. Some people would describe this as God being present in the room. Others would describe it as the power of the group. Others might describe it as the small self, merging with the greater Self. To connect with this feeling of being part of something greater than oneself one does not have to be in the constant company of a crowd of people, any more than a Christian has to be in a congregation in order to connect with God.

The second idea in Step 2 that some people take exception to is the implied judgement that they are insane. Many addicts, after looking realistically at their using behaviour in Step 1, will cheerfully admit to having been crazy while under the influence. Going alone into dangerous places at night is crazy. Taking the dog out for a walk at midnight so you can put your empty bottles in other people's dustbins is crazy. The woman who went for her eye test when she was drunk and could only see out of her expensive new glasses after she had had a bottle or two of wine admitted that was crazy. The postman who hid whenever the post was delivered because he didn't want his colleague to know he was in rehab, when he'd been receiving letters with his name and address on for weeks, realised one day how crazy hiding was. Admitting you have been irrational is not quite the same as admitting you are insane. Also bearing in mind that many addicts have a long history of involvement with psychiatric services, having drug-induced psychosis, being sectioned and being sedated against their will, I have removed the words 'restored to sanity'. I completely agree that addicts have been cognitively damaged by their addiction and need cognitive recovery, but I do not want to alienate people who may feel judged or insulted by talk of sanity or the lack of it.

Addicts at the end of Step 1 need hope. Step 2 is essentially about how to get hope. In the original version the hope is that there is a Power that can heal you. For many addicts even this is a step too far. They don't believe there is a Power or, if there is, it's not going to do anything for them now when it hasn't done anything for them so far. In the re-phrased version the hope is that recovery is possible, and we know this because we can see other addicts who are recovering. Addicts on Step 2 are at the beginning of a long recovery journey. They need the Steps to be as simple as possible. The prime aim is to get them to come to their first meeting and keep coming back.

The original version of Step 2 begins with the words 'Came to believe'. This is important and I have left these words in, although in a re-structured sentence. Step 2 does not say 'We believed'. It does not tell you what you have to believe. I do not know of any addicts who first came to the 12 Steps, either in rehab or in the meetings, full of hope that they could recover from their addiction. Most people came in despair and fear that they could never recover. Most people had tried all kinds of interventions before and none of them had helped. They arrived in a 12 Step group because it was a last resort and they didn't think this one was going to work either.

Traditionally meetings close with an invitation to everyone to 'Keep coming back.' If newcomers are not put off by the wording of the Steps and do keep coming back, they start to become aware of what is happening in the group. They may not have said anything yet but they are listening. After a while of listening they notice a common theme being shared by their peers in the group. They hear how people are getting well. They hear how alcoholics haven't had a drink for days, months, years. They hear how addicts have been reconciled with their families now they are no longer using. They hear people laughing in the meetings. They see them making friendships and having a social life. They get invited to go for coffee after the meeting. They see with their own eyes that addicts are not only not using but also enjoying life. Over time, faced with this evidence, they come to believe that recovery is possible. Over more time they come to believe that it may be possible for them too. They are just like me. If they can do it, maybe I can do it. They say they will help me do it. Maybe I will ask them.

> You get beyond the words when it's explained to you
> by someone who's done it. *Nick*

The addict is now ready to move on to Step 3.

Step 3

Made a decision to turn our will and our lives over to the care of God *as we understood Him.*	We made a decision to stop acting on impulse and instead to be guided by the principles of the 12 Step programme.

Step 3 is usually where the non-religious mentally jump ship. Some will get this far and have all their doubts confirmed. 'This really is about God and you have been conning me all along.' In vain AA members try to explain, 'No, it doesn't have to be about God. Look it says *in italic letters* than it's God *as we understood Him.* That means it can be any god you like, or any Higher Power you like.' I think the writers of the Steps were aware that not everyone would share their Christian beliefs so added the words 'as we understood Him' in an attempt to make the Steps inclusive. For the majority of non-believers, however, this simply does not convince. Narcotics Anonymous, a fellowship which came into being some years after AA, re-phrased Step 3 by replacing 'Him' with 'God', thinking that 'God, *as we understood God*' would avoid the Christian connotation of 'Him'. This made Step 3 slightly less off-putting for me but I still could not embrace it.

I recall a conversation I had with my counsellor. His name was Joe. He was a recovering addict and founder of The Rehab. I had worked my way through Step 1 and admitted all the damage I had done to myself and others, and accepted that addiction was more powerful than me. I had attended lots of meetings and had come to believe that recovery was possible, and that there were lots of people who could help me recover as they were recovering themselves. So far so OK. I hadn't had to think about God at all yet. Joe told me it was time for me to move on to Step 3. I had to be honest and told him I really did not think this was going to be possible. I did not have faith in God. I did not understand what it meant to turn my will and my life over to God's care. It did not make sense to me at all. 'But what does it *mean*?' I asked Joe, 'How do you *do* it?' Joe said that if I wanted to work the 12 Steps I had to do Step 3 before I could any of the others. That was why it was called Step 3. I couldn't leave out the ones I didn't like. The thing that really annoyed me was when he said 'Well if you haven't got a higher power you'd better get one fast.' There followed a couple of weeks in which I felt resentful, self-pitying, and finally, when that wore off, afraid. If I couldn't carry on with the 12 Steps I was going to return to the desolate state from which I had just emerged. I really could not stand the thought of that.

People in the meetings told me about their ideas of God or Higher Power. They said it made no difference what you believed about God, the important thing was that you accepted that you were not all-knowing and all-powerful and that you .needed someone or something else to guide you. The important action in Step 3 was making a decision to put your life in the care of someone or something who knew better than you did. You couldn't steer the car so you had to get out of the driving seat and let someone else do the driving. I said that, in my view, if there was a God He must be cruel and punishing; I didn't want to have anything to do with a God who stood at the gates of Heaven and said, 'You can't come in'. 'Look at the words,' they said in the meetings, '"turn our lives over to the *care* of God", not a punishing God.' One bit of feedback struck a chord with me, 'If that's your idea of God, you need to get a new one!' So I could sack the critical Father and get a loving one? But you can't sack God, even if you don't believe in him … I had to think hard about this. I was being asked in Step 3 to trust something outside of myself and agree to do what that thing willed me to do. I really, honestly, deeply distrusted the whole notion.

It does not come easily to addicts, who have kept secrets and misused people for so long, to trust anyone else. There is also strong resistance to doing what you are told. Now I was going to have to do what I was told by some all-powerful cosmic being I did not believe in. At the same time I was supposed to be entirely honest in my dealings with people. 'It's an honest programme,' I was told in the meetings. 'So how can I do it when I don't believe in it?' I asked in a petulant voice. 'Fake it to make it!' came the reply. There were a lot of slogans quoted in the meetings. That one I particularly disliked. I had been faking it for years, feeling like a phoney and living in fear that one day someone was going to see through the masks and reveal the inadequate me underneath. I didn't want to fake anything anymore. I felt a hunger for integrity. I didn't want to comply, to pretend. I wished I did have faith in God, I envied those who did; I tried to have faith but I didn't. The early stage of Step 3 was disturbing and upsetting for me because I was hung up on the idea of God, like a person tangled in barbed wire, in pain and unable to get myself free.

By the time of my next appointment with Joe I knew I had to do Step 3. It didn't matter that I did not understand it. It did not matter that I did not believe it. I just had to do it. I just had to make the decision. Joe told me to write some words to the effect that I was now handing over my life and will into the care of a loving power greater than myself and, in the company of a recovering peer, read this aloud in the spirit of asking for help and being willing to accept it. 'Like in the marriage ceremony, "Do you take this man ...", when you say "I do", that's when you do it. When you say "I am now handing over", that's when you hand over.' I went away and I did it. In my reading I used the word 'God'. Nothing dramatic happened, no thunderclaps or lightening. Afterwards I did feel some sense of relief though, as I no longer had to bear the painful burden of addiction on my own any more. I recently heard a saying which describes my situation at that time, 'Without a higher power I will get high. Knowing I am powerless is reason enough for me to give God a try.'[6]

It was not until some time later that I realised I had made a decision to put my life and my will into the care of someone more powerful than myself, when I first made the decision to trust Joe and do what he told me to do. I had not understood when I had heard people say in the meetings, 'Any higher power will do. Just choose one for now. You can choose another one later.' Now I understood what they meant. I had chosen to do what Joe told me to do because I believed he cared about me and could help me get well. Joe wasn't God but he knew how to do recovery and would do very well for now.

Only with trust in something can there be a permanent change in behaviour, thinking, and emotional well-being. *Richard*

---

[6] Attributed to April P., member of an anonymous Fellowship.

Later, when I was asked to share how Step 3 was for me, I said I felt as if I was standing at the top of a precipice. The land behind me was falling away and the ground beneath my feet was crumbling. I could not go back, nor stay where I was. I took the only option available to me and took a running leap into empty air. I felt like the cartoon character Wile E. Coyote in pursuit of the Road Runner, who runs off the cliff and hangs in mid-air with his legs still running before he drops like a stone to the canyon floor below. Unlike Wile E. Coyote, however, I have not hit the canyon floor yet. I suppose something must have caught me.

Every one of the 12 Steps is important but Step 3 marks a radical and crucial change in a person's attitude. It is the beginning of humility, which is the natural progression from the change of thinking which occurred in Step 2. At the end of Step 2 addicts stand at a crossroads and a decision as to which path to take is necessary. One path goes back to the using life which is painful, but where everything is familiar and addicts know the rules of the game. The other path leads to a future which is believed to be better, but which is also unknown, where everything is changing and addicts don't know the rules. They know how to lie and hide and manipulate, and they know the codes and conventions of the using world; but they don't know how to be open and honest, to trust and be intimate, and they don't know how to fit into a world where people act morally and value each other.

I have been surrounded by love ever since I surrendered and the other route has always been unthinkable since I did Step 3. *David*

Step 3 is hard enough to do without the added complication of the God element. This is crunch time. Are you just going along complying with the programme, or are you actually going to change? It really is a simple decision but it is fraught with doubt and fear. Many addicts drop out of the programme at this point because they are too afraid to re-evaluate everything about themselves. They prefer the devil they know to the devil they don't. The excuse they most frequently give for not facing the fear is that Step 3 talks about God and so is not for them.

I knew it was important to remove the God words from this Step but had to think long and hard before I found a form of words which I thought was suitable. Often in meetings people who don't use the word God do use the term Higher Power. 'For years addiction was my Higher Power. Now I've chosen a new one, one who cares about me.' For these people, a group of addicts in recovery is a power greater than themselves that they can turn to for help. 'God' has been interpreted as 'Group of Drunks' which is down to earth and immediately accessible. When you are at risk of relapse you can ring a member of the group and talk through the cravings without acting on them. This is a lot easier to understand, and to do, than trust God to intervene to get you through a crisis.

This morning I handed over my life and my will. I felt emotional as I am now having a second chance to start a new life coming from that dark place that I have been living in for the last few years, and now seeing the light and looking forward to my clean and sober life in the future with the help of my Higher Power and going to AA meetings. *Sian*

In the end I decided to take the focus off the idea of who or what was going to be in the driving seat and just state what the decision is. From now on I am not going to do whatever I like whenever I feel like it. From now on I am going to do what the 12 Steps and my peers in recovery advise me to do. From now on, if something is not compatible with the Steps I am not going to do it. I am making this decision of my own free will and I am going to stick to it, come what may.

This is a big decision and requires commitment. It does involve being willing to let go of many things to which you are attached but which are not compatible with a life in recovery. You do really have to want a drug and alcohol free life. Making this decision starts a process of change which can continue for the rest of your life. The longer you do it the better you get. The more whole-heartedly you do it the wiser you get. I believe that it is more effective to start this change simply so that, as it is done daily over months and years, a deeper understanding of its significance develops. Many recovering people do come to find meaning in the idea of 'God as we understand God', but this is an eventual outcome and not a necessary pre-condition of working the Steps.

While on the topic of Step 3 I would like to share some thoughts on the nature of prayer. Many people who say they are not sure if they believe in God or not will use the word in times of shock or crisis. You read in the newspaper that someone you know has been attacked and robbed: 'Oh my God!' Your family member has been involved in a car crash: 'Oh God, no!' Your loved one is critically ill in intensive care: 'Oh God, don't let him die!' When asked to pray for the safe return of hostages, millions of agnostics will tick the Like button and add their prayers to those of the believers. How many of you have tried to bargain with the God you don't believe in? 'Oh God, please let such-and-such happen (or not happen), and I will be good for the rest of my life, I promise!' 'God, I do my best to be a good person; please don't let this happen to me!'

Prayers like these to God are interesting. I see these as acknowledgements of the helplessness of the individual. I cannot accept this is happening and I am totally unable to prevent it. I have no power to change anything in this situation and neither does anyone else. Everything that can be done has been done and no one can do any more. Spontaneously I make the leap to the hope that there is something above and beyond helpless humanity who can stop this happening. 'Oh God, grant me this and I will never ask you for anything else again.' It is not only believers who pray this way. I don't think I am the only person who has ever thought 'Oh God, I beg you, do this or that and if you do I promise to believe in you.'

I mention this because in the meetings when people talk about Step 3 they talk about 'handing over' and about a 'handover prayer'. Traditionally individuals, when acting on their decision to hand their life and will into the care of something other than themselves, will do this verbally and address their words to some named entity. They may call upon God, Nature, the Spirit of the Universe, Fate, Destiny, or any of the thousands of names for a supreme being. They are advised to hold a simple ceremony when they say it and be accompanied by a recovering friend. Saying words aloud and before witnesses are fundamental components of ritual, and ritual adds gravitas to the most important occasions in life. Marriages, funerals, coronations, the swearing of oaths, testifying in court, bestowing honours, receiving university degrees, initiation into gangs, all are made more solemnly binding by the presence of ritual and the spoken word.

One important difference between a handover prayer and a request-type prayer is that the latter is asking for a specific outcome and a handover prayer is not. A handover prayer is not a list of requests, not even when they are good requests for the benefit of others. A handover prayer does not ask God to do your will. It asks for the understanding and strength necessary for you to do God's will. This is the beginning of the handover prayer I used: 'God, I am now willing to put my life into your care. Align my will with yours and help me recognise and carry out your will ...' As I have said, at that time I did not know what I believed about God. I used the word 'God' and mentally addressed it to 'Whoever you are'.

'Handing over' your will implies putting it into the hands of someone, but if you want to take Step 3 and avoid all mention of God and prayer then you can. You can write a different form of words confirming your commitment to change and say that with your witness. You can still mark the occasion with a flower floating down the stream, or a goodbye letter to addiction, or whatever ritual is meaningful to you. Using the re-worded version of Step 3, the words you use are more a promise than a prayer. You could, for example, begin 'From today I will ...' and put into your own words the decision you have now made. I still recommend some kind of simple ceremony. If you make a decision in your head and don't tell anyone, it is all too easy to change your mind and abandon your decision as soon as you feel like it. It is also a good idea to make a version which is short and simple. Once you have made the decision and marked the occasion, handing over or affirming your commitment is best done every day.

I have heard it said in the meetings 'Be careful what you pray for,' and 'Sometimes prayers are answered in ways you don't expect.' One share I particularly liked was 'I prayed for wisdom and I was given problems so that in solving them I could become wise. I prayed for courage and was given fear so that in facing it I could find my courage.' Once you accept that life is for the most part beyond your control you come to realise that your task is to find the resources to manage it as best you can. Every problem that befalls you is an opportunity to develop your strengths. Hand over your life and see what happens. It can't be worse than the addiction you have come from. The very worst that can happen is that nothing changes and you feel a bit silly. If in time you find series of events occur and doors open to opportunities you had not dreamt of, it may be coincidence, it may be Destiny, who knows what it's called. What we do know for sure is that it happens.

If you make the decision and take the Third Step your life will never be the same again. As Joe said to me, 'Enjoy the wild ride!'

Step 4

Made a searching and fearless moral inventory of ourselves.	Made a searching and fearless moral inventory of ourselves.

At first glance this appears to be the simplest of the 12 Steps. Taking inventory is stocktaking. An inventory is a list. Anyone can make a list. It does not require any particular belief, there is no mention of any Higher Power, and no promises have to be made. It is not necessary to be knowledgeable, educated, or especially intelligent. To make an inventory you just have a look, see what is there, and write it down. The thing you are going to have a look at is yourself. Although you may overlook some aspects of yourself and miss some things off your list, you cannot actually get an inventory wrong. There is no need to re-phrase this Step, it is simple enough as it is.

It may be simple but it is not easy to do. It is a Step which involves a rigorous examination of oneself and requires scrupulous honesty. Most people find it extremely painful. Step 4 asks you to be 'searching'. You need to dig deep. You need to look beyond the superficial and look right down into yourself, beyond the masks and pretences and self-illusions. You need to keep an open mind and be willing to let yourself acknowledge truths about yourself which you may find hard to face. You need to take your time and have a good look. This is not a Step to be rushed. You are asked to be 'fearless'. This means you need to face facts however unpleasant they may be. You need to stop deluding yourself and stop making excuses. It is natural to have some fear about doing this. Step 4 does not mean you must not have fear: that would be unrealistic. To be 'fearless' is to have fear and not let it stop you. You have to find the courage and honesty to overcome your fear to look at and into yourself.

Searching and fearless describe how you need to be when you are making your inventory, but what is a 'moral' inventory? 'Moral' refers to your values and principles. What do you think is right, and wrong? What is good, what is bad? What do you believe in? What are your attitudes? What do you find acceptable, what unacceptable? What is important to you, what is not important? In making a moral inventory we take stock of our strengths and weaknesses, our attitudes, beliefs, and values. At the same time we make moral judgements about ourselves and identify the things about ourselves we need to change.

Residents struggling with Step 4 have asked, 'Why do I have to do this?', 'What has this got to do with me stopping drinking?', and 'What will happen if I miss this one out?' It's a fair question. Of course the simple answer is, 'You can't do Steps 5 – 12 if you haven't done 4.' This is not as glib as it sounds. For addicts to recover from addiction they need to make some radical changes. They don't need just to change their environment and social group; they also need to change aspects of themselves. They need to minimise the attitudes and character traits they currently have which put them at risk of relapse, and they need to develop and enhance those attitudes and character traits which are conducive to their growth in recovery. My answer to their questions is 'You need to change. Until you take inventory of yourself you will not know what you need to change. In doing Step 4 you will discover what you need to change and Steps 5, 6, and 7 will tell you how to do it.'

The *AA Big Book* says 'though our decision (Step 3) was a vital and crucial step, it could have little permanent effect unless at once followed by a strenuous effort to face, and to be rid of, the things in ourselves which have been blocking us'. Whether we have made a decision to turn our will and our lives over to the care of God, or have made a decision to stop acting on impulse and instead to be guided by the principles of the 12 Step programme, we are not going to be able to keep to it indefinitely unless we get rid of the personal characteristics that are going to take us back to using.

Step 4, however, is not all about looking for the bad bits of ourselves. This is a fact sometimes overlooked at first glance. Half an inventory is useless. It gives a distorted picture of the real state of affairs. A really thorough inventory has to be balanced; it has to include all the good bits too. This means that in making a moral inventory of ourselves we have to acknowledge our good character traits, our positive attributes, our good attitudes and beliefs, our sound moral principles. Some addicts find this part of Step 4 much harder than the other. They are all too aware of the bad and find it almost impossible to see any of the good.

Residents at The Rehab would come to me, sometimes in tears, saying they could not do this inventory. They had spent weeks looking at the ways in which they had hurt other people in the course of their using drugs and alcohol. They had been searching and fearless in acknowledging their dishonesty, cowardice, selfishness, arrogance and violence. They had seen how they had behaved without kindness, without pity, without respect, without love. They had come to see that in order to get their hands on drugs or alcohol they would break any promise, tell any lie, break any moral code they had. When they were out of control there was nothing they would not do. They may have thought there were some lines they would never cross, but to their horror they had found that they had crossed them; and if there were some lines they had not crossed, they only had not crossed them yet. And now, having done all that, they were being asked to identify their good points. 'I haven't got any assets,' was a common theme. 'I'm just evil.' 'I'm just a piece of shit. I act like shit and I feel like shit.' 'I hate myself.' 'I don't deserve to get well.'

These comments show why it is necessary to do a balanced inventory. Change is not going to be possible unless I have some assets upon which to act. These assets may be few and small at present but they have to exist. Even in the most hardened addict there is some goodness, some ability to feel regret, some part remaining of the person he was before addiction took hold and stripped him of his conscience. They may not be so immediately obvious as the negative qualities but the good qualities are there and a thorough search will reveal them. To residents who believed themselves without assets I pointed out that doing the work they had done so far was evidence of their courage. Sharing with others the damage they had done was evidence of their honesty. Learning about and acting on the 12 Steps was evidence of their open-mindedness. Carrying on with the Steps when the going got tough was evidence of their willingness to recover. So that was at least four assets they had, and they were enough for now.

A further benefit of Step 4 is that it provides an opportunity for you to start the process of letting go of emotional pain which may be grounded in the past but which you are still experiencing in the present. If, for example, you find that you are carrying a burning resentment against your brother which is destroying your relationship with your whole family, you can write resentment on the list of personal qualities that are preventing you from being drug free and content. Later you can decide whether you wish to hold on to this resentment or do something to change it. If you suffer from low self-esteem amounting to self-hate, which makes it impossible for you to live with yourself unless you are medicated with drugs or alcohol, you can write self-hate on your inventory. If you have done things, or had things done to you, which cause you to feel unbearable shame, you can write shame on your inventory. It is huge block to your recovery and will almost inevitably lead you back to using. Don't be afraid of it. Put it on your list of things you want to change. You might not know how to change it yet, but you can put it on your list.

It may not feel like it at the time but this Step is for healing. First you have to expose the wound to the light, only then can you see what needs to be done to make it better. Completing a personal inventory promises you six benefits:

1. Reducing your denial.
2. Reducing the power the past has over you.
3. Freedom from the burden of keeping secrets.
4. Increasing self-awareness.
5. Reinforcing your belief that change is possible.
6. Laying the groundwork for further Steps.

Contrary to popular belief, Step 4 is not a beat-yourself-up session. It asks you to take a good, honest look at who you have been, who you are now, and who you would like to be. It is a time to take stock of yourself, to assess your personality traits, and become aware of what can block or jeopardise your recovery. Step 4 also allows you to recognise your strengths and qualities and see how you can use these to develop your recovery and your self-respect.

We have seen how addiction damages the person on four levels: physical, emotional, cognitive, and spiritual, and that recovery on all four levels is needed. Step 4 brings the focus onto spiritual recovery. I have to make a 'moral' inventory. I have to assess and evaluate. I have to judge my actions against moral principles.

Addiction has damaged my value system. I therefore have to take into account the values and moral principles not just of myself but of the wider community. If recovery lies in integration within something greater than myself, I need to see whether my values are compatible with those of the community of which I wish to become a part. If they are not compatible I need to decide whether I want to change them or not. At every stage I am required to make a decision. I don't have to do any of this. If I want what they have, I can do what they did. They took moral inventory. I had better get on with it. The next question is where do I start?

There are various guides to writing a Step 4 inventory. The *Big Book* describes how the writers of the 12 Steps did it. Al-Anon has a Step 4 guide for family members of alcoholics. At the back of this book is the guide designed for use in The Rehab. I have put it at the back in case, like me, you may be tempted to get stuck into Step 4 before understanding Steps 1, 2 and 3. After a cursory glance at the 12 Steps I thought I could easily skip the first three, but I was keen to make a long list of all my defects of character. Had I done this, I would have completely failed to understand the significance of the three foundation Steps: 'I am an addict. When I use, I am out of control. When I use, I break my moral code and everyone gets hurt. I cannot stop this by myself. I need someone or something to help me. Now I will take stock of myself and discover what I need to change and what resources I have which will enable me to change'. This is entirely different from 'I have done many bad things. This is a list of all my character defects. Any good qualities I have are far outweighed by my bad ones. And yes, shame and self-hate are major issues for me'.

The Rehab's Step 4 guide is simple to follow and pretty comprehensive. To get the most benefit from this inventory residents were told to be specific and not generalise. Generalising can degenerate into exaggeration and self-condemnation, which is definitely not called for in a balanced appraisal of one's strengths and weaknesses. For example, while it is honest to say 'I hurt my loved one when I lied to her' it is not honest to say 'I always hurt my loved ones'. I have to admit I have the trait of dishonesty, because I was dishonest in this way, on that occasion, to these people. It is not true that I am always dishonest, that I am never truthful, that I lie about everything to everybody all the time.

Generalising in statements including 'always' and 'never' serves only to reinforce the false notion that I cannot change. Yes, I was frequently dishonest when I was using; I don't have to be dishonest now I am in recovery. I will put it on my list of things I want to change.

Another reason for writing specific examples of times you have acted on particular traits is that once you have done this it is more difficult for you to slip back into denial about the truth of it. Consider intolerance or prejudice: this is a character trait on the negative side of the list. Most people do not like to think of themselves as being prejudiced. We like to think of ourselves as open-minded and not much bothered by the differences between people. When we dig deeper and examine our conscience we can ask: How do I really feel about people who do not look like me? Who do not dress like me? Who have different values and lifestyles from me? If at first you say to yourself 'I am tolerant of all these groups of people' ask yourself this: Who of these do you fear? Who do you resent? Who do you make assumptions about? Are you sure you have no prejudices?

If you are ready to undertake a moral inventory of yourself, or if you just want to get an idea of what is involved, have a look at the guide in Appendix 4. It is divided into five sections:

1. Blocks to your recovery
2. Principles/values
3. Assets
4. Faith, hope and love
5. Attitudes/responsibilities

There is also an additional section for members of the resident group: Peer feedback on changes made while in treatment.

Addiction damages every aspect of a person's life and personality, and Step 4 is your opportunity to have a good hard look at each part. As you progress through your inventory the parts come together to make a whole. You see how you have been caught in vicious circles where one negative character trait leads to another as addiction takes hold. The descent into despair is not a straight line, it is a downward spiral, one thing leading to another, until you arrive at a rock bottom morally bankrupt, broken, and hopeless. The good news is that as you work the rest of the Steps and start acting on your assets you are on an upward spiral, where each asset enhances the next, and the upward journey can go as far as you like.

Recovery isn't about always getting it right but it is about growing, learning, and feeling a sense of achievement. Writing about your assets in Step 4 is your opportunity to acknowledge your positive qualities and assess some of the changes you are already making, to be justly proud of what you are already achieving, and to set some goals for the future.

So you have completed your inventory. You have been searching and fearless and held nothing back. All your shameful secrets are in there, all your hopes and fears. You are now ready to move on to Step 5. Now you are going to share it.

Step 5

Admitted to God, to ourselves, and to another human being the exact nature of our wrongs.	Admitted to ourselves and another person the exact nature of our blocks to recovery.

If you thought Step 4 was asking a lot of you, you are likely to think Step 5 is asking too much. It is one thing to be searching and fearless when you are the only person who is going to know what you have written. To share your inventory with someone else is to lay yourself open to the scrutiny of another in total vulnerability, which many people, and not just addicts, would regard as incredibly risky if not plain reckless. Clearly, Step 5 is going to require great courage and great trust. If you have conscientiously worked the preceding four Steps you may be surprised to find that courage and trust are two of the things you have acquired along the way.

I have made two alterations to the wording of Step 5. First, to make it more appropriate to non-believers I have simply removed the word 'God'. I have not attempted to replace it with anything else because I think the Step does not require it. People who do believe in God may think it necessary that they admit their wrongs to God, even though they believe that God already knows the secrets of their heart. Whether it is more meaningful for you to admit to 'God and another human being', or simply to another human being, is a matter for you alone to decide. It is the admitting which is important in this Step, not necessarily to whom. In my inventory I have identified my personal attributes, positive and negative. Writing them down was the beginning of admitting them. Now I am required to admit them out loud and in the presence of a witness. Again we see the importance of ceremony and the spoken word. I am admitting this. I cannot un-admit it. I cannot fall back into denial. From now on I am responsible for taking action to change what I know is unacceptable. I cannot just forget about it.

It is important to bear in mind that in Step 5 you are not asking for forgiveness. Even if you are admitting to the God of your understanding, you are still not asking for anything. Sharing your inventory with someone is not like confessing your sins to a priest. You are not judged, not given a penance, and not given absolution. It is less like confession and more like house cleaning. In Step 4 you clean your house. You open up the dark cupboards and clean away the cobwebs. You have a good look at all the contents and decide what you want to keep. All your useful and beautiful things are given a polish, appreciated, and put back ready for use. You find you are left with a pile of old junk that is no use to anyone and you no longer want to keep in your clean new house, so you box it up ready to take to the tip. In Step 5 you show another person all the stuff you are getting rid of and all the precious stuff you are going to keep.

The second change I have made in Step 5 is to replace 'our wrongs' with 'our blocks to recovery' because I want to remove the judgemental overtones attached to 'wrongs'. People in active addiction behave in many ways that are morally wrong. 'Wrong' is an adjective that describes an action or behaviour: stealing is wrong, cheating is wrong. I am not comfortable with turning 'wrong' into a noun and saying it is something I have. What are 'my wrongs'? This sounds too much like 'my sins' or 'my trespasses'. It implies judgement and the need for forgiveness. Addicts do need to make amends for the damage they have done, and may be judged by a god of some kind, but this is not part of Step 5. Every addict has certain attributes, or character traits, call them what you will, that need to be changed if they are to stay drug and alcohol free. Step 5 refers to these as 'wrongs', Step 6 as 'defects of character', and Step 7 as 'shortcomings'. I prefer the simpler and non-pejorative term 'blocks to recovery'. My dishonesty is a block to my recovery. My self-centredness is a block to my recovery. My resentment is a block to my recovery, not a 'wrong' I have.

Similarly, I do not like the term 'defect of character' because it does not fit with the understanding I have of addiction as an illness. Anyone can suffer from addiction, whether they are 'defective' or not. I object to the implication that because I have an addictive illness I have 'defects of character'. 'Defective' is a judgemental and insulting description. People used to be called 'mentally defective' as well as 'morally defective' and this is no longer acceptable. When I first heard the word 'defect' in the 12 Steps I imagined a beautiful, fine, porcelain vase with an ugly crack down it. No matter how you try to paint over it the crack remains. The beautiful vase will always have a defect. People are not like vases with cracks. Their 'defects' can be removed. It makes more sense to me to call them 'blocks to recovery' or 'blocks' for short. On the road to recovery there are obstacles in the way. Some are big, some are small. They stand between you and your goal. You have to find a way to overcome them before you can make progress. They are not sins, they are just roadblocks.

This is particularly important with regard to blocks such as shame and self-hate. Both of these can be so deeply rooted that they do feel like an integral part of the person. I have met many people who are so full of shame or self-hate that they cannot form relationships, cannot try to attain goals, and who are in such unremitting emotional pain that they unable to tolerate life without the numbing effects of drugs or alcohol. They have suffered from shame for so long that they have forgotten what life is like without it. To refer to this shame as a defect of character is to reinforce the idea that shame is a part of their very being. To these people I have said, 'Shame is not the truth of who are you. It is not a defective part of you. It is a just a block on your road to recovery. Put it on your list of things to be changed.'

In Step 5 you share with another person the insights you have gained in Step 4. You read your inventory aloud as you have written it, missing out nothing. It may be tempting to edit it as you go, but for the most benefit total honesty is required. Obviously, if you are going to trust another person with all this information about yourself, you are going to have to choose your 5th Step listener carefully. At The Rehab each resident was introduced to a listener who was in recovery and had some identification with the resident. This person was usually unknown to the resident and unlikely to meet them again but had been carefully selected by staff as a suitable person to hear their inventory. The fact that they were not likely to meet their listener outside of The Rehab often allowed residents to share their inventory without reservation.

A Step 5 listener should have certain qualities: good listening skills, non-judgemental attitude, absolute discretion, empathy, and personal experience of working a 12 Step programme. If possible the listener should be able to identify with the sharer's drug or alcohol use and using lifestyle. Most people approach Step 5 with dread. It helps reduce the fear to some degree if your listener has had similar experiences to you. This is not essential, though, as any recovering addict who has been working the Steps for some years will be able to identify with the thoughts and feelings of another addict even if their circumstances have been very different.

More important is the ability to keep what is shared confidential. If someone is going to trust you with their secrets they have to know that you will honour the expectation of confidentiality which is fundamental to 12 Step meetings.[7] It can be deeply distressing to hear the secrets of others. It can be hard to forget some of the things you are told. A Step 5 listener has to maintain a non-judgemental attitude while hearing about acts of cruelty and being witness to the sharer's emotional state while talking about them. In short, Step 5 listeners need to be able to take care of themselves emotionally. They need the ability to be wholly present in the Step 5 shared experience and wholly unaffected by its negative aspect once it is finished.

Step 5 is an intensely personal experience and is different for every person who undertakes it. The sharer and the listener are equally involved. A thorough Step 5 may last for hours or even all day and at its best is a time of extraordinary intimacy. When sharing person to person, as equals, both parties acknowledge their less-than-perfect humanity. It is not a counselling session. The listener is there to listen, not to give feedback, not to ask why, not to give advice. He may give identification but only if the sharer asks for it. His role is to make it possible for the sharer to complete Step 5. He will be the receiver of the searching and fearless moral inventory of the sharer, and this is a great and rare privilege. When the day comes for you to do Step 5 remind yourself that it is not often in life that you get the chance to say anything you want, for

---

[7] Confidentiality is not absolute, however; there are limits which are defined by law: for example, if a listener is told of an impending terrorist attack, or has reason to believe a child is at risk, they are obliged by law to disclose it. The limits to confidentiality should be made clear to the person sharing their inventory before the Step 5 begins. Other than that, the listener keeps the information to themselves.

as long as you need, without being interrupted or criticised. So make the most of it.

Over the years I have heard many 5th Steps. I have forgotten the details – there was no need for me to remember them – but I retain the memory of how I felt during and after someone else's Step 5. I have shared my own inventory in my own Step 5 and I know how afraid I was and how difficult it was for me to trust another person with the dark side of myself, and how difficult it was to admit my good qualities for fear of sounding arrogant. I know the amount of courage and commitment to recovery I had to find in order to do Step 5. So when I took the role of listener I knew how courageous this person in the room with me was, how big a deal it was for her to trust me. I knew what she needed from me as a listener, as I had needed from my listener: loving acceptance. In 5th Steps I have been fully present with addicts as they experience regret and grief and shame, and their painful feelings have touched my own. Later, while sharing their assets and describing how they are finding faith and love and hope in recovery, feelings of joy and wonderment are expressed and these too have resonated with me. It is these moments of emotional intimacy in the course of a 5th Step that define for me what recovery is all about. Addiction isolates, empties, and starves the spirit. Recovery is the opposite: it nourishes, warms, and fills what was empty with a sense of shared humanity which transcends the individual self. Time after time, in a 5th Step, when sharers start to share their assets, the sun comes out. I have many of these golden moments in my 'recovery bank', resources I can call on when the going gets tough, when two people in recovery are focused on joy and even the weather affirms it.

After my own 5th Step I felt as if I was floating two feet above the floor and wondered how I was going to drive home. I had a 'pink fluffy cloud' feeling and couldn't stop smiling. Of course it did not last, which was a good thing because I could not live at that level of intensity for long. Next day when I came down to earth I was aware that I had taken a big step forward in my recovery. I had admitted what I needed to change and shared it with another person. Now it was time for me to start acting on these insights and making the changes. It was time to start Step 6.

At The Rehab, first-stage treatment ended with the completion of Step 5. Residents who were not going on to work Steps 6 – 12 in second-stage treatment were told to go to meetings and continue working the Steps with a sponsor. Step 5 is a milestone, but without Steps 6 and 7 relapse remains a high risk. Steps 6 and 7 are the Steps of change and if nothing changes, nothing changes.

Steps 6 and 7

Step 6

Were entirely ready to have God remove all these defects of character.	By acting always on our strengths and assets we saw our blocks to recovery diminish.

Step 7

Humbly asked Him to remove our shortcomings.	We asked for help, to accomplish what we could not achieve alone.

Step 6 logically precedes Step 7 and is a preparation for it. This is a repeating pattern in the 12 Steps. In Step 2 we came to believe, in preparation for making a decision in Step 3. In Step 4 we took personal inventory in preparation for sharing ourselves with another person in Step 5. In Step 6 we become entirely ready to have our defects removed and in Step 7 we ask for them to be removed.

No doubt about it, Steps 6 and 7 are specifically about God and humbly asking God to intervene on our behalf. For Christians who have faith in God, Steps 6 and 7 are quite straightforward: become entirely ready, humbly ask, and presumably this prayer is answered when God removes your character defects. It is hard to see how people without a theistic faith can do Steps 6 and 7. People who have chosen to take Nature or the Spirit of the Universe as their higher power are at a loss to see how these powers can intervene on a personal level to alter their character. People who have chosen the members of AA or NA as the power greater than themselves wonder how they are going to ask their peers to remove their shortcomings and how their peers might be expected to achieve this. As a result, many people are inclined to skip over Steps 6 and 7 which have come to be referred to as 'the forgotten Steps'.

I think this is dangerous, as these Steps are at the heart of the twelve and crucially deal with the personal changes a person needs to make in order to lessen the risk of relapse. I thought there had to be a way to make Steps 6 and 7 understandable and doable for non-believers, but struggled to see a way to re-word it without losing its moral relevance.

As written, Step 6 sounds as if I do not have to do anything much except 'be ready' and then some external Power will magically transform me. It gives no clue as to how I am to become ready or when I will know if I am 'entirely' ready. There is plenty of literature written about the Steps and how to interpret them, but I am thinking from the position of addicts seeking help and seeing the 12 Steps for the first time. If they walk into their first meeting and see a poster of the 12 Steps on the wall there is a high chance they will look at these Steps and decide the programme is not for them.

The 12 Step programme is above all a programme of action: we admitted, came to believe, made a decision, made an inventory, admitted, asked, made a list, made amends, sought to improve, continued to take inventory, tried to carry the message. The only Step not written as an action is step 6 'Were entirely ready ...' where the active participant in this Step is not 'we' but 'God'. It is frequently heard said in the meetings, 'If it ain't practical, it ain't spiritual.' In my search for an appropriate re-wording of Step 6 I therefore decided to focus on the practical and make this Step an action Step like the others.

The question I asked myself was: As a recovering person, what am I trying to achieve at this stage? I have spent time and effort identifying my blocks to recovery and the assets I have which I can act on to overcome my blocks. My aim is to clear the way to recovery. Step 6 therefore must be about me making changes which will reduce the blocks that stand in my way. I know what the blocks are so I know what changes need to be made. If I act on the assets I have, over time I will see the blocks get smaller. So if, for example, dishonesty has been a big block to my recovery and I need to reduce it, I will choose always to act on my asset of honesty. If I do this consistently, my dishonesty will become less and less. Similarly, if self-pity has been a block to my recovery and I need to overcome this block in order to be well, I will consciously choose to cultivate an attitude of gratitude for what I have. Over time I will become more grateful and less self-pitying. Thinking about Step 6 in this very simple way led me to find the solution to the problem of how to write this Step without reference to God. 'By acting always on our strengths and assets we saw our blocks to recovery diminish,' is simple and straightforward. As I behave well, my blocks to recovery get less. The more I act on my good qualities, the less my irresponsibility and self-centredness become. I can't at the same time act on sound moral principles and lie, steal, cheat, and hurt people – all the things one does in active addiction.

Step 6 is a Step which recovering people do in the course of their daily lives. It involves being aware of the decisions they are making and choosing to act on the positive. We are all faced with a multitude of choices every day and usually act without thinking. If we pay attention to the choices around us we will find many opportunities to strengthen our assets and diminish our blocks. Some time after I had done Step 5 I was standing in a supermarket queue. It was a long queue and moving slowly. At the front was a customer who was rather slow in finding the right money. It was a supermarket which only accepted cash and they were running out of change. It was a hot day and I was tired and fed up. I found myself getting impatient and intolerant of the customer who was holding up proceedings. Because I was now on Step 6 I took stock of myself. My old behaviour would have been to show my irritation by looking at my watch and huffing or muttering complaints under my breath. I would have made myself angry and resentful over something so petty as a few minutes delay. Applying the programme, I realised I had a choice to make. I could either leave the queue and not buy the goods or, if I really wanted the goods, I could stay in the queue and practise diminishing my blocks. Impatience and intolerance were blocks to my peace of mind. If I chose to, I could instead practise patience and tolerance. I made a mental adjustment of my attitude. My behaviour changed accordingly. Instead of muttering I smiled. When I eventually reached the checkout I saw a handwritten notice stuck to the till: 'Your change is much appreciated.' It made me smile for days.

So far so good. I am behaving in accordance with sound moral principles and my blocks or negative character traits are getting less and less. They haven't gone away, though. I can still slip back into irresponsibility or self-centredness or dishonesty or any of the other self-defeating ways of behaving that were so habitual in active addiction. The question now is 'When am I going to be "entirely ready" for them to be gone?' I think the answer to this depends upon the particular block and upon the individual whose block it is. A person may have some blocks he wishes to be rid of straight away and others which he feels he needs to retain for the time being. Some qualities which are blocks to recovery can be turned into qualities which help to improve life. For example, although anger can be a significant block to recovery there are some people who have only recently allowed themselves to acknowledge their anger and who appreciate its ability to make them feel empowered. People who have felt like a helpless victim can use the feeling of anger to motivate them into taking action which transforms them into a survivor. Similarly envy, which can be corrosive, can be used as a motivator: I want what he has got, so I will work hard to get one too.

In my case resentment was a big block to recovery. I had been angry for so long that my anger, which could have motivated me had I acted on it when it was hot and fresh, had become hardened into a deep resentment. This in turn triggered self-pity and blaming and a lot of negative thinking which was on the verge of becoming obsessive. Irrational revenge fantasies are not conducive to a healthy and happy life. When I came to work the 12 Step programme I was quite attached to my resentment. As the years went by, however, I became sick of it. I was sick and tired of going to meetings saying 'I'm so angry! I'm so angry!' and my peers patiently telling me 'Keep coming back. Keep coming back.' I saw no end to it. I thought I would be eaten by resentment for the rest of my days. Maybe this was what 'becoming entirely ready' meant? Maybe I was entirely ready to have a block removed when I had done all I could to reduce it and in spite of my best efforts I still was not free from it. Maybe I was not entirely ready to let go of it until it hurt me enough. I got angry with the Steps. No matter how hard I practise I must always fall short. How can my shortcomings ever be gone? Do I have to become perfect? How

60

can a human being be perfect? My peers reminded me of the existence of Step 7. Step 7 was a real obstacle for me. It didn't make sense, I didn't believe it and I wasn't going to do it.

'Humbly asked Him to remove our shortcomings.' There has been much discussion about the terms 'wrongs', 'defects of character', and 'shortcomings'. One school of thought is that there are subtle differences between the three. Another is that the writers of the Steps varied the words for the sake of style and they all mean much the same. 'Shortcomings' makes sense to me because if I have assiduously worked Step 6 over a long period of time my blocks are lessened but I am still not one hundred per cent good or well. The difference between the best I can achieve and the ideal is the shortfall, or shortcoming. I have no difficulty with this part of Step 7 – I know I have many shortcomings. The bit I have great difficulty swallowing is the idea that God is going to take them away if I ask Him properly. It is very tempting to think, 'Well, that's what you did. I can't do that, so I'm going to miss this one out.' My fear, though, is that if I miss out a Step there is a hole in my recovery, and a hole in my protection against relapse. I had to find a way of making sense of Step 7, of making it doable.

Eventually I decided upon, 'We asked for help, to accomplish what we could not achieve alone'. I realise this does not entirely convey the spiritual depth of the Step as written. Humbly to ask God to remove one's imperfections, one's negative character traits, one's blocks to recovery, is asking for a miracle. God is being asked to intervene directly to change me into a better person. For a person to make this humble request of God must involve a great deal of faith, and trust and hope. The request, made in a form of prayer, is an act of reaching out to God. This is a spiritual as well as religious communion with God and I do not underestimate its deep significance for Christians. But there has to be a Step for people who have no belief in any god and, while it may lack the sense of communion with the divine, it can still contain the essential aspects of asking for help and asking appropriately.

It is interesting that there is no mention of whether or not this request was granted. There is no Step that begins, 'Having had our defects removed by the grace of God ...' Indeed I doubt that the writers of the Steps did consider themselves to be without shortcomings. This leads me to believe that the important aspect of Step 7 is not the shortcomings being removed but the humbly asking. If I don't have a god whom I can humbly ask, I do have people I can humbly ask. And if I can't expect them to remove my shortcomings, I can ask them for help, to accomplish what I cannot achieve alone. In its simplest form Step 7 says I will do the best I can, but I will never be perfect and there is a limited amount to what I can achieve by myself. I am going to need some help from others to build myself a firm and lasting recovery, so I am going to ask for help and act on it.

Asking for help is a fundamental and recurring theme throughout the 12 Step programme. Addicts need help from other addicts if they are going to get well and stay well. In Step 3 we decided to be guided by those who had successfully worked the programme before us. In Step 7 we ask these people to help us achieve our goal of recovery. In Step 12 we help other addicts as we have been helped. There is a huge and ever-growing community of recovering addicts who help each other. In Step 7 I am going to ask members of this community to help me when I am struggling with the blocks in my path, when I lose hope, or when I have urges to use, or when life just seems too hard to manage. There will always be help for me if I just pick up the phone and ask. There will always be someone there who will listen to me when I need to talk, or hug me if I need to cry, or remind me that recovery is possible if ever I start to doubt it. I just need to swallow my pride and ask. It might not be communion with the divine, but it is a sense of belonging to a community of mutual aid, wherein each person enhances their recovery by helping others with theirs.

I will add a postscript to the story of my resentment. Much later I had reason to re-assess the state of my resentment. It had not been removed and every now and again gave me a stab of pain. I looked again at the original wording of Step 7. It still did not fit with my rational frame of mind. 'What the hell', I thought, 'what harm will it do to ask?' To make the asking more real I felt the need for some kind of ceremony. I went to the beach and picked up the heaviest rock I could lift. I staggered to the shore and heaved the rock with all my strength into the sea. 'This is my resentment, God,' I said, 'I cannot carry it any more. Please, I ask you, take it from me.' I went home and thought no more about it. With hindsight I can see that that particular resentment has not troubled me since then. I do not trouble my head with wondering why.

This completes the middle block of Steps which started with Step 4. These are the Steps of change, where Steps 4 and 5 prepare for the actions of Steps 6 and 7. As a clean and sober person, willing to act in accordance with sound moral principles, I am now ready to face up to the damaging consequences of my actions when I was in active addiction, and do what I can to put things right. I am ready for Steps 8 and 9, the amends Steps.

Step 8

Made a list of all persons we had harmed, and became willing to make amends to them all.	Made a list of all persons we had harmed, and became willing to make amends to them all.

Step 8 is a simple action Step and requires no re-wording. In it the focus shifts from myself, my loss of control over chemicals, my strengths and weaknesses, my beliefs and values, and looks outward to the community. In the course of my addiction I have done things which led to harmful consequences for myself. My addiction has also caused pain and distress to my loved ones and damaged a whole range of other people in a variety of ways. Now that I have re-discovered my conscience and made a commitment to behaving well I have to consider my responsibilities and obligations. I am now to be held accountable. It is time for me to put right as much as I can of the damage I caused in the past. Once again Step 8 is the preparation for the actions in Step 9. Making amends is a process which happens over time. It begins by making a list.

In working Step 1 residents at The Rehab had gained insight into the damage they had done to others. By writing examples of powerlessness and consequences, sharing with peers, and listening to the feedback from family members' questionnaires, they had come to see how addiction had serious unwanted consequences in every area of their lives, so when they arrived at Step 8 they had a pretty good idea of who needed to be on their list. For some residents the result of all this focus on loss of control and its consequences was that they came to feel so guilty and ashamed that they believed everyone they had come into contact with, and even some people they had not, was owed an amend.

For example, a resident who had had an alcoholic seizure and been admitted to hospital shared that he had become aggressive towards nurses and shouted obscenities at them. When his parents arrived at his bedside he told them very rudely to clear off and tried to assault his father. He then discharged himself against the advice of doctors, and went to buy alcohol and Valium which he took in the company of other addicts. When asked who, beside himself, had been damaged by this behaviour the resident made a long list: his mother who was worried sick at being summoned to the hospital only to be more frightened and hurt when she got there, his father because he was similarly worried and had to avoid a punch in the face, the nurses who were verbally abused when trying to help him, the doctors whose advice he ignored, the ambulance crew who wasted time and effort taking him to hospital when he did not want to be there, any seriously ill person who could not get an ambulance when they needed one because he who did not need one was using it, the passers-by who were upset to see him having a fit in the street and called the ambulance, his brother and sister who had to reassure their parents that none of this was their fault, the other patients in the ward who were disturbed by his drunken aggressiveness, the girl in the shop who had to sell him alcohol when he was already drunk and foul-mouthed, his dealer who sold him the Valium because dealing is immoral and he was enabling the dealer to do wrong, the addicts he used with because using was damaging to them all, and the landlord whose house was being used as a place to sell and use drugs.

While it is true that the harmful consequences of addiction spread outward like ripples in a pond, it is unrealistic to say that this resident can make direct amends to every person on this list plus the community at large for being drunk in public. In the great scheme of addiction this is a comparatively minor example of unwanted consequences. It is certainly serious enough but there are many far more complicated examples where people have died and other people's lives have been shattered forever. A list of all persons you have harmed is likely to be very long indeed and include groups of unnamed people as well as known individuals, especially if you have been addicted for many years. It does not matter how long your list is. At this stage you are not making a plan, you are just writing a list of all the people who have been adversely affected by your addicted behaviour. Step 8 itself is not about making amends, it is about preparing to make amends. The essential requirement in this preparation is to become *willing* to make amends to everyone on your list.

Difficulties arise not so much with writing a comprehensive list but with becoming willing, and especially with becoming willing to make amends to them all. What if I don't want to make amends to them all? What if I am so full of resentment or hatred towards some people that I have no intention ever of making amends to them even if I have hurt them while I was using? These are some examples from residents who were having difficulty becoming willing to make amends to them all. 'My father was a violent alcoholic. He used to beat me with his belt when I wet the bed. Five years ago when I was drunk I punched him down the stairs and broke his ribs. I'm not making amends to that bastard. I haven't seen him for years anyway.' 'My husband was always having affairs. I found the receipts for jewellery and hotel bills. I emptied all the money from our joint account and ran up eight thousand pounds debt on his credit card. I spent it all in a couple of months on booze and cocaine. I'm not making amends to him, it serves him right.' 'I fucking hate the police, the fucking racists. Yes I was throwing bottles at them in the riots. I'm not making amends to them.'

Reasons for being unwilling to make amends to particular people are usually emotional. If I hate someone and I have hurt them I am likely to feel glad, not sorry. I will not be inclined to ask for their forgiveness. Many people suffering from addiction have been using drugs and alcohol in a destructive way for most of their lives. These people have been stigmatised and rejected by society. They have been brutalised by the counter-culture in which they live and de-sensitised by the chemicals they take. They have lived in a dog eat dog world where different rules apply. Making amends for having hurt someone is a concept alien to many. It is important to bear in mind that Step 8 does not say you have to feel anything in particular towards the people on your amends list. It describes a rational state of willingness to take action. Furthermore, it does not say you need to make amends for other people's benefit; you need to become willing to make amends for the sake of your recovery. When you make amends to the people you love, you may hope for forgiveness from them, but you do not make amends in order to be forgiven. The question you have to ask yourself is, 'Am I going to make myself willing to make amends to this person whom I hate, or not?' or, to put it another way, 'Am I going to let my resentment towards this person prevent me from completing my 12 Step programme?'

Step 8 is another example of a Step which appears simple but can be very difficult to do. For some people it will involve a great deal of soul-searching. Can I find the strength to be willing to make amends to someone who has harmed me? Does making amends to them mean I first have to forgive them for what they did to me? It can help to clarify some of these questions when I consider why the 12 Steps contain these two Steps about amends. In active addiction I have behaved badly. Now I am in recovery I have made a commitment to act in accordance with moral principles and behave in ways that respect the rights and feelings of other people. Now my conscience is alive again I will at some time feel guilty for the bad things I did. Guilt for past actions is a block to recovery; it can grow so big that it puts me at high risk of relapse. I need to do something to lessen this block, indeed I need to become entirely ready for it to be gone. The Steps suggest that the best way to lessen guilt is to be willing to do what you can to put right what you did wrong. This logical approach does not depend upon feelings. I have a moral obligation to make amends. I don't do it in order to be forgiven, I do it because I ought to do it. When I do what I ought to do, I may in time become free from guilt. As I live 'in good conscience' I become less likely to relapse on unbearable feelings of guilt, shame, regret and remorse. I make amends because to do so strengthens my recovery. Becoming willing is a big step forward in my spiritual development.

In Step 8 you do not have to worry about how to make amends, or what kind of actions would be appropriate, or whether an attempt to make amends might do more harm than good. These are all questions to be addressed in Step 9.

Step 9

Made direct amends to such people wherever possible, except when to do so would injure them or others.	Made direct amends to such people wherever possible, except when to do so would injure them or others.

Like Step 8, Step 9 is self-explanatory and does not need re-phrasing. I have made my list of those people I have harmed and have become willing to make amends to them. If I was not willing to make amends to them *all* I identified what was blocking me from becoming willing and worked Steps 6 and 7 to diminish that block. If after this I still have some unwillingness to make amends to one or two people, I can nevertheless start to make amends to the people at the top of my list, the people who are most important to me.

Regarding any people I still bitterly resent, sometimes the best I can do is to hope that at some point in the future I may become willing to make amends to them too. It is often the case that, over time, as people work the 12 Step programme they find it gets easier let go of their past. They come to accept that the past cannot be changed and that the anger and hatred they are still carrying is hurting no one but themselves. As they grow in recovery the past has less power over them and eventually they become less resistant to making amends. A person may have harmed me, but that does not alter the fact that in my active addiction I harmed him and I owe an amend for what I did. I have to accept that. He may never admit that he did wrong to me or want to make an amend for it, and I have to accept that too. I may never forgive him for what he did to me. That does not alter the fact that where I have done wrong I need to be willing to make it right. If I want to be well and I want to prevent relapse I need to live in peace with my conscience. I keep my focus on what I have done, not what was done to me, and put right what I can.

Step 9 tells me I need to make direct amends. I take this to mean that the amends should be made person-to-person. Whether face-to-face or by letter I need to admit I have done wrong to that person. He needs to know that I am aware of the harm I caused him and that I regret it. Making some kind of anonymous amend gesture is not sufficient. I have to face up and apologise. I also need to be specific. 'I'm sorry my addiction hurt you,' is probably not going to cover it. Making a direct amend requires a good deal of courage and an appropriate amount of humility. You are going to admit what you did and sincerely apologise for it, and, if appropriate, offer restitution. Bear in mind that the person you will be facing has been badly affected by you and probably has strong feelings towards you, not all of them warm. You do not know how your amend will be received. It may be met with anger, or indifference. No matter what the outcome, you owe it to the person you have wronged to allow them their feelings. Do not apologise and then try to justify your behaviour if you don't get the response you were hoping for. If the person will not accept your amend, that is their right; you have fulfilled your obligation to be willing and to take action. You have done what is required of you, whether the person feels better or not. Bearing this in mind, you can understand why it is a good idea to plan what you are going to say when you make the amend, and to ask for feedback and suggestions from peers in recovery who have worked Step 9 themselves.

The next element in Step 9 concerns amends which are not able to be made directly. In these cases indirect amends are to be made. This does not mean getting your friend to apologise on your behalf. As I understand it, indirect amends can be made when the person you hurt is not known to you by name, or their location is not known, or they have died. During their stay in The Rehab some residents suffered feelings of grief and regret when they became willing to make an amend to a parent or grandparent, only to find that they were too late and the person had died. When family members died while their addict was resident in The Rehab but before they had reached the stage of making amends, this was indeed a heavy burden of grief and guilt to bear. For these residents only indirect amends could be made. All these residents felt a need to say sorry to their deceased loved one. Some wrote a letter and read it at the funeral, others shared their letter with their fellow group members in The Rehab. Their desire to make amends and say goodbye in some sort of ceremony was very strong. After leaving treatment some decided to take on voluntary work being helpful to elderly people in their neighbourhood. If they could not make amends to their own grandmother they could instead mow the lawn for another old lady.

Bearing in mind the point that you need to make amends for the sake of your own recovery, you can appreciate the need in certain circumstances for indirect amends. They may not be the same as direct amends but they are the best you can do and are better than no amends at all. I mention this as a warning. We all think we have all the time in the world to say we are sorry and put things right. We don't. If you have become willing to make an amend, act on it as soon as you can. If you leave it too late you will regret it.

The last part of Step 9 is a qualifier and advises caution. There are situations in which an attempt to make a direct amend will cause harm. If that is the case, do not attempt to make the amend. You will have to find another way, an indirect amend, to put right what you have done wrong. Consider this example: If in active addiction you have been unfaithful to your wife, you owe your wife an amend. If your wife does not know about this you will not be able to make a direct amend without telling her, which will cause her pain. This is not to say that it is OK to be unfaithful and keep it a secret. It simply means that in this situation you will have to think hard and ask for advice about what is the right kind of amend to make. If you honestly believe that a direct amend would do more harm to your wife than good, an indirect amend may be the best you can achieve, for example being a better husband from now on. If you have committed crimes you may not be able to make direct amends to the people you hurt. There are times when you have to take a step back and look at the wider view. If you have damaged society by living the addict lifestyle, maybe the best amend you can make is to leave that life behind you and stay clean and sober. Where you have taken from the community, you can make a positive contribution to the community.

Damage due to addiction is vast; sometimes individual acts cannot be redressed. Maybe this is why so many recovering addicts working a 12 Step programme are drawn to do voluntary work, or take up careers in the caring professions, and offer to do service in the meetings. They all say the same thing, 'I want to give something back.' Without Steps 8 and 9 addicts may be free from chemicals but they would not be well. They would still feel guilty and bad, and relapse would not be far away.

The amends Steps, 8 and 9, mark progress in an addict's spiritual recovery. They are no longer isolated and withdrawn, living in accordance with addiction's own rules for survival. They are on a recovery journey accompanied by other travellers and guides who know the way. They are experiencing a return of clear thinking and of emotions which were frozen. Their conscience has woken up and lets them know what is right and what is not. When they carry guilt for past behaviour they accept that they ought to make amends. In becoming willing to apologise they have swallowed their pride and put aside their resentment. They start to see themselves as one person among equals, all of whom have the right not to be abused. They are coming to experience real humility, which is a core element of spiritual development.

Do not confuse humility with humiliation. Humiliation happens when one person feels belittled, mocked, or shamed by another. There is no place in spiritual recovery for humiliation. Humility, however, is the state of being which follows the realisation that one is of equal worth as anyone else. Humility does not debase; it takes one off one's pedestal and makes one equal with one's peers. It does not elevate; it brings one out of the pit of low self-esteem and shame and sets one on an equal footing with the rest of imperfect humanity. Real humility is a blessing and a relief. Thank goodness I am not so special and different. I am not the ruler of the world, neither am I toxic. I am no better and no worse than any other human being. I am a tiny part of something more huge than I can even comprehend. I am at the same time infinitesimally small and vitally important. Without this grain of sand the beach would not be the same. Without this star the universe would be missing something. I am unique and precious – and so is everyone else. I ought to act accordingly and make amends for when I did not.

Step 10

Continued to take personal inventory and when we were wrong promptly admitted it.	Continued to take personal inventory and when we were wrong promptly admitted it.

Having worked Steps 1-9, my recovery is well under way. Step 10 is about maintaining recovery and preventing relapse. This is a simple and practical Step. I keep a check on myself and when I make a mistake, or slip back into old ways of thinking or behaving, I lose no time in admitting it, stopping it, and putting it right. If I keep a check every day, I won't go far wrong before I get back on course.

As I have said before, being alcohol and drug free is not a normal state for an addict whose default setting is using. If I don't pay attention and make a conscious effort to be aware of myself I can slip back into old patterns without even noticing. My peers will usually notice before I do, which is why I need to be open to feedback from others in early recovery. The easiest way to keep a check is to take personal inventory at the end of each day. A simple guide can be found in Appendix 5.

Continuing to take personal inventory does not mean doing Step 4 every day. All that is required is a short but honest self-assessment of one's recovery that day. You don't have to share it in a Step 5 and you don't have to write it down if you don't want to. The aim is to keep an eye on your physical, emotional, cognitive, and spiritual health, and flag up any warning signs of a return to ill-health before they become a problem. The slide away from recovery and into relapse is sometimes so insidious it is all too easy to miss the early signs. If we don't check frequently enough we can find ourselves right back in our old ways of thinking and acting before we know it. So many alcoholics who have relapsed have said words to the effect, 'I don't know how it happened. I went out to buy milk and the next thing I knew I was in the pub buying a drink.' Addicts who have let their resentments build up have a relatively minor disagreement with their partner and the next thing they know they are on the phone to their dealer. Recovering people who fall back into inactivity and hopelessness when life gets hard find they have little resistance to relapse. By the time they realise that they have isolated from their group of recovering peers and are relying only on their own resources to stay well, they may be on the very verge of using again and not consciously aware of it.

It may be useful here to point out some relapse warning signs which can be discovered in the course of working Step 10. Contrary to the way it seems, relapse does not happen suddenly. It is a process and if you are aware of it you can intervene at any point and get yourself back on track. If you find any of this happening to you, take action before it gets any worse:

I'm getting pretty stressed and I'm having mood swings. I put on an act and look OK from the outside, but on the inside I am not right. I do not want to talk about this. I say to myself and other people that I am adamant I will never use alcohol or drugs again. I start acting on impulse instead of thinking about what I am doing. Because I make poor judgements my plans start to fail. I exaggerate my failures and ignore my successes, so I have feelings of guilt and worthlessness. My thinking becomes confused. I start to feel crazy. I am usually irritable and get angry with everyone so I prefer to avoid people. I abandon my usual daily routine and my life is without structure. I eat fast food and sleep poorly. I become deeply dissatisfied with life in general and start to feel hopeless. I reject all offers of help and lie to those people who want to help me. I have thoughts of drugs and alcohol and think if this is what life in recovery is like I might as well be using. I think I can control it this time so it will not get so bad. I pick up again and feel so ashamed, guilty and weak that I lie about it and stop contact with my peers in recovery. I am now back where I started, only worse, because I know what recovery was like and I think I have lost it now.

The point of taking daily inventory is to prevent this happening. If for a few days you have been stressed, irritable, and down on yourself, and you have a strong reluctance to talk about this with your peers in recovery, you are at risk. You need to stop this process before it gets worse. No matter how much you don't want to talk to someone about it, this is exactly what you need to do. You do not need chemicals to take these feelings away. You need the support of a power greater than yourself, in this case your group of people in the meetings. This is one of those times that, even if you don't believe it will help, you should just do it. Work Steps 2 and 3 again. Admit you need help and ask for it. There is never any shame in asking for help, and you have absolutely nothing to lose if you do.

One important point to remember is that if you do relapse, all is not lost. Addiction is a relapsing condition and recovery is not a straight line upwards. The path to wellness can meander about, go round in circles, forwards and backwards, while heading in a general upwards direction. If you are conscientious about doing Step 10 you lessen your risk of relapse but relapse can happen to anyone, no matter how long you have been in recovery. I have said to many people who relapsed and came to talk about it that the most important thing is what you do next, not what you have just done. You can recover from relapse. You take yourself back to Step 1 and ask for help from your peer group. Step 10 does not expect anyone to be perfect, and anyone who relapses and comes back to ask for help is very brave and deserves compassion, not condemnation.

The second part of Step 10 suggests that when we were wrong we promptly admitted it. People can have difficulty with this for one of two reasons. The first is that some people have a big block about admitting they are wrong and never want to admit to anything. The second is that other people feel guilty all the time and want to admit to everything whether they have been wrong or not. Step 10 is the realistic middle ground between these two extremes. No one is right all the time and no one is wrong all the time. *When* I am wrong I should promptly *admit* it. I don't have to commit ritual suicide, and I don't have to admit to being wrong when I am not.

Steps 10, 11, and 12 are the Steps which keep me in 'right relation' – with myself, with something greater than myself, and with the community. Working Step 10 keeps me in right relation with myself. I am now ready to enter into right relation with my 'power greater', which I do in Step 11.

Step 11

Sought through prayer and meditation to improve our conscious contact with God *as we understood Him*, praying only for knowledge of His will for us and the power to carry that out.	Sought through mindfulness and meditation to develop our spiritual and ethical selves.

Step 11, like Step 3, is a tough step to swallow for a non-religious person. In it I am told that the writers of the 12 Steps had conscious contact with God and used prayer and meditation to improve it. Also that when they prayed they asked God to let them know what He wanted them to do. Included in the prayer was a request for God to give them the strength to do whatever it was He wanted them to do.

'If you want what we have, you can do what we did'. Well, I do want what you have, but every rational bit of me is protesting, 'What on earth does Step 11 mean?! How do I do that?' To begin with, it presupposes an already existing conscious contact with God. What is conscious contact with God? Is it like having a telephone connection, a hot line to God? What kind of relationship can I have with the divine Creator of everything? How can my little consciousness contain an understanding of God? At a time like this it does not help to have an academic background in philosophy.

Secondly, I have to improve this conscious contact by praying. Do I have to keep ringing God, and asking him to let me know what He wants me to do next? What if I ring but no one answers? Because that is what it feels like to me when I try to do it. Thirdly, how is God going to let me know His will for me? I know I can pray using words, but how does God answer? Please don't say I'm going to hear voices; I know where that leads and I don't want to go there again. If the answer is going to come to me as a thought or a feeling that this is what I should do, how can I know whether this is an answer from God or just my own self-will telling me what I want to do? What if all I am really doing is doing what I want and justifying it by telling myself that this is God's will? If I have handed over my life and my will in Step 3, and now in Step 11 I am asking God to let me know His will, surely I can attribute to God's will any idea that comes into my head about what I want to do. Throughout history people have committed all kinds of atrocities and claimed they were doing God's will. That can't be right.

Another set of objections arise when I am to pray only for knowledge and strength to do God's will. What about my responsibility to make decisions? What about being proactive, setting my own goals and facing my fears? What about gaining wisdom by making mistakes and learning from them? If all I have to do is wait for God to let me know his plan for me, does that mean I just remain passive and then do what I'm told, safe in the knowledge that it has to be the right thing because it is God's will? And if somehow I do discover what is God's will and I do my best but cannot achieve it, where does that leave me? Have I failed because I did not get the strength I asked for, or I am I just an irredeemable failure no matter how much I am given?

I'm sure Step 11 was perfectly simple for the people who wrote the Steps, and will be for all the people nowadays who have a theistic faith. It is over-analytical people like me who complicate it to the point of absurdity and then complain it is impossible to understand. I accept this. At the same time I really want (or is it God's will?) to find a way of making Step 11 accessible to non-believers. Simply to cut it out is not an option as it expresses a core component of the 12 step programme. I have spent much time pondering the meaning of Step 11, looking for non-religious words which convey its spiritual nature. What I have come up with seems to me to capture it:

Sought through mindfulness and meditation to develop our spiritual and ethical selves.
When looking for the meaning of Step 11 my reasoning went something like this. I understand the notion that God is good. God therefore would want only good for me. In working Steps 4, 5, 6,

and 7 I have been searching and fearless and identified in myself some aspects which are good and some which are not good. I have already decided to enhance my good qualities and reduce my not good ones by choosing in my daily life to act on the good ones. If God only wants good for me it must be the case that in developing my good points I can be described as acting in accordance with God's will. Furthermore, if I am acting on my good qualities I can be said to be developing my ethical self.

Now comes the leap into spirituality. If I am in the process of becoming a better person, acting in ways that are honest and courageous and respectful and loving towards others, and I am doing this in the company of, and following the guidance of, others who are in the same process themselves, then I am part of a progression towards good which is greater than just myself. This I think is approaching the concept of a 'power greater' or 'higher power' than myself. When I allow myself to become part of a transformative movement of change toward the good, maybe I can be said to be improving my conscious contact with the spiritual. Maybe in committing myself to a journey of recovery in the company of my peers I am transcending my small self and developing my spiritual self. Whether this makes sense to anyone else, it makes a kind of sense to me. So that can be the end of my worry about what Step 11 means and now I can look for the words that will tell me how to do it.

'Prayer and meditation' caused me some difficulty. Whatever I thought of as a possible replacement for 'prayer' didn't quite cover it. One morning, when I was thinking of something else entirely, the word 'mindfulness' popped into my mind and I knew that was the word I had been looking for. Step 11 suggests I be mindful. It suggests I pay attention and stay aware of everything I have learned so far about myself, about my limitations and need for help, and about my nature as one among equals. It asks me to take this into consideration when deciding what to do and how to behave.

By 'meditating' I understand quieting the mind and being open to experiencing a connection between myself and the wider powers of life. Step 11 tells me that the way to develop my spiritual and ethical self is by mindfulness and meditation. When I reflect on recovery and addiction, communion and isolation, love and numbness, joy and despair, I know what I want and I know there is no room in my life now for addiction. In its simplest form Step 11 tells me I have already chosen which side I am on, whose gang I belong to, where my true self stands. Staying mindful and allowing myself to experience oneness with something greater than myself will reaffirm my choice.

If I am not sure what to do, I can ask myself, and my peers, 'Is this good for my recovery?'. 'Does this fit with the 12 Step programme?', 'Is this in accordance with my values and moral principles?' and 'Does this enhance the general good?' are variations on the same question.

Step 10 keeps me in right relation to myself. Step 11 keeps me in right relation to a power greater than myself. Now I can look to Step 12, which keeps me in right relation to the wider community.

Step 12

Having had a spiritual awakening as a result of these steps, we tried to carry this message to alcoholics, and to practice these principles in all our affairs.	Recovering from addiction as a result of these steps, we shared our experience with others seeking recovery and continued to practice these principles in all our affairs.

After the intellectual struggles of Step 11, Step 12 is pretty straightforward. As a result of working the previous eleven Steps I have experienced a 'spiritual awakening'. I take this to mean that I have had a moral awakening, insofar as I now have an active conscience which makes me unpleasantly uncomfortable when I do something I know is wrong. In active addiction I could lie with no discernible ill effects because mood-altering chemicals had become my higher power and I was acting in accordance with addiction's will for me. I was also in a community of peers who were on the same journey as myself. Lying was normal and for the most part was not painful. Now I am awake and mindful my conscience is once again my guide. If I am morally uncomfortable at the thought of doing something, then it is likely to be not a good thing, so I should not do it. As for spiritual awakening, I take this to describe my growing realisation that I am a small but integral part of the flow of life. If this is what I have learned from working Steps 1-11, I am obliged to behave in accordance with this knowledge. I think I can accept the wording of Step 12 as it stands, but I have chosen to make some alterations for the sake of those who might react negatively to some of its associations.

The words 'spiritual awakening' and 'carry the message' are redolent of Christian terminology and can conjure up images of evangelists seeking converts. If there is one thing that is going to make many hardened addicts run a mile it is images of 'the God squad' inviting you to come and join them. I know the *Big Book* specifically says that AA works by attraction rather than promotion, but if people are put off by their first glance at the Steps they are not going to get as far as reading the *Big Book*. In looking for a replacement for 'having had a spiritual awakening' I found it helpful to remember what the 12 Steps are for. They are a means to recovery from addiction, not necessarily to communion with God. We may experience a spiritual awakening, however you want to describe that, but that is something that happens along the way. The real and simple aim of the Steps is recovery from addiction. 'Recovering from addiction as a result of these steps' is a simple statement of what has been achieved regarding addiction and is not going to frighten anyone away because that is just what they wanted in the first place.

The second amendment I have made is to change 'we tried to carry this message' to 'we shared our experience'. In meetings all over the world recovering addicts share their experience, strength, and hope. They are not trying to tell anyone what to believe or what to do. They are there to share what they have done and are still doing to stay drug and alcohol free. They are not trying to convert anyone and they do not preach. In exactly the same way as the founders of AA and the writers of the 12 Steps shared with others how they were managing to live in recovery, so people today continue the tradition. They go to meetings to keep in touch with their recovery community, their power greater than themselves. The way they behave when in the meetings demonstrates how well they are. They share openly and honestly, and that is what still-suffering addicts find attractive.

Using addicts seeking recovery can go to any meeting and hear people sharing their experiences. At their first meeting they may be amazed to hear these clean and tidy, humorous, confident people talking about how they were out of control addicts and alcoholics just like them. When they hear their shares and see their good health they may think 'I want some of that'. If they do, they can take the first step, Step 1. This is the beautiful simplicity of the 12 Step programme. Everyone starts as a lonely, using addict and in working the Steps becomes a role model for other lonely, using addicts.

You will notice I have replaced 'alcoholics' with 'others seeking recovery'. This is because I believe addiction is the same no matter what your drug (or behaviour) of choice. Drug addicts, alcohol addicts, food addicts, self-harm addicts, overwork addicts, gambling addicts, and all the rest, suffer from addiction. Although they were written by alcoholics for the benefit of alcoholics, the 12 Steps set out a recovery pathway from the disease of addiction which is effective irrespective of which specific behaviour has become obsessive-compulsive. Indeed many addicts transfer their dependency from one chemical or behaviour to another, and Step 1 means admitting you are powerless over the lot. I have met many drug addicts who stop using illegal drugs and compulsively use alcohol in its place because it is easily available and legal. Instead of being 'addicts' they have now become 'alcoholics'. For this reason I use the words 'addict' and 'alcoholic' interchangeably throughout this book. Alcoholics are addicts who prefer alcohol. The 12 Step programme works for anyone seeking recovery from addiction, not just alcoholics, so I have altered Step 12 accordingly.

I have made another small amendment to the second part of Step 12. I have replaced 'we *tried* ... to practice these principles in all our affairs' with 'we ... *continued* to practice these principles in all our affairs'. We didn't just try, we actually did. We started to act on our moral principles as soon as we became aware of what they were, and in Step 12 we continued to do so. We can't say 'I did *try* to be honest (but dishonesty got the better of me and I ate your cake and blamed it on the dog).' We need to *be* honest. Fortunately for us there is Step 10, for when we are wrong, and Step 9 for when we need to make amends.

Step 12 is an action Step in which we are asked to do two things: to share our experience of addiction and recovery, and to continue to act on sound moral principles in all areas of our life. The latter maintains my recovery and benefits the community in which I live, and the former is my contribution to the recovering community of which I am a part. Sometimes members of a meeting receive a request from a non-member for a 'Step 12 call'. This is a request for someone in recovery to visit an addict who wants help but is unable to attend a meeting at present. For example, if an addict is admitted to hospital and talks to a nurse about his addiction and his despair that he is unable to do anything about it, that nurse may ask him if he would like to talk to someone who is in recovery. If he does, the nurse may contact someone in a meeting and request a visit. Two people from the meeting will then go and visit the person in hospital. They do not go to tell the person what to do or get them to enrol in anything. They go to share their experience, strength, and hope and give the person a contact number to ring if he wants to talk with them again. A 12 Step call is an opportunity for a recovering addict to give back what he has been given. There is such a thing as a never-ending free gift, if a person who was given one gives it to someone else.

Step 12 looks towards the future. It implies that recovering is a continuing process. There is no point at which I can say, 'There, I have arrived. My recovery is completed. So I don't have to practise these principles any more.' By continuing to act on these principles I make 12 Step recovery a way of life. Over time it becomes more than a set of Steps to take to achieve abstinence from mood-altering chemicals. It becomes a journey which leads me ever closer to personal fulfilment, an awareness of my true nature, and an experience of integration with a power greater than myself.

> I love my new life, I will always be so grateful to everyone who helped me to find it and who continues to do so every new day that I enjoy the privilege of living it. *Tim*

Step 12 also contains within it the guarantee that the 12 Step fellowship will continue and grow. Without Step 12 it would have been all too easy for the original recovering addicts to have got well and gone their separate ways. They could have just got on with pursuing their own clean and sober lives and in time their experience and wisdom would have died with them. Instead they decided to write down the steps they took, kept going to meetings, made known their existence, and attracted more suffering addicts to their way of life. By writing Step 12 they ensured the continuation of the fellowship. As more and more recovering addicts practise Step 12 they attract more and more people stuck in the hell of addiction to take their first steps towards recovery.

The moral precept found in many spiritual and religious movements is contained in Step 12: the practice of giving unconditionally. It is perhaps the mark of a truly spiritual man that he will share what he has with another who needs it and ask for nothing in return.

This brings this section of the book to a close. In later chapters I will discuss addiction in its different forms and how the 12 Step programme provides a route to recovery from all of them.

> When I looked at the Steps and saw 'God' I couldn't accept it at all. When I looked at both versions together and was told they mean the same thing then I could comfortably accept both. *David*

I am not suggesting that my version of the Steps is an improvement on the original, it is simply an alternative. I believe the 12 Step programme is one of the greatest gifts given to mankind in the 20th Century and would not ever seek to better it. This book is actually my way of working Step 12.

These are the thoughts of Helen S:

> I was a part-time staff member for a year at The Rehab. My role was teaching the twelve Steps. I used the twelve Steps myself and had been sober for six years in the fellowship of Alcoholics Anonymous. I'd got sober through the fellowship alone and not had any 'treatment' or 'counselling' for my alcoholism, so was 'AA' through and through.
>
> At the time of what I hope was my rock bottom, I had been suicidally depressed. I was unable to manage any of the difficulties in my life. It had taken me four months in AA to put the drink down long enough to realise that I was an alcoholic and that the people I'd met there might have something to teach me about how to deal with that fact. I got a sponsor and began to work the Steps. I listened to others, went to Step meetings, read the *Big Book*, the *Twelve & Twelve*, and other AA literature. I did written work, and I tried to apply the Steps to the particularities of my life. Once I got beyond some initial

resistance to some of the language, I realised that the Steps were for me the perfect toolkit for changing my life into the kind of life I had always wanted. I had had years of counselling (for 'other' issues) and 'sitting with feelings'. I'd understood a lot about myself, but nothing had changed. The Steps offered me a programme of action, and that made all the difference.

Although I was a bit of a spiritual seeker, I definitely wasn't religious, so I had to find my own way of understanding the Steps. I did that simply by listening to people who had similar beliefs to me, and hearing how they had made the Steps fit them. I used to tell my sponsor (in quite strong terms) that no one, but no one, could make me believe in anything. My sponsor agreed! After I'd worked on Step 1 and was absolutely sure of my own powerlessness around alcohol, she said 'do you think that you will get and stay sober through your own will power?'

'No!' I replied. 'That's obvious. That's what powerlessness means. My will power is no good.'

Then she said, 'Do you think you will get sober?'

I said, 'Well, I haven't had a drink for a couple of months now, and if people in the meetings can do it, I don't see why I can't.'

'In that case,' she said, 'you already have a power greater than yourself that is keeping you sober. You've admitted it's not you and your will power. It must be something else.' I couldn't fault the logic. For me that power was the group, my sober friends, being around people who talked about sobriety, working on the Steps. A Higher Power? Certainly. It worked for me and my life got better.

I became convinced that AA had preserved a very precious technique for people like me to be able to build sober lives, and had carefully passed it down the generations. I loved that sense of oral tradition, ordinary people teaching other ordinary people extraordinary things that would change their lives. At first the language was an obstacle, and I couldn't understand, when the very Bible itself had been re-translated several times to make it less sexist, *why* in the world the *Big Book* had to remain in its original (to my mind, honestly, offensive) language. I did begin to see, however, that there was something that worked about the 12 Step programme and I could understand, even if I didn't agree with, the reluctance to 'tinker' with it.

A couple of years on I went on a 12 Step Buddhist retreat for women, and there I encountered women who strongly hated the language of the *Big Book* and other fellowship literature. One woman said that she thought AA was 'a patriarchal outrage and all women should boycott it.' I found it very hard not to agree with her, and suspected I had been a bad feminist all this time. I took my worries back to my sponsor, whose view was that I needed to be careful not to let 'political' views, no matter how deeply felt and righteous, let me lose touch with the power that had kept me sober all that time. She suggested that perhaps the woman I'd met might have been looking for an 'excuse' to drink, and reminded me what was at stake for me. I felt very conflicted. I could see that my political views had in the past had contributed to my alcoholism. I'd used alcohol to fire up my anger about issues, and once angry, needed more alcohol to get any mental relief.

However, I was deeply and authentically committed (drunk or sober) to the belief that the downgrading (degrading) of women in every aspect of culture, including in language and in theology, was absolutely wrong and should be fought. But how could I balance that with my sense of loyalty to the formula that had given me my life back, and that I shared with others as a sponsor myself by then? How could I square it with my sense of the sacredness of fellowship members passing on truths from the past into the future that seemed to be so effective for the suffering people who heard them? It remained a concern, and I got something of a reputation in the meetings I attended for adding to readings words that weren't there; like 'and women'; or saying 'she or he' when the reading just said 'he'. At the beginning of the chapter on Step 6 in the *Twelve & Twelve* it says 'This is the Step that sorts the men from the boys.' I would always say 'the sheep from the goats' or the 'wheat from the chaff.'

In some meetings I attended I met residents of The Rehab, the treatment centre on the hill with a reputation for being very challenging. I was glad they went to meetings, as I knew that after their three or six month stay, they would need to have built a strong sense of identity with their appropriate fellowship(s) in order to stay clean and sober long term. No point having treatment if afterwards you think you're cured and can drink and use again. In those meetings I heard about some of the methods used at The Rehab, but I didn't know that they used a different version of the Steps until I was exploring the possibility of working there part time.

I looked at their version of the Steps online and felt rather shaken. They had been significantly altered. How would people in this treatment centre come to trust the 12 Step programme and pass it on effectively to others if they believed it could be improved upon? If the Steps could be changed in this way, then they could be changed in all sorts of other ways, and the whole idea of a 12 Step programme was being undermined. Could I work in an organisation which was willing to do this? Not being a trained counsellor, the only thing that I was in any way qualified to do was to teach the Steps, as I had done with sponsees. But could I teach *these* Steps? What most alarmed me was that there was no mention of a higher power at all. I had been told over and over again in AA that I needed a higher power. And it wasn't only that people told me, it was my own personal experience (far more powerful than being 'told') that until I surrendered and accepted that, I had been unable to put the drink down. To me, a higher power was non-negotiable, and was one of a few key factors that set the 12 Steps apart from other, in my view more limited, treatment interventions such as CBT or MI.

At my interview it was explained to me that The Rehab was a 12 Step rehab, but that the re-worded Steps were offered as an 'alternative' to those who struggled with the traditional language. Slightly reassured, I decided to take the risk, and The Rehab decided to take the risk with me. It didn't take me long to realise The Rehab's re-worded Steps were just a semi-formal way of expressing an interpretation of the Steps which was in fact much closer to my own than the original words.

Whenever a person seeking 12 Step recovery attempts to make the Steps part of their life, some interpretation is involved. People talk about 'the *Big Book* Way' as if orthodoxy is fixed, and language and interpretation is not something culturally embedded, personal, and ever changing. Even the so called '*Big*

Book fundamentalists' are 'interpreting' the language. They are, after all, not 1930s wealthy male American members of the Oxford Group. They are finding a way of giving the Steps power in their own lives to effect recovery. That is what works for them, and will work for many others. But that does not mean that they have some Rosetta Stone which gives them access to the 'true meaning' of the Steps for everybody (even though they often seem to think it does). I realised that I had been interpreting the literature in my own way all along. I had been reading with a feminist filter – and thank God I had been. If I had been unable to do that, I would have walked away.

I did spend a long time thinking about the 'on the other hand' questions. If the Steps mean whatever you want them to mean, is that not putting 'self' back in the driving seat? I'd been taught to mistrust my own thinking, because this had brought me to my rock bottom. Should I be careful about trusting my own interpretation of the Steps? I concluded that the main thing that had been wrong with my thinking previously was my denial, self-justification, and minimisation around my drinking. The most important thing was to keep my clarity on that. Other aspects of my thinking may not be quite so faulty. However, I was also wary of interpreting the Steps in such a way that I disempowered them as tools. Step 11, for instance, is, on the face of it, a huge order. Might my interpretation of it water it down into something meaningless? Could I end up thinking I was doing the Steps, but really not doing them?

I concluded that so long as I endeavoured to keep these questions alive in my mind, did not become complacent, and had the humility to listen to others with a view to seeing the value in interpretations which were different to mine, I'd be trying to work a spiritual programme of recovery, which was really the best I could do.

So what happened at The Rehab? Just like with sponsees, I tried to help residents come to their own meaningful ways of using the Steps to understand their own experience of addiction, and as a framework for building a recovery that would make sense to them. Many of them who had been afraid that 'God' was going to need to be part of the picture were relieved by the alternative wording, and found recovery just like others. In any seminar on a Step I used both wordings. After all, residents would encounter the traditional wording out in the fellowships, so they needed to become familiar with it. The alternative wording gave them some room to understand that these Steps had to make absolute sense to them personally, and some authority to trust their own understanding. 'You can look at is this way, or you can look at it that way. How do you look at it?' I saw people take their first steps on the path of recovery in The Rehab. Recovery is a marathon, not a sprint, and treatment can never do more than point people in the right direction. However, I saw people beginning to trust their peers and to consider that the strength of their shared aims might legitimately be seen as a higher power which would be transferable to the context of life beyond The Rehab. In the end, I saw The Rehab's wording as a valuable method to help people who would otherwise have run a mile from the anonymous fellowships to see their worth, and their relevance to them. Most recovery research shows that social networks and not 'beliefs' are the crucial mediating factor of recovery. You can believe all the orthodox propositions, but still be active in addiction. It is, however, hard to be active in addiction if you are in caring and reciprocal close relationships with other people seeking recovery. The founders of AA itself had beliefs and spiritual experiences galore, but could not stay sober without their relationships with each other.

I've come to respect the courage of those at The Rehab who were prepared to go against the grain of 12 Step orthodoxy in order to retrieve (12 Step) recovery for a population who would otherwise not have found it. In doing so they have ensured that their alumni have the tools they need to develop those crucial, hopefully life-long, positive relationships within the naturally occurring contexts of the fellowships, or wherever else they may find them.

Helen S.

Chapter Three

Transference of dependency

After more than twenty years of meeting and working with addicts I have no doubt that addicts have more in common than they have differences. People may raise an eyebrow at this, wondering what a thirty-year-old male heroin addict with a long prison history has in common with a sixty-year-old grandmother who drinks all day in her home, or what a twenty-five-year-old university postgraduate with an eating disorder has in common with a twenty-five-year-old sex worker living in a crack house. I would argue that as addicts they share certain character traits and that when in active addiction their behaviour has common characteristics. Furthermore, when in recovery their values, aims, and needs are basically the same.

The idea that all addiction is the same irrespective of the sufferer's drug of choice is one that underpinned the work at The Rehab. If all addiction is the same then the 12 Step programme shows the way to recovery from all addiction, whether the addict is dependent on drugs, alcohol, over- or under-eating, gambling, sex, spending, exercise, social networking sites, working, or trying to control other people. It is interesting how this idea of addiction has crept into the language when people talk not only of alcoholics but also of workaholics, chocoholics, and shopaholics. Adding '-holic' to a behaviour indicates that the behaviour is excessive, in the same way as '-gate' indicates a scandal. It may not be a scientific or precise term, but it is has become part of common parlance and is generally understood. Some people can get addicted to anything. They can be any-kind-of-holic.

In this chapter I will look at the character traits that addicts have in common, and at the characteristics of dependency. Putting these two elements together I hope to show how people who are dependent on one chemical or behaviour can easily transfer dependency to another. This is important information for addicts and for those professionals working with them. Recovery is about living free from addiction, not just living without one particular mood-alterer.

These are the **character traits of a dependent personality**. It is probably not a comprehensive list but it works as a rough guide to who is likely to have a predisposition to experience loss of control over mood-altering chemicals or behaviour. I used it at The Rehab as part of the assessment of a potential resident's suitability for our treatment programme. It was also useful to bear in mind when a particular resident was resisting offers of help or fighting against the requirement to abide by the unit expectations. It helped staff to respond rationally instead of react emotionally to an apparently hostile resident when they remembered that addicts share these character traits and in stressful situations, like rehab, are likely to act out on them.

If you suspect you may have a dependent personality see how many of these character traits you identify with:

- Weak ego
- Lack of openness
- Hyper-sensitivity
- Guilt proneness
- Melancholia
- Emotionality

Weak ego

In one sense this can mean that you are not sure who you 'really' are. Sometimes you judge yourself in a positive way and secretly feel you are better than other people, but more often you judge yourself in a negative way and feel that you are not good enough or flawed in some way. Occasionally you feel confident that your ideas and opinions are authentic and your own; at other times you may feel inauthentic, a phony, agreeing with what other people think, putting on a compliant mask in order to fit in. If this is the case you are likely to live in a permanent low-level state of anxiety because you fear exposure. Because you are never quite sure of yourself you can become anxious about how other people see you.

Because you need to feel acceptable in the eyes of others you tend to try hard to be seen to do well. All too often you set your targets unattainably high and, when you fail to achieve them, judge yourself harshly. You may take this further and ascribe this judgemental attitude to others, seeing yourself as not good enough in others' eyes when actually the only harsh critic is yourself. You can become so self-conscious in the negative sense that you feel strangers in the street look at you and see your manifest defects. Sometimes you don't want to go out at all unless you have a little 'fortifier' first.

Lack of openness

Because you are fundamentally uneasy about yourself you are wary of letting other people get too close. In your attempts to protect yourself against what you fear will be critical scrutiny you are often dishonest. You will say you are fine when you are distressed. You will say it does not matter when it does. You will not willingly ask for help because if you did people would know you have problems. You prefer to lie rather than be honest and assertive. You will make up excuses for why you cannot join in social gatherings that make you uncomfortable, rather than simply saying you don't want to go. You don't openly tell people how you feel. Sometimes you expect them to guess and resent them when they do not. Mostly you prefer to bottle up your feelings, which is why at times they burst out of you in ways that take people by surprise. To reduce the risk of this happening you pretend you have no strong feelings at all. You are often deceitful. You keep secrets. You can become devious. If you don't want people to know what you are doing you may make up a whole fictional lifestyle, like people who 'leave for work' every morning at the usual time with their usual packed lunch then sit in the park all day because they were made redundant weeks ago and don't want anyone to know. There are different approaches to keeping people at a distance: you may be shy and defensive, or go to the opposite extreme and act in a grandiose way. Both are defences and not authentic. Having successfully kept people from knowing you for so long, you wonder why you are lonely and have so few friends.

Hyper-sensitivity

Although you pretend not to have strong feelings you are in fact over-sensitive and can all too easily be hurt. Sometimes you feel physically sensitive as well as emotionally sensitive. Sometimes you feel as if you do not have enough skin on, as if you need another protective layer between you and the world which can so easily wound you. As well as over-sensitive in this sense, you are hyper-sensitive in the sense of being intuitive. You are in the habit of scanning for potential threats because you have been doing this for so long that it has become second nature and you do it without thinking. You can read people, pick up on their feelings, get a sense of whether they are lying or hiding something. You have 'gut instinct'. You can walk into a room and pick up on who is creating an unpleasant atmosphere, who has a false smile, when to watch your back. Of course your gut instinct is not infallible and sometimes gets it wrong. This can lead to internal conflict because you want to trust your gut but have become afraid to do so. Gut instinct can be seen as an asset by addicts who want to identify danger and take avoiding action fast. It can, however, be a curse for other addicts who identify danger and are attracted by it. I have met women who could walk into a crowded room and within minutes pick out the most dangerous man there and find him irresistible.

Guilt proneness

Guilt is usually experienced when a person has done or is thinking of doing something which they believe to be wrong. If you are guilt prone you feel guilty whether you have done anything wrong or not. Even if you are driving a wholly legal car in a wholly legal way, when you see a police car in your rear view mirror you worry about whether you have done anything to feel guilty about. When there is discord in the family and everyone is blaming someone else, you are the one person who feels guilty even if you weren't even there at the time. You may feel guilty *because* you were not there at the time. When other people ignore their responsibilities, you are the one who takes their responsibilities upon yourself because you feel guilty if you don't. You feel guilty when your adult children get into debt, or get divorced, because you were not a better parent. You feel guilty when your dog looks at you with sad eyes because you are not a good enough dog owner. Your guilt feelings are not confined to wrong actions; you can suffer intense guilt about your thoughts and feelings even if you have not acted on them.

Guilt is useful as an indication to you that an action is wrong: if you have done it, you need to put it right, and if you have not yet done it, don't. Being guilt prone, however, can grow into living in a perpetual state of pain and anxiety which takes up all your energy and yet achieves nothing. It is like living with constant backache – sooner or later you are going to need a painkiller to take the edge off it.

Melancholia

People don't often use this word any more but I think it has its merits. In this context I prefer it to the word 'depression', which is the name of a medical condition but generally misused to refer to a state of being unhappy or sad for no apparent reason (which is what melancholia is). Of course some people have two illnesses at the same time, addiction and depression, which both require some kind of treatment; but 'depressed' has become as inappropriately used as 'paranoid' to describe an unpleasant frame of mind. You may be sad all the time but you are not necessarily suffering from depression.

In fact if you are suffering from depression you are more likely to feel nothing at all. You are melancholy if you have all the things you want but are still unhappy, if, in spite of all the good things around you, you still feel sad. You may feel as if there is something missing that you can't quite identify. You may try to alleviate your unhappiness by buying new things, or starting new relationships, but these new acquisitions do not take the sad feeling away for long. You start to feel demoralised. If you get stuck in melancholia you will be lonely as well as sad because no one enjoys the company of someone who is usually miserable. This may not be the most dramatically painful character trait but it a slow insidious killer of joy. It can also get very boring.

Emotionality

This is similar to hyper-sensitivity but specifically in the realm of emotions. If you have this personality trait you find your emotions overwhelming. Whereas 'normal' people go through life having moderate ups and downs in proportion to events and circumstances, you can go from ecstatic highs to the depths of despair in a matter of moments in response to relatively minor events. When someone annoys you, you don't just get irritated, you get angry. Sometimes you feel so overwhelmed with rage you feel afraid of your potential for violence. When you feel resentful you can hold a bitter grudge for years until it poisons your life. When you feel fear it can be so petrifying that you refuse to acknowledge it and get angry instead. When you suffer loss your grief can be so overwhelming that you feel literally heartbroken and need to medicate it before you die of it. When you feel happy you feel ridiculously happy. When it wears off you come down with a crash. When you desire something you feel you have to have it, and you have to have it now. Living in such emotional intensity is exhausting. It also makes it very hard to stop and think. You are on an emotional rollercoaster and it is hard to make rational decisions when you are screaming at the top of your voice. Because you feel at the mercy of feelings which are too intense for you to manage, and because you cannot selectively feel only the happy ones and cut off the rest, after a time you would prefer to have no feelings at all.

Adding these six character traits together you can see why people who have all of them are likely candidates for addiction. As one trait leads into and enhances another, a complex and troubled personality emerges. As some people feel physical pain more than others, some people feel emotional pain more than others. If you have a low tolerance level for emotional pain and your default emotional setting is fear and guilt, you are going to be in pain more than you are not. If your brain chemistry provides you with less internal painkillers than other people, you are more likely than others to seek relief in the form of external chemicals.

Most people do not set out to become addicts. It is not a career choice. They may start using chemicals for fun, for pleasure, because it is socially expected by their peers, to rebel against authority, or to belong to a particular group. Starting to use alcohol is often regarded as a rite of passage, becoming old enough to drink. People who can 'hold their drink' are admired. People who get drunk quickly or do not enjoy the sensation are seen as weak or killjoys. Starting to use drugs is often regarded as initiation into a special group of peers, who may see themselves as rebels, or artists, or seekers after truth. For whatever reason they start to use chemicals, people who have these particular character traits discover that the chemicals modify the feelings which trouble them. Some turn fear into excitement, some replace low self-confidence with boundless belief in one's own abilities. Some take guilt and shame away completely, for a while. They discover that different chemicals have different effects. It does not take long for people to discover what, out of the various options available in their environment, works best for them.

Once they have found their drug of choice, these addicts in the making use it more and more frequently. Whenever they feel anxious they use it. Whenever they lack confidence they use it. Whenever they want more energy, more fun, more sexual prowess, more whatever, they use it. Whenever they just want to escape from all the intolerable pressures of life they use it. Before long, using their drug of choice has become normal for them. It has become their way of coping. In time they become dependent on this way of coping. They cannot cope without it.

At this point they have crossed a line. They are dependent on a drug to complete the most mundane of tasks. They cannot go shopping without taking a drink or a drug. They cannot make a telephone call without taking a drink or a drug. They become unable to cope with interactions with other people. They cannot go to a social gathering without taking a drink or a drug. When they get good news they celebrate by taking a drink or a drug. When they get bad news they try to avoid the pain by taking a drink or a drug.

Although it is often blindingly obvious to everyone else, they may be in denial about the fact that they cannot function without alcohol or drugs. They may insist, too frequently, that they can stop using whenever they want to. They may concede that even if they are using a bit too much they are not hurting anybody and anyway they are free agents and can do what they like. None of these statements is true, but they will not believe it. Sometimes they will not accept that they are dependent on their drugs until the drugs run out. Then they will move heaven and earth to get more, often still denying that they are addicted. For this reason addicts go to great lengths to minimise the chances of running out.

This brings us to a clearer understanding of what it is like to have an addictive personality. If you identify with these character traits, you fit the profile of a person who is at risk of developing a dependent way of coping. Now we will look at what a dependent way of coping involves.

These are all **characteristics of chemical dependency** and if your use of alcohol or drugs has crossed the line from over-use into dependency you will be able to identify with them:

- Preoccupation
- Using alone
- Using for effect
- Using as a medicine
- Protection of supply
- Using more than planned
- Increased tolerance
- Withdrawal symptoms
- Memory blackouts (for alcohol only)

In addition to these, an addict will be experiencing:

- An erosion of moral values
- Serious unwanted consequences

Preoccupation

You spend a lot of your time thinking about your drug of choice. As addiction progresses your thinking becomes obsessive. It is your first thought in the morning and your last thought at night. You think about where to get it, how to afford it, how to conceal it, and when you are going to use it. You think about who might try to stop you using it and how you can avoid them. If you cannot use your drug of choice as soon as you have it in your possession, you watch the clock and count the minutes until you can. If you are in the company of other people, you think about how to get away so you can be with your drug of choice. You think up stories and excuses for why you have to go now. You do not pay attention to anything anyone is saying because you are thinking about your drug of choice and how much you want to use it. You have to think ahead and take precautions to lessen the chance of running out. You constantly have to think of new places to hide it. You have to think about how to dispose of empty bottles and used paraphernalia, especially if there are legal constraints upon you. If you don't have enough money you have to think about how to get some and whether this will involve committing crime or borrowing from loan sharks. If it does, you will have a load more worries to think about. You will also need a lot more drugs to cope with your obsessive thinking.

Using alone

You may be one of the great number of alcoholics who protest that you are only social drinkers. You drink in company and you do it in order to be sociable. I think it was Billy Connelly who joked that sometimes he became so sociable he fell down. You may have started as a social drinker but by the time you have become dependent you will be quite happy to drink alone. Indeed you usually prefer to drink alone for two reasons; one, no one will try to make you stop, and two, you won't have to share. If you use illegal drugs you may have started out by using in the company of peers and enjoying the sense of shared risk taking and drug using ritual, but as addiction progresses you will use alone whenever you can. Addiction is a lonely business. You are secretive and devious when you need to use. You may use alone in public lavatories and car parks. You may lock yourself in your bathroom to use away from the eyes of your family. However you do it, you lock yourself in and you lock others out. You go alone into dangerous places and hide in dark corners to be alone with your one remaining friend, the only one you want to be with: your drug of choice.

Using for effect

How do you take your first drink? If you are an alcoholic you will not savour it and sip it appreciatively. You will get it down you as fast as you can because you want to feel the effect. Downing a pint in one is sometimes regarded by hearty drinkers as a sign of manliness or of being a good-sported gal who can keep up with the guys. In fact, rapid intake is a classic characteristic of addiction. Intravenous drug addicts take this to the extreme. You love the immediate sensation as your drug flows into your arm, or leg, or wherever you have a vein left to inject into. You don't want to wait minutes before drugs in tablet form take effect. You want to get something in your bloodstream or up your nose as fast as you can get it to your brain. Long-term drug addicts want a quick result and will not wait for it any more than alcoholics will take a taste of wine, swill it round, and spit it out.

As well as rapid intake, another feature of using for effect is that you are not fussy what you take. If your drink of choice is gin and tonic you will readily drink a bottle of murky home-brewed beer if that is all you can lay your hands on. You may prefer wine but you will drink all the dregs in other guests' glasses before you leave the party. In the same way, if your drug of choice is crack cocaine you won't say no to a bag of heroin if that is on offer. If you like to use alcohol to get off your head you may well like to take a bit of someone else's methadone or Valium, just to speed the process up a bit. You are using for effect, not necessarily because you enjoy the taste, and sometimes even if you no longer like the effect. You use because you have to, because you suffer unbearable withdrawal symptoms if you don't. When addiction reaches an advanced stage the effect you are using for is merely the absence of withdrawal. The days of using for pleasure or to change mood are gone. I have met many alcoholics who describe the agonies of drinking at the start of their day: the dry retching, the vomiting, the uncontrollable shaking and sweating, the inability to pour the alcohol into a glass and drink from it. If you are now at the stage where you need to get the first one down you as fast as you can, bear in mind that addition is a progressive disease. Alcoholics dying of liver disease or alcohol-induced seizures and strokes started out just like you.

Using as a medicine

This is similar to using for effect but with the focus specifically on changing mood. Using as a medicine means you will use anything available to change the way you feel. As we have already seen, the feelings which addicts most usually want to medicate are painful ones like fear, anger, grief, and guilt. If you are a using addict you will be having these feelings most of the time, as a consequence of the lifestyle you are leading and the effect this is having on the people around you. If you do not know how else to deal with these feelings, you will experience an urgent need to medicate them away. In The Rehab residents frequently shared that, while they may have had many reasons for starting to use drugs and alcohol, in the later stages of their illness they were simply drinking to oblivion[8]. Addiction is a vicious downward spiral. You take drugs to make yourself feel better. Instead of feeling better, you feel worse. You take more drugs to make yourself feel better. The time comes when the drugs don't work. Eventually you feel so ill and get so little relief that you think death would be a rest.

Protection of supply

So you've found the money and you've got your drugs. You'll be able to use very soon and satisfy your craving. You can start to feel a sense of relief. Now all you have to worry about is not running out. Have you ever felt that everyone around you is making it their mission in life to come between you and your drug of choice? Does your partner pour your alcohol down the sink or flush your drugs down the toilet? Do your friends want to use your precious drink and drugs while you are asleep? Do addicts break into your home or search your pockets to steal your stash? In active addiction the worst thing that can happen to you is to have nothing to use. You may lose your home, your family, your possessions,

---

[8] This was memorably shared by one alcoholic whose command of words was not what it once had been, when he announced to his group that for years he had been drinking to Bolivia. I always thought this would be a splendid name for a book about the funny side of rehab but feared it might be taken for a guide to South America.

and the clothes off your back, but if you lose your drugs that's a real crisis – everything else can be made OK once you've had something to sort your head out. So whatever else you need to do today, you have to protect your supply.

Often this is not as simple as it sounds. If you have a partner who is trying to save your life you are going to be locked in a battle of wills, which you will need to be deceitful and cunning to win. You hide your supply in the garden shed, behind the bath panel, under a floorboard. You partner searches until they find it. You hide it in the bushes near your home, in a public lavatory, in a gym locker. Your partner follows you and finds it. They don't tell you they've found it, they just get rid of it. When you can't find it you feel crazy because you are not exactly sure where you hid it last time. As well as having to think of more and more bizarre places to hide your drugs once you have got them, you have to do whatever it takes to keep on the right side of your supplier. You can buy alcohol in many places but, if your partner asks all the shops and bars in your neighbourhood not to serve you, you may have to come to a friendly arrangement with one of them to serve you in secret, or travel quite a distance to get out of the prohibition zone. If you are addicted to illegal drugs the most important person in your life is going to be your dealer. You must not upset your dealer.

If you don't think you are an addict because you are not that bad, ask yourself this: how do you feel about sharing your last bottle of wine with someone else? If there was one drink or drug left would you offer it to someone else because you had had enough? If you dropped your last bag of powder on the carpet would you just brush it up and throw it away? The greater your reluctance the more likely you are to be addicted.

Using more than planned

This means loss of control and is a defining characteristic of addiction. It is neatly described in the well-known saying 'One is too many and a hundred not enough'. The very first Step on the journey of recovery says 'We admitted we were powerless over our addiction', or 'We admitted our addiction was more powerful than we were'. Being powerless, or being in the grip of something more powerful than you are, means that you are not in control of the situation. It means you cannot exercise your free will. You have to do what you are made to do, whether you want to or not. This does not mean that addicts have to use because they cannot help it, so they cannot be held responsible or punished for their behaviour when intoxicated. It means that once an addict starts using, addiction is triggered, brain chemistry changes, and the addict loses the power to decide when to stop.

Once addicts have stopped using and started working the 12 Step programme, they know it is the first drink or drug that does the damage, not the tenth or twentieth, so they are responsible for not picking up the first one. It's a bit like having an allergy. If you know from your own experience that every time you eat nuts you go into anaphylactic shock, then you need to abstain from eating nuts. If you know from your own experience that every time you use a mood-altering chemical you get so intoxicated that you act against your values and cause chaos, then you need to abstain from mood-altering chemicals. If you can't stop once you start, don't start. You may not be able to control when you stop, but you can control whether or not you start. This is particularly relevant after an addict has been detoxified. As we have seen, addiction develops over a period of time. People do not start as addicts. They start using mood-altering chemicals because that is what people in their culture do to enjoy themselves. So when they start using they do not believe they will become addicted. It is only when they have stopped using and are free from the chemicals that they can choose whether or not to start again. The 12 Step programme begins with the addict admitting that he is an addict – something which he did not realise before. The 12 Step programme does not detoxify you. It tells you that when you have stopped you need to abstain from starting again.

The definition of 'powerlessness' used at The Rehab was 'loss of control', which in turn was defined as 'the inability to consistently predict if or when I will stop using once I pick up my first drink or drug ...' (or first use of whatever else I am addicted to). 'To *consistently* predict' is important. It means that sometimes, but I cannot be sure when, I might be able to stop using when I plan to. If you are an addict you know from past experience that you have ruined birthdays, Christmases, weddings, funerals, holidays, and most social activities you have been invited to, by your using more than planned. How many times have you promised your family to take it easy and not make a spectacle of yourself, or cause a fight, or generally bring shame on the family? Nevertheless, once in a while, you just might promise to restrict yourself to three glasses of wine and be able stick to it. Unfortunately this causes problems in more ways than one. First, because you have been able to do it once, you ignore the countless times you were not able to do it and convince yourself that you are not addicted. Secondly, you cannot be sure whether or not you can stop when planned on any particular occasion. You managed to control your using at your daughter's wedding, so how could you have been so selfish as to get so drunk and ruin your son's? With your denial reinforced by a rare exception to the norm, you make more promises you cannot keep and cause more and more harm. Eventually you don't get invited any more and you resent this because you are not an alcoholic are you? An occasional, inconsistent ability to predict when you will stop using does more harm than good. If you cannot consistently stop when planned, you are somewhere on the downward slope of addiction.

Increased tolerance

Have you noticed that recently you are using more of your drug of choice than you used to? Do you use it more frequently? Do you need more and more to get the same result? Do you sometimes mix it with other things to get a better effect? If so, you are showing another characteristic of dependency, increased tolerance. Have you ever joked with friends about how when you first started using it made you so sick and ill that you had to persevere until you got to like it? And now it takes ten times as much before you feel sick and ill! Ha ha ha! Needing a greater quantity to get the same effect is evidence that your body is adapting to the chemical. You are building up tolerance. This happens naturally with any kind of chemical, be it alcohol, street drugs, prescribed antibiotics, or over-the-counter painkillers. If you take them too much they don't work as well as they did at first, so you tend to take more. Tolerance and resistance are two sides of the same coin. If you take heroin for years your tolerance for it goes up. If you take antibiotics for too long you build up a resistance to them.

Changes in tolerance are dangerous. If you have been using heroin for years you will have built up a high tolerance level so you will be able to use relatively high doses without going into a coma. If you then stop using heroin for a while your tolerance level will fall. This means that if, after a period of time without using heroin, you use it again, and use the same amount you took before you stopped, you are at very high risk of a fatal overdose. The risk for users of street drugs is always high, first because you may not be aware of what your tolerance level is these days, and secondly because you never know what street drugs actually contain. If you are used to using heroin bulked out with inactive powder and unknowingly get sold some unadulterated heroin, without urgent medical assistance you are highly likely to die. If you are using alone your prospects are grim.

The situation regarding alcohol is different. For a long time tolerance to alcohol will continue to rise. There comes a time, however, when tolerance falls even though the alcoholic continues to drink. This reduction in tolerance can happen quite suddenly and drinkers who have been used to drinking prodigious amounts of alcohol on a daily basis and still manage to stand up find themselves getting drunk and incapable after a couple of pints of beer. If this is happening to you, you need to know that this is a symptom of liver damage. Your liver has had to work so hard for so long to clear the toxins put into your body by alcohol that it is wearing out. As your liver function decreases, toxins build up and even a small amount of alcohol will produce symptoms of alcohol overdose.

Reading this you may think that anyone who fits this description surely cannot be in any doubt that he is addicted. Do not underestimate the power of denial. Denial is not lying; it is a psychological resistance to accepting an unbearable truth. It is also a feature of addiction. Addiction is an illness that tells you that you do not have it. Everyone around you knows you are addicted, but you think they are wrong. You also think that they don't know half of what you've been up to, because you are so convincingly dishonest, but you are probably wrong about that too.

103

Withdrawal symptoms

In British culture nowadays it is considered an asset to be able to consume vast amounts of alcohol; paradoxically, at the same time there is great stigma attached to being an alcoholic. Perhaps this accounts for the way in which people are quite happy to talk about hangovers they have had but no one wants to call them withdrawal symptoms. After a 'good night out' have you benefitted from a hair of the dog that bit you? Do you find that a nice little glass of something the morning after will settle your stomach and steady your nerves? Do you need a 'livener' before you are ready to face the day? If you feel ill after one night of over-drinking how do you imagine you would feel after ten or twenty years of over-drinking? It is not necessary to list all the symptoms of withdrawal; suffice to say it is a painful and horrible experience. Excess followed by sudden absence of any chemical will cause a body to experience withdrawal symptoms. Whether the chemical is alcohol or street drugs, caffeine or sugar, if you take too much of it for too long your body is going to miss it when it's gone; and it's going to cause you pain until you give it some more.

There are two important things you need to know about withdrawal symptoms. The first is that while withdrawal from many drugs such as opioids is extremely, nightmarishly painful, you don't die of it. For some drugs you may be over the worst in a matter of days, for other drugs it will take longer. Medication can be prescribed to lessen the pain of the detoxification process. The second thing you need to know is that you *can* die from alcohol withdrawal and if you are alcohol dependent you should not attempt to stop suddenly or without medical intervention. I find it amazing and shocking that people subject their bodies to such devastating, life-threatening damage and do so with such breezy unconcern. It's like battering your television with a hammer and then being surprised when it won't work. Of course I only think this now I am in recovery and thinking clearly. Again, I am in awe of the power of denial. It has often been said that you won't know you've got a problem until the drugs run out. If you think maybe you have a problem but you are not sure, see what happens when you stop. You might want to get honest with your doctor first.

Memory blackouts

This applies to alcohol only. Although many family members of alcoholics don't believe it, it is true that alcoholics can have memory blackouts. People tend to think of a blackout as being collapsed and unconscious and so cannot understand how a person can walk about and hold conversations with people and genuinely have no memory at all of what they did. Many a spouse has accused their alcoholic of deception and infidelity when they ask where the alcoholic has been all night and the alcoholic says he can't remember. Alcoholics do wake up in places unknown to them and ask 'Where am I?' and 'How did I get here?' Sometimes they also have to ask 'And who are you?' I found this hard to believe until it started happening to me when I could not remember how I had managed to get home after a night out drinking.

As we saw in Chapter One, periods of alcohol-induced amnesia are the result of damage to brain cells. Some memories may come back but others do not. It is as if the brain has stopped recording memories for a time. At the same time, however, other areas of the brain allow the body to move about and the rational part of the brain allows conversations to take place. The alcoholic may appear to be functioning fairly well, if a bit unsteady and talking rubbish, but there is nothing to indicate to an onlooker that memory is not being formed. This caused me a good deal of pain and confusion when I had an alcoholic partner. He would come home drunk and say things which were deeply hurtful and the next day would behave as if nothing had happened. With what I know now, I can see that maybe from his point of view nothing had happened because he had not remembered it. I just thought he was deliberately cruel. These periods of memory blackouts may be another reason why alcoholics and their spouses either do not talk to each other about the problems caused by the drinking, or have furious arguments with accusations and denials flying back and forth. The alcoholic does not want to admit to being out of control and in blackout and the spouse thinks 'blackouts' are a lie.

Erosion of moral values

In Chapter One we looked at how addiction causes damage to a person's body, emotions, ability to reason, and spirituality, and at how the concept of spirituality is intrinsically linked with the concept of morality. Addicts may have certain character traits which make them more susceptible to becoming chemically dependent but being without morals is not one of them. Addicts, like anyone else, start out with a sense of morality which is usually determined by the culture in which they have been raised. Whatever the particular ethics may be, they believe that some actions are right and some are wrong and that there is a difference between good and bad.

Addiction can afflict anyone, good or bad. Most addicts are fundamentally good people who do bad things when they are out of control. It is crucial to differentiate between the person and the behaviour. If addicts who have behaved badly believe that they themselves are bad, they find it hard to believe that they can become good; consequently they doubt that they will be able to recover. With little or no hope the battle is lost before it is begun. This is another reason why seeing addiction as an illness is helpful to recovery. In The Rehab residents introduced themselves in group therapy with the words 'My name is ... I have an addictive illness', which implies I can get well. It is entirely different from the thought 'My name is ..., I am a bad person' which is what most addicts actually believe. My view on the nature of humankind is diametrically opposed to the concept of original sin, which holds that man is born bad and should strive to become good. I believe that man is born good and should strive to stay that way. It is a sad fact that addicts are stigmatised and looked down upon when they need and deserve the respect and care due to any other person. It is hard enough to recover from addiction without the added handicap of being regarded as a pariah.

It is a characteristic of addiction that the sufferer experiences an erosion of moral values. They do not start out with no moral values. They have moral values but as addiction escalates their compulsion to use becomes so powerful that they are not able to withstand it. They have no choice but to use and, in the course of doing it, will if necessary act against every moral value they ever had. If you are possessed by a truly irresistible craving you will do whatever is necessary to satisfy that craving. If you have to do things which you believe are wrong, you will do them because you have no power not to. You will feel guilty afterwards, but the chemicals will quieten your guilt for a while. Over the years you will see yourself breaking your own moral code in every way. When you act against your values so frequently that it becomes a way of life, gradually you start to care less. Your conscience is exhausted and gives up the fight to get your attention. 'Erosion' is a most apt term: like a coastline being washed away, over time your moral boundaries are breached by degrees and eventually it matters less and less.

Non-addicted members of the public see addicts in advanced stages of addiction and find it all too easy to believe that these are bad people, essentially selfish and without respect for anyone. They have no idea what it is like to be addicted, nor of the internal conflict of addicts who act against conscience in order to satisfy their need. Addicts would come into The Rehab emotionally numb and morally bankrupt, sharing some of the damage they had done and implying that they did not care. After six weeks intensively working Step 1, most were suffering acute guilt and shame. Some took this as a sign that the programme not working, 'I came here to get better, not to feel worse', but I saw this as evidence of the beginning of spiritual recovery. Moral values were not gone. As they re-affirmed their presence conscience came back like a flood.

If other people are suggesting that you have a problem with drugs or alcohol, examine your conscience. Are you entirely comfortable with your behaviour? Your financial behaviour? Your sexual behaviour? Have you started doing things you once thought you would never do? Do you ever need a drink or drug to take away guilt feelings? Remember that once erosion starts it gets worse unless action is taken, and the sooner you start the better.

Serious unwanted consequences

If you are an addict and you let your addiction progress untreated, be prepared to lose whatever you hold dear. There is no need for me to list everything you stand to lose because you stand to lose everything. It is often said that addicts will not be ready to undertake the challenge of recovering unless they have reached 'rock bottom'. There is some truth in this, in the sense that most addicts will continue to use until the real pain of using becomes greater than the feared pain of stopping. However it is not true to say that all addicts must be on the verge of losing everything before they are ready to stop. Rock bottom is a personal matter and is different for everyone. There are some alcoholics for whom losing their driving licence – and the prospect of consequently losing their job and their income and their home – is enough. There are some addicts for whom neglecting their children on one occasion – when the child could have suffered an accident as a result – is enough. You can decide enough is enough when you are about to lose any one thing you are not prepared to lose, whatever that thing may be. Having decided that you want to stop, you will probably not be able to stop on your own but you can ask for help at any time. You do not have to wait until you have lost all your family and friends and are lying in intensive care again.

If you are starting to feel uncomfortable reading about these indicators of addiction and are getting worried that I may be talking about you, check it out. Ask yourself, what has your use of alcohol or drugs cost you so far? Have you lost anything precious yet? What do you think you are likely to lose next if you carry on as you are? Are you willing to lose that? Is there anything which you are not prepared to lose? How far are you going to let this go before you become sick with grief over all your losses? Addiction is all about loss and all about grief. It isn't what you thought it would be when you started. You thought you could handle it, that you were in control, that it wouldn't do any real harm. The truth is you cannot use without consequences. The longer you use the worse the consequences are. Maybe you should make the decision to face reality while you still can.

So far we have looked at the character traits of a dependent personality and the characteristics of chemical dependency. If you use drugs or alcohol on a regular basis and wonder if you may be addicted, see how many character traits you identify with. For easy reference I include a simple checklist in Appendix 1. The more traits you tick, the more likely you are to be one of those people who are predisposed to become chemically dependent. If your score is high, consider next how you use in relation to the characteristics of chemical dependency. If you identify with all of these, you are probably in an advanced state of addiction and an urgent intervention is needed. If you identify with three or more you are likely to be addicted and I recommend that you seek help without delay. If you don't want to approach a medical professional you can go to a 12 Step meeting where you will hear people who are addicts share their experiences. If you identify with them they will help you if you ask. I will talk more about meetings later in this book.

Transference of dependency

I hope by now it will have become clear that it is not the chemical itself that is the problem. The problem is the relationship the user has with the chemical. Some users can use when they want to and stop when they choose to; they are not addicts and they do not share the character traits of a dependent personality. Non-addicts have control over their using. If they get very drunk very often it is because they choose to, not because they have to. Addicts are in a dependent relationship with their mood-alterer, and if they get very drunk very often it is because they are not in control.

Alcohol itself is not evil. It is a social lubricant much enjoyed by millions of people and, when taken occasionally and moderately, probably does no more harm than any other of the activities enjoyed in the 21st century. Heroin itself is not evil. It is a blessing when administered appropriately to people dying in agony. It is how you use them that is the problem, and that lies in the relationship of dependency that the person has with the drug.

This reinforces my belief that some people can get addicted to anything. It also explains how an addict can stop using one thing and become dependent on another, and how some people can be addicted to different things at the same time. I will now take this idea further and say that the object of dependency does not have to be a chemical, it can be a behaviour.

Of the addicts admitted to The Rehab in the last few years the majority were dependent on more than one chemical and a high proportion on a chemical and a behaviour. The proportion of residents who were 'multi-addicted' increased dramatically in recent years. It is important to know about transference of dependency for two reasons. First, it has implications for addiction services. It is usual among service providers to treat clients for one addiction depending on the primary drug of choice. Alcoholics are treated for alcohol addiction and the fact that some also use high doses of benzodiazepine drugs like Valium on a daily basis goes disregarded, usually because the client does not disclose it. Consequently when treatment for alcohol dependency is over, the dependency on benzodiazepines remains. If an addict continues to take a second-favourite drug after treatment it will not be very long before he is back taking his first-favourite drug, alcohol, as well. This is why at The Rehab we had a programme of complete abstinence from all mood-altering drugs and behaviour. For a person with a dependent personality it is no use giving up one dependent way of coping if you are going to persist with another. The focus may have changed but the characteristics of addiction transfer to the new mood-alterer of choice and the serious unwanted consequences continue to accumulate.

Here are some examples of multi-addicted residents: The heroin addict who was also addicted to gambling. The alcoholic who was also addicted to tranquillisers. The amphetamine addict who was also an obsessive-compulsive under-eater. The crack addict who was also a sex addict. The alcoholic who was also a co-dependent. The alcoholic who was also addicted to shopping. The alcoholic who had managed to stop drinking but was dependent on over-eating. The cocaine addict who was also addicted to working. The alcoholic who was also addicted to prescribed and illegal drugs, and sex, and shopping, and when not compulsively over-eating was compulsively under-eating. For these residents, treating their problems singly would not have been successful. The Rehab's holistic programme tackled addiction in its entirety and kept the focus where it needed to be: on the dysfunctional relationship of person and mood-alterer, which may explain why it had such successful long-term outcomes with clients whom other service providers had been unable to help.

Secondly, it is important to know about transference of dependency because this has implications for service users. Addicts themselves are usually not aware that they are multi-addicted. By the time they get to rehab they usually know, even if they don't admit it, that they have a destructive relationship with their drug of choice. They are much less likely to realise that their second or third favourite way of coping is going to cause just as many problems for them if they don't give that up too. Because they have never had to go without their drug of choice, their lesser dependencies will not appear to be so damaging. If you see your life falling apart because you are drunk all the time, you are not going to realise how your gambling is causing problems too. So if alcohol is your drug of choice and gambling is your second favourite, what is going to happen when you leave treatment and do not drink? You yourself will be fundamentally unchanged and you will still be unable to cope with the normal stresses of life. If your number one drug of choice is no longer an option your second favourite will quickly take its place.

This is exemplified by a resident I shall name Jon, a heroin addict in his late thirties. He grew up in a district where the rate of addiction and associated crime was high. Everyone in his family was addicted to drugs or alcohol with the exception of one sister who had moved away because she could not cope with the demands of her addicted family. Jon started using drugs and alcohol at the age of twelve and stealing at the age of thirteen. When he was admitted to The Rehab he had spent most of his adult life up to that point in prisons for violent offences and identified himself as a heroin addict. He had lived by a set of rules appropriate to the culture in which he lived and found it hard to adapt to the rules of The Rehab which were for the most part the direct opposite of what he had been used to. Instead of being closed, defended, and self-reliant he was expected to become open, vulnerable, and willing to be helped. Instead of being hostile to authority and protective of his peers' using secrets, he was expected to respect the rules and to confront peers who were dishonest. Within a short time Jon had a change of attitude; he started to identify with peers in recovery and to put effort into working his Step 1 assignments. In his work it became clear that he suffered from what in the trade is known as 'junkie pride'. He saw heroin addiction as somehow being different from mere alcohol addiction: it was more real, more dangerous, more stigmatised than just getting drunk and falling over. In his eyes he was a hard, bad man with the worst addiction one can get. This was the persona he had built up over his years of pain and isolation; it covered his fear and gave him an identity he could, in his home environment, be proud of. He was playing a game of 'best worst' and he wasn't about to give it up easily.

Working Step 1 in the Rehab involved sharing the consequences of addiction and then in each example tracing back to the time of the first use of a chemical which had triggered that episode of powerlessness. Jon had been arrested and sent to prison for grievous bodily harm when he attacked another addict over an alleged drug debt. He identified heroin as the activating cause of his behaviour on that day. When we looked more closely at this example however, it came to light that on that day Jon had started drinking litres of strong cider as soon as he woke up. He was on his way to buy heroin when the assault took place. Further examination of his examples of powerlessness and consequences showed that all his acts of violence had occurred when he had been drinking and his arrests directly related to the use of heroin were limited to possession. Jon was offended when I told him he was an alcoholic. It did not fit with the way he had aggrandised his addiction as being something special and different.

Jon had the potential to make a very good recovery and I was sad when he decided to leave The Rehab prematurely. As he had started to recover, his emotions had returned. He had felt overwhelmed by strong feelings of loss and anger and could not bring himself to show vulnerability to staff or his peers by sharing the sadness of his addiction-riddled lonely childhood and years of imprisonment. Jon discharged himself from treatment after one month drug and alcohol free and the next day was using again. The chemical he chose to use was alcohol.

There are many, many examples such as Jon's. I believe it would be interesting to find out what proportion of addicts who relapse during or shortly after finishing treatment are dependent on more than one chemical or obsessive-compulsive behaviour. Addicts, when they feel their addiction is under threat, become very protective of it. When their loved ones insist that they get help to stop using their street drugs or their alcohol, they may well comply and manage to give up using their drug of choice, at least for a while. At the same time they will do their utmost to retain one dependent way of coping which they can indulge in secret whenever their stress level gets too high to bear. This leads to behaviour which is sometimes quite bizarre, like the alcoholic who would stare at the wall throughout group therapy and never seem to be paying attention, because he was making bets with himself about which fly would buzz first. Or the alcoholic who persuaded her visitors to bring into the unit bars of chocolate which she hid in her rain hat and binged on in secret when she was supposed to be gardening. Or the heroin addict who was spotted going into the broom cupboard a bit too frequently because he had hidden pornographic magazines in there. We had one alcoholic resident who kept complaining of severe bowel pain, for which he had been prescribed painkillers. Eventually we sent him to the local hospital for a colonoscopy, after which all his symptoms and need for painkillers miraculously disappeared. After that I thought all residents who insisted they needed opioid painkillers while in a drug and alcohol free rehab should be given a colonoscopy but usually the suggestion was enough.

This brings me to my concluding point in this chapter. If addicts share certain distinguishing character traits, and relationships with a chemical or behaviour both share the same characteristics of addiction, then it is reasonable to draw these conclusions: that fundamentally all addiction is the same, that any addict can become addicted to anything, and for recovery from addiction to be sustained all one's focuses of addiction need to be addressed. To this I will add: if the 12 Steps of AA provide a proven pathway to recovery from alcohol addiction, then they will also provide a pathway to recovery from any addiction; and if they are proven to promote the psychological and spiritual healing of alcohol addicts, they will promote the psychological and spiritual healing of all addicts. We shall explore this idea in the next chapters.

Chapter Four

Eating Disorders

You may wonder what a chapter about eating disorders is doing in a book about addiction. There have been numerous books written about eating disorders, especially overeating. Bookshops are crammed with diet books, exercise and fitness manuals, and healthy eating cookbooks. Magazines are full of advice on how to lose weight, which clothes can make you look thinner, how to fight the flab, how to prepare for summer in a bikini, and does my bum look big in this? If you are shaped like a pear you ought to wear this. If you are shaped like a banana add a belt and a pair of high heels and hello happiness. This chapter is not about food and is not about weight. In it I wish to put forward the theory that the eating disorders anorexia and bulimia are obsessive-compulsive relationships with food, that is to say, they are addictions. More precisely they are specific manifestations of addiction, which is one and the same thing irrespective of its focus. Moreover, as they are addiction, the 12 Step programme offers a way to recover from them. I shall test this theory against what we already know about addiction and the 12 Step programme and see if it stands up to scrutiny.

This is important for everyone who thinks they may be an addict, even if you do not think you have a problem with food at the moment. From the previous chapter, Transference of Dependency, you will be aware that addiction is characterised by certain criteria and affects those persons who have certain personality traits which render them predisposed to loss of control over any dependent way of coping. If you have identified those personality traits in yourself and are aware that your use of chemicals is becoming obsessive-compulsive, then you need to be aware that when you stop using your chemicals you are at risk of developing the same kind of relationship with food. This is not to say that you will develop an eating disorder, only that you should remain aware of your behaviour around food, just in case you start to transfer dependency from one thing to another. It has happened to many other addicts and you do not want it to happen to you.

There are lots of theories about eating disorders. Doctors, psychiatrists, and service providers agree that it is a fascinating condition but disagree about what it actually is. When I put the idea to residents in The Rehab that eating disorders are addiction, the alcoholics and drug addicts looked sceptical. This was especially true of some of the drug addicts who (with some honourable exceptions) tended to think that nothing was as bad as drug addiction and even alcohol addicts were somehow not real addicts. They could not see how food could be addictive and felt a bit insulted at the suggestion that food addicts suffered as much as drug addicts did. Their first thoughts were along the lines of: 'Food is not actually dangerous, is it? Not like heroin.' 'You don't need to get detoxed from it, do you? Not like alcohol,' and 'How are you going to abstain from food, then? You can't, can you? Or you'll die.' The more they looked at the differences the less they were able to understand it. It was only when they came to look at the similarities that the idea started to make sense.

First it is important to make the point that people who go through phases of eating too much or eating too little are not necessarily addicts, any more than people who sometimes drink too much are alcoholics. There are very many people, particularly in the developed nations of the world, who at some time in their lives go through a phase of overeating, or dieting, or switching from one to another. They may do this in response to events in their lives which they find stressful. For example, a middle-aged man who is made redundant and cannot find another job may respond to this by drinking too much or by snacking all day while he watches daytime TV at home. A woman who fears getting old and lonely when her children start to grow up and leave home may try one diet after another in an attempt to regain her slim figure and sense of confidence and optimism she had in her twenties. A person who experiences the loss of a loved one may eat very little for the whole time they are grieving. A schoolgirl who is being bullied may comfort eat and then diet for the whole time she remains in that school. What these people have in common is that their changed eating pattern is a response to their external circumstances and is a temporary phase which comes to an end when their circumstances change. When the redundant man gets a job or a new interest, when the woman starts to enjoy life without resident children, when the grief fades, when the girl leaves school, these people tend to change the way they eat. Their changed life has no room in it for overeating or dieting. One day they realise that they have done it long enough and are now bored with it. They may be fed up with feeling unhealthy or sick of counting calories. They don't usually give it much thought or make a considered decision, they just feel like a change and they stop it when they feel like it. These people have the power of choice. They are not addicts.

Food addiction may look similar but is different. It is not a temporary condition which stops when the original distressing circumstances cease. Food addicts do not just grow out of it, or wake up one day and decide 'No more dieting for me.' Food addicts use food as drug addicts use drugs, and alcohol addicts use alcohol. For whatever reason they started using, the time comes when they discover that what they do with food enhances their mood, or numbs their feelings, or gives them that euphoria that nothing else gives them. Their particular behaviour with food becomes the way they cope with any sign of stress. They become dependent on doing it. While they are experiencing serious unwanted consequences as a result of doing it, at the same time they feel they cannot function adequately unless they do it. They have entered into an obsessive-compulsive relationship with food, which is long-term, progressive, and, if left untreated, can result in serious harmful consequences including ultimately death.

People who have an obsessive-compulsive relationship with food think obsessively about food and calories and weight and body shape, and act out compulsively with their 'drug of choice' by starving, bingeing, vomiting, purging with laxatives or colonic irrigation, or burning off calories by exercising. Whether they eat ritualistically, cutting their food into tiny pieces and chewing each piece twenty times, or whether they stuff food into their mouths with their hands, they suffer from the same illness. It can take different forms but it is the same addiction. I will use the term 'compulsive overeater' to mean a food addict who experiences a

116

loss of control when he takes the first compulsive bite. I will use 'bulimia' to refer to the bingeing and purging syndrome which is how some food addicts act out with their drug of choice. By 'anorexia' I will mean obsessive-compulsive under-eating which is the pattern of other food addicts' active addiction.

Of these three food addicts, compulsive overeaters and anorexics who are in an advanced state of their illness are relatively easy to spot – they wear the effects of their addiction on their bodies. The compulsive overeater who has not developed a purging behaviour may gain a lot of weight and become dangerously obese. The anorexic gets thinner and thinner as he compulsively starves himself. Bulimia, however, is not obvious. Because an over-eating binge is followed by purging, the sufferer's weight may remain average and stable for years. Like all addicts, food addicts who don't want to stop using are protective of their addiction and will discount any attempts at confrontation by arguing 'I can't possibly be a food addict; I'm the perfect weight for my height and I've weighed the same for the last four years.' They may not only be trying to convince other people they don't have a problem. They may also be in denial about their own addiction, and the fact that they are neither gaining nor losing weight is a powerful block to their facing reality.

In the same way as being an alcoholic is not necessarily related to the amount a person drinks, being a food addict is not necessarily related to the amount a person weighs. In both cases it is the nature of the relationship between person and mood-alterer that determines whether something is an addiction or not. This has particular relevance to the treatment of food addiction. Dieticians who focus on the effects of over or under-eating may advise diets designed to decrease or increase weight. When weight is lost or gained and a target weight reached, they may say 'Your weight is now down to, or up to, normal. Now you just watch out for that over or under-eating.' This to my mind is analogous to a doctor saying to a seriously ill patient 'Your temperature is now down to normal. Now you just watch out for that pneumonia.' Moderating the effects of obsessive-compulsive over or under-eating does not address the underlying condition, which is a primary addiction, does not go away on its own and needs to be treated.

I shall introduce you now to a food addict whom I shall call

Julie. I have chosen her[9] because she exemplifies many of the characteristics which food addicts share and she shows how the acting out behaviour can change while the underlying addiction remains the same.

Julie is twenty-four and has been in active addiction since the age of fourteen. In her second year of secondary school she started to feel that, no matter what she did, she did not feel attractive or successful. She worked hard at her studies and always handed in her homework on time; she got higher than average grades but she did not feel clever or bright. She tried her best to please but her teachers never seemed to notice her efforts. She longed for special recognition from them but she did not get it. Her friends started talking about boys and it seemed to Julie that all the other girls in her class had boyfriends. Julie was interested in boys but felt that boys were not interested in her. She looked at her developing body in her bedroom mirror and did not like what she saw. She decided she was much too fat. She started to believe that if only she could lose a bit of weight she would be attractive: boys, teachers, parents would notice her more and value her. If she could lose a few pounds she would be just like her friend Kate who was tall, confident, clever, popular, and very slim.

Julie became an avid reader of magazine articles on healthy eating. She went online and read about all the latest diets and 'secrets of the stars' who had lost weight. She learned the calorific value of just about everything edible and she persuaded her mother to buy a new, more accurate, set of bathroom scales. Her mother was quite keen on trying new diets herself so did not need much persuading. Julie refused to eat anything fried, cut out all dairy produce and told her mother she was now a vegetarian. She stopped buying crisps and sweets at school. She ate fruit and salads and sometimes fish for essential fatty acids. She weighed herself every morning and every night. She was delighted to see that she was gradually losing weight. Unfortunately for Julie, none of this calorie counting and dieting made her feel better for very long. The scales told her she was losing weight but every time she looked at

---

[9] I am using Julie as an example as the majority of food addicts are women. Note that, contrary to popular belief, men do suffer from food addiction too.

her body in the mirror she saw herself as unpleasantly fat. She did not want breasts and a bottom and rounded hips; she wanted to be thinner. So Julie started exercising. She didn't just jog, she ran. She bought aerobics CDs and worked out to them every day in her bedroom. She walked the family dog so far and so fast that the poor dog was exhausted. The bathroom scales continued to show weight loss but Julie did not believe them; she could see she was as fat as ever.

Julie's parents started to complain that she was always late or out at mealtimes, that she was awkward and finicky, picking at her food, criticising it, and contriving to leave most of it. They were bored with the way she talked about new diets all the time, and annoyed with the way she cut her dinner into tiny pieces, pushed them all round her plate for half an hour, and then said it was cold and left it. Whenever her parents complained Julie ignored them. When she could not ignore them any more she shouted angrily at them, accusing them, 'You just want to make me fat!' Julie is fourteen and is in the early stage of anorexia. She compulsively under-eats at breakfast time and after that she is not able to choose how she eats; she is experiencing a loss of control. Paradoxically Julie believes that she is demonstrating how powerful she is by not eating food. She may feel powerless to get what she wants from the world but she feels powerful enough to withstand hunger pangs. She may not be able to control how the world treats her but she can control what she does or does not put in her mouth. As Julie is about to find out however, this feeling of being in control is an illusion. She is in the early stage now but her addiction will progress and the time will come when her loss of control will be ever more hard to deny.

'Anorexia', derived from Greek, literally means 'loss of appetite', but this is a misnomer. Julie does not experience a loss of appetite. She spends most of her time feeling very hungry. What she does experience is a distorted way of thinking and behaving around food. She is preoccupied with thoughts of food and dieting and weight loss to the point of obsession, and she acts out compulsively, denying herself food whether she feels hungry or not. She is developing a dread of eating. To Julie it feels as if every morsel she swallows sticks to her insides like tar, filling her, bulking her up. She longs to feel empty and clean and light, and she starts to hate her body because it is lumpy and heavy and all too solid. As hate and shame colour the way she regards herself, Julie isolates from others, becomes more secretive and refuses to talk to anyone about her deeply painful thoughts and feelings.

By the time she is eighteen Julie has grown to five feet six inches and weighs seven and a half stone. She passes her A-levels and leaves home to go to university where she studies to become a P.E. teacher. Her parents are actually relieved when she leaves. Their once loving and happy little girl has grown into an angry and critical young woman who does all she can to avoid them and reject their love and concern. They are hurt, worried, and confused. They miss her, but they breathe a sigh of relief when she is not around. In her hall of residence Julie is frightened of being away from her family. She avoided them at home when they questioned her eating but now they are not there Julie feels insecure. She is in a new town, where she knows no one, and feels overwhelmed with the pressure of university studies and the responsibility of having to manage on a student loan. The only way Julie knows to deal with stress is to under-eat. This is increasingly difficult in her new environment where her peers are not as easy to avoid as her parents. She is thinking about food most of the time now and is still very hungry.

Julie starts to change her eating behaviour. She compulsively under-eats all day, then 'gives in' to her hunger and binge eats in the privacy of her bedroom every night. Sometimes the only way she can manage not to eat during the day is to promise herself a binge reward later that night. She makes sure she has a supply of easy to eat binge food ready to use, and she can't wait for night time to come. Julie is now frantic that she will put on weight. Her ability to go without food is leaving her and she finds herself in the grip over an overwhelming compulsion to binge. The more frantic she feels the greater her compulsion. She is terrified that she is losing the control she believed she had over food. She is now caught in binge-eating hell, where every mouthful fills her with fear and disgust yet she can't stop gorging every day. Then, as if in answer to a prayer, Julie discovers she can vomit. This means she is going to be able to binge as much and as often as she likes and vomit up every last bit, so she is never going to have to put on weight no matter how much she eats.

Julie has now entered the bulimic stage of her illness. Within a matter of weeks her addiction escalates to the point where she is bingeing and vomiting five or six times a day. She retreats from the real world of university life, friends, lectures, essays, and spends most of her time hiding, furtive, guilty, using. She goes shopping in supermarkets where her bulk buying of binge foods will not be noticed. If the person on the checkout makes a passing comment, Julie says she is having a party. She makes excuses for missing lectures by saying she is depressed or suffering from stress, so her lecturers do not confront her. Her friends stop inviting her out because she makes it plain that she does not enjoy their company as she always has one eye on the time and says she has to leave early. She spends a good deal of her time locked in the lavatory. She has to spend a lot of money on toilet cleaners, air fresheners, toothpastes, mouthwash, and deodorants, because she is never really sure if the smell of vomit is lingering on her, and she does not want anyone to guess what she is doing in there.

In Julie's case bulimia is not just a psychological problem based on a fear of being fat. Julie has learnt that when she binges and then purges she experiences, for a short time, a relief from the intolerable pressures of life, a numbing of the emotions which confuse and distress her, and a brief feeling of euphoria. When she binges and purges she feels good, everything's OK and life's problems recede. Julie's response to any kind of stress, any new situation, indeed to any feeling, is now to binge and purge. This has become the way in which she deals with life and she has become dependent on this behaviour. It doesn't matter that the moments of euphoria are getting less and that she has to binge and vomit more and more for less and less relief. The worse she feels the more she is compelled to act out on her addiction. Julie is out of control. She is powerless over her addiction. Her urge to binge and vomit is more powerful than she is. She is experiencing serious harmful consequences, to herself and to the people around her, but she does not know what is happening to her and she is unable to stop her behaviour.

As her food addiction escalates and progresses, Julie begins to develop new compulsive behaviours. As well as purging by vomiting she purges with laxatives. She does not just take one or two and wait for them to work. She takes them compulsively, sometimes by the handful; on some days she may take forty or fifty. They can never work enough for Julie; no matter how many times or ways she purges herself she can never feel empty and clean enough. Doctors will not prescribe slimming pills for Julie but now she is at university she becomes aware that drugs are available to buy illegally. Some of the students use amphetamine and cocaine when they go to clubs and parties and it is not difficult for Julie to get hold of some. Julie discovers that these drugs give her plenty of energy, so she can exercise harder, and take away her appetite so she is not tormented by hungry feelings any more. Julie takes to stimulant drugs like a duck to water. She loves them. She can't get enough of them.

With the artificial energy provided by stimulants, Julie perks up and goes shopping. She discovers that she feels good when she buys herself something nice and new to wear. She has got a cupboard full of little Lycra outfits to wear when she is working out. She has got more pairs of trainers than one person can use, but she can't resist buying more and only the best brands will do. She doesn't let the fact that she can't afford it stop her. She's got a credit card. Every time she gets a letter from the bank she puts it unopened in a drawer and feels so frightened that she has to binge and vomit. In her frantic efforts to escape reality Julie is totally out of control. In spite of serious and mounting consequences she cannot stop.

As we saw in Chapter One, addictive illness harms the sufferer physically, emotionally, cognitively, and spiritually. This is a list of the damage being done to Julie **physically**. In the anorexic phase of her illness Julie loses a quarter of her body weight. She stops menstruating. Her skin becomes dry and flaky and her hair starts falling out. As she becomes more malnourished and starved she starts to develop a fine growth of hair over her body – her body's attempt to stop her dying of hypothermia. In the compulsive overeating phase she becomes obese, which increases her risk of developing diabetes and puts extra strain on her heart. In the bulimic phase of her illness Julie experiences fatigue, weakness, aching muscles, faintness, chills, and cold sweats. These symptoms are caused by fluctuations in her blood sugar levels as a result of bingeing and vomiting. She has bowel problems as a result of her laxative abuse and suffers what the laxative manufacturers refer to as 'anal leakage'. When she is not having diarrhoea she is constipated. Her teeth are decaying because vomited stomach acid has eroded their enamel. She has frequent throat infections and lesions where she has damaged the delicate skin at the back of her throat by inducing vomiting with her fingers. Vomiting has caused the fine blood vessels in her face and eyes to rupture so her eyes are bloodshot and her complexion is red and blotchy. She is deficient in the hormone oestrogen so her bones are deteriorating and becoming brittle. In her mid-twenties Julie has the bone density of a seventy-year-old woman. She has an imbalance in her electrolyte levels and her low level of potassium is causing her heart to beat irregularly. If any drug or alcohol addict thinks food addiction is not dangerous, they are wrong.

Emotionally Julie suffers all the painful feelings that chemically dependent people feel. In her case the feelings of shame and self-hate are especially strong. People who are addicted to chemicals are able to see themselves as separate from the chemical: the drug is over there on the table, in a bottle or a pill or a powder. For food addicts it is more difficult to make this conceptual differentiation. Our relationship with food is primal: straight after birth the baby is put to the breast. At the beginning of life taking food comes second only to breathing. Food is ingested into the body and becomes part of it, in a way that alcohol and drugs do not. It is harder for a food addict to say this is me, and that is my addiction, when the food has become part of the body and is seen as part of the self. Heroin addicts can come to hate their heroin. Alcoholics can come to hate their alcohol. Food addicts can come to hate the food on the plate and the food which constitutes their body. To recover from addiction addicts need to be able to distinguish 'the person I am' from 'the addiction I have'. They can hate the addiction they have, but they will find it very hard indeed to make an emotional and spiritual recovery if they hate the person they are. Because food addiction feels like an intrinsic part of the sufferer's self, self-hate can be a big problem for food addicts. It is, however, just a block on the road to recovery and not, as food addicts may believe, an essential part of who they are.

Regarding **cognitive** damage, a food addict's ability to concentrate, process information, and retain it are severely compromised by their preoccupation with food. As well as general preoccupation, anorexics in particular suffer damage to their thinking processes when their weight falls below a certain level. As starvation approaches the body goes into survival mode and all functions not essential to life are gradually shut down in order to keep the heart and lungs functioning. At The Rehab we did not admit anyone in the anorexic phase whose weight had fallen below five stone because their cognitive ability at that time had been reduced to the point where they were not able to meet the intellectual requirements of our treatment[10] programme.

The **spiritual** damage done by addiction, including food addiction, is severe. As we have seen, its main features are: withdrawal from community, isolation, alienation, sense of emptiness or meaninglessness, erosion of moral values, and deluded sense of power or control. The addict is out of right relationship with other people and with the community at large and is locked in a love-hate relationship where only they and their addiction are present. For the food addict who identifies their physical self with their addiction, the alienation is from themselves as well as from other people. The bulimic who stuffs their body with junk food whenever they get the opportunity has a gnawing sense of spiritual emptiness which nothing can fill. The anorexic who feels so in control that they can deny their body food until they starve to death is actually unable to control any aspect of their life. Repulsed by lumpen reality they seek to become transparent and disappear like a soap bubble.

In the chapter Transference of Dependency I suggested that if someone is concerned about something they are doing more and more frequently and fear that it may be becoming an addiction, they can check it out against the defining characteristics of addiction and see how many boxes it ticks. To strengthen my theory that anorexia, compulsive overeating, and bulimia really are addiction, I will apply the test to Julie and see how well it fits. The defining characteristics are these: preoccupation, using alone, using for effect, using as a medicine, protection of supply, using

---

[10] The 12 Step programme itself does not require any particular level of intelligence or cognitive ability. The Rehab's treatment programme, however, did.

more than planned, increased tolerance, withdrawal symptoms, an erosion of moral values, and serious unwanted consequences. As we shall see, Julie scores positive on all counts.

Julie is certainly **preoccupied** with food, whether avoiding it or stocking up for a binge. Like any addict with their drug of choice she is unable to get on with the daily tasks of life because she is constantly thinking about calories, body weight, where to buy her binge food, where to hide it, how to avoid eating with other people, and how to dispose of the evidence after bingeing and vomiting. It seems that everywhere she looks there is food, or an advertisement for food, or people eating. When she turns on her television there are programmes about food and cooking competitions and famous cooks telling her how to make death by chocolate. Thoughts of food fill her head and she gets no relief until she acts on them.

She certainly **uses alone**. For years she has been unable to eat in the presence of other people. In her overeating and bulimic phases there is no way on earth she is going to let anyone see how she eats. From residents in The Rehab I have heard many accounts of bingeing behaviour. Julie's account is one of these: 'I would prepare everything carefully. I had all my binge foods lined up in order of colour. I would eat something red first. That's so that when I threw it back up I could see the red and know it was all out.' 'My binge foods were sugar and margarine. I used to mix a bag of sugar with a tub of soft margarine and scoop it all in with my hands. It was easy to throw up.' 'I would start off with my biscuits and chocolate, then move on to anything else I could find. One day last week I ate six packets of biscuits then ate all the stuff in the fridge whether it was cooked or not. I stood at the fridge and ate with my fingers, I didn't cut it up or anything, I just crammed it in my mouth as fast as I could.' 'When I'd eaten all the food it wasn't enough. I went through the rubbish bin and ate all the scraps that had been thrown away.' Julie doesn't just eat alone because she thinks an onlooker would find her way of eating disgusting; she eats alone because this is her special time when she can be alone with her addiction. Addiction has become her primary relationship, her lover, her soulmate. She is not going to let anyone else get a look in.

Julie **uses for effect**. She does not choose her binge foods because she particularly likes the taste of them. She chooses them because she can vomit them up easily. She does not eat to satisfy hunger or to socialise, or even to provide the nourishment she needs to live. She eats to excess because that is her way of getting relief from the cravings that overwhelm her. Julie is different from someone who is simply greedy. There is a difference between a greedy person who loves the taste of cream buns, buys three to share with her friends but eats them all herself, and Julie who will eat as many cream buns as she can lay hands on whether she likes them or not. Julie **uses as a medicine**, to numb emotional pain or to get high. I cannot believe that anyone would eat a whole tub of margarine mixed with a kilo of sugar and then make themselves vomit because they enjoy it.

Like any addict Julie **protects her supply**. At the back of her wardrobe or under her bed is a box of binge foods. If she shares a house these foods are not kept in the kitchen and are not for general consumption. Julie feels anxious and insecure if she does not have ready access to a supply of special foods which she keeps for when the urge to use overcomes her. With her supply safely hidden Julie can relax a little. She will on no account share these foods and woe betide anyone who tries to take them from her. One food addict at The Rehab became hostile to the point of threatening violence when I confiscated her last packet of sweets which she had hidden in one of her Wellington boots.

In the bulimic phase of her addiction Julie plans her binges. She makes sure that everything she will need is ready to hand: binge foods, toilet cleaned and ready to be vomited into, drink of water, tissues, hair band to tie back her hair. She has been doing this many times every day for a long time so knows what she will need. At this point '**using more than planned**' does not apply to the amount of binge food she uses but to how frequently she uses. She may plan to binge and vomit once, but when she starts bingeing she cannot consistently predict how many times she will binge that day. Sometimes she carries on bingeing and vomiting until she is exhausted and falls asleep surrounded by the empty packets and cartons of the food she has compulsively eaten. Compulsive overeaters who are not bulimic will use more than planned in the sense that once they take their first compulsive bite they cannot consistently predict when they will stop eating. These are the people who once they start can eat until the food cupboards are empty, or who graze constantly throughout the day. 'Using more than planned' describes loss of control and is the mark of addiction. Nobody eats out of rubbish bins without a pretty compelling reason to do so. In spite of her compulsive spending on clothes Julie does have some money left to buy food and she is not starving. She eats other people's leftovers in the same way as an alcoholic drinks the dregs of other people's drinks, because she's out of control and her addiction is more powerful than she is. Looking at Julie's story we can clearly see that she is not in control of her eating. She starves herself to get high and she binges to get numb. She is using food to mood alter in the same way as any other addict uses their drug of choice to mood alter, and until she learns a different way to manage her emotions she will be dependent on using it – unless she finds a more efficient way of mood altering, which Julie is about to do with cocaine.

Julie ticks the '**increased tolerance**' box too. Food addiction escalates like any chemical dependency. Julie may start bingeing and purging once a week. This soon becomes once a day. In a short time she is making herself sick ten, twenty times a day. No matter how frequently she does it she cannot achieve the euphoric high she had the first time she did it. She is putting her body under tremendous strain and her stomach muscles are not going to recover from this abuse for a long time, if ever. She vomits now automatically and no longer needs fingers or other implements down her throat to induce it. As her tolerance increases she can vomit on demand. Her body is so used to it, it does it by itself with minimum effort from her.

While it is true that Julie does not have physical **withdrawal symptoms** in the way that drug and alcohol addicts do, she does have very painful emotions when she first stops acting out with food. Physical withdrawal symptoms can be minimised with the right doses of prescribed medication, but there are no painkillers which will medicate the emotional agony of losing your only way of coping with life. Like any addict Julie found in addiction a way of taking the edge off emotions that she felt unable to bear. Now her addiction is taken away Julie is left missing it, craving it, and grieving for it. On top of that she has to experience the re-emergence of the original pain she was trying to escape from in the first place. Withdrawal from dependency is hellish. I think sometimes that emotional withdrawal can be even worse than physical withdrawal. At least with physical withdrawal you know what is happening to you, you understand that this is withdrawal and will not last forever. With emotional withdrawal you feel mad and raw and desperate but you don't know why. If you don't see eating disorders as addiction you will not be able to understand your experience as withdrawal and therefore temporary. You feel like you're going to die and that there will be no end to it.

As with any other addict there is an **erosion of** Julie's **moral values.** A well brought up, intelligent girl from an affluent family, she grew up with a set of moral values. She believed in love, equality, fair play, honesty, loyalty, being kind and respectful. In the course of her addiction she has been dishonest, deceitful, manipulative, unkind, and utterly self-centred. She has lied, stolen, broken the law, abandoned her responsibilities, and hurt a lot of people. Another box ticked.

The final characteristic is **serious unwanted consequences**. Nothing of any good whatsoever is coming from Julie's behaviour. Every aspect of her life is falling apart as a direct result of her obsessive-compulsive behaviour. Anybody can get things wrong sometimes and get serious unwanted consequences as a result. I would suggest that the only people who carry on doing something for years on end in spite of getting ever more serious unwanted consequences are addicts.

I hope that by now the theory that anorexia, compulsive over-eating, and bulimia are food addiction is looking more convincing. It may be hard to understand why this behaviour should relieve stress or numb emotional pain. On the face of it this behaviour seems irrational and bizarre. Why would anyone choose to behave like this, living a secret life, starving, or bingeing and vomiting five, ten, twenty times a day? The way I have come to make sense of it is to see it as addiction. When I see how the symptoms and the personality profile fits, it all becomes quite simple. If we consider Julie, with her weak ego, lack of openness, hyper-sensitivity, guilt proneness, melancholia, and emotionality, we see a person who fits the profile of someone predisposed to become addicted to something; and if we consider her behaviour we see it measures up perfectly to the defining characteristics of addiction.

Eating disorders cause a huge amount of suffering and are

notoriously difficult to treat. In Britain now there is increasing concern by health professionals and the government about the rise of obesity and consequent cost to the National Health Service. The medical response to this looming health crisis is to focus on eating less and exercising more, or cutting out sugar and eating more vegetables. I'm afraid to say that this response is likely to have little success with the at risk people who are addicted. Their problem is that they are in an unhealthy relationship with food and to get well they need to change themselves and the way they attempt to get their emotional needs met. They are already obsessed with food; they need to think about it less, not more. Doctors who perform stomach stapling surgery on the most morbidly obese patients find it hard to understand why, even after this drastic life-saving intervention, their patient lapses back into destructive eating patterns. It makes sense to me: they are addicted and while their body may have been treated, their addiction has not been addressed at all.

I will now look at how the 12 Steps of Alcoholics Anonymous have been adapted for use by food addicts and describe how we developed a treatment plan for food addicts at The Rehab. My aim will be to show that understanding this condition as addiction, and treating it as such by applying the 12 Steps, offers a pathway to recovery and freedom from this distressing and destructive illness.

The 12 Step programme has been adapted widely by groups of people recovering from various addictions, compulsive behaviours, and mental health problems. This is because while the programme itself is proven to be effective for any addiction people feel more comfortable attending meetings where addicts similar to themselves are sharing their experiences. Of the thirty-six or more Anonymous groups in Britain, at least four are focused on food addiction. The ones I know of are Overeaters Anonymous (OA), Food Addicts in Recovery (FA), Food Addicts Anonymous (FAA) and Anorexics and Bulimics Anonymous (ABA). The way to distinguish the different beliefs of each group is to look at its Step 1 and see what you need to abstain from.

Step 1 of **OA** says 'We admitted we were powerless over food' and defines abstinence as 'the action of refraining from compulsive eating and compulsive food behaviours while working towards or maintaining a healthy body weight.' Furthermore the OA program suggests that members identify the particular foods that 'trigger' overeating and abstain from them.

FA believes that food addicts have an allergy to flour, sugar, and large quantities. This allergy results in an uncontrollable craving, which can be arrested one day at a time by the action of weighing and measuring food and abstaining completely from all flour and sugar. So FA defines abstinence as weighed and measured meals with nothing in between, no flour, no sugar, and the avoidance of any individual binge foods.

FAA believes that there is sometimes a link between alcohol addiction and food addiction, and has a suggested a food plan that calls for abstinence from sugar, flour, and wheat, but says this is not designed as a diet or weight loss programme.

ABA's Step 1 says 'We admitted we were powerless over our insane eating patterns' and believes that the 'drug' over which members are powerless is 'the feeling of being in control of our food, exercise, and body weight and shape'. In order to recover therefore 'we need to surrender all control of our food, exercise, and body weight and shape to a higher power', where the 'higher power' at first works through other recovering people.

Of these four groups the one closest to my understanding of food addiction is ABA, so it was upon these beliefs that we developed the treatment plan for use in The Rehab with food addicts like Julie. Throughout the different stages in her food addiction Julie had been obsessed with her weight. She weighed herself numerous times a day, before and after purging to see if there was any tiny weight gain or loss. At one stage she had been obsessed with calorie counting and weighing and measuring food. She had been obsessive about one diet after another and cut out or added particular foods as the latest diet demanded. For Julie weighing and measuring food and cutting out certain items are not going to give her relief from her addiction as these are the very things she cannot control once she starts. Nor is 'working towards or maintaining a healthy body weight' going to help her. She has been trying to control her body weight and shape for years without success. Furthermore she now has no idea what a healthy body weight looks like because she thinks she looks fat even when the mirror shows her to be thin.

If Julie decides to work the OA programme she is going to be met with a big problem in the very first Step. Whatever she is powerless over, she needs to abstain from. OA's Step 1 tells her 'We admitted we were powerless over food', but Julie cannot abstain from food or she will starve to death. The OA position is that, in the same way as alcoholics need to drink but do not need to drink alcohol to live, so food addicts need to eat but do not need to eat trigger foods to live. The difficulty with this is that Julie may have favourite binge foods but these are not necessarily the triggers to active addiction. Her active addiction, when she experiences a loss of control, is when she first become preoccupied with planning a binge. In this sense she is out of control before any 'trigger foods' touch her lips. To maintain the simile, alcoholics may favour whisky but it is not necessarily the whisky which triggers their out of control drinking. Alcoholics who are preoccupied with drinking are out of control before they open the bottle, in the sense that nothing is going to come between them and alcohol once they get the determination to use it.

ABA's Step 1, 'We admitted we were powerless over our insane eating patterns', avoids all mention of weighing and measuring and body weight and trigger foods, and to my mind hits the nail right on the head. Julie is powerless over her insane eating patterns, so she needs to abstain from her insane eating patterns. It is not food that is the problem for Julie, it is what she does with it that is the problem. Just like any other addiction, the problem does not lie in the substance or behaviour itself, but in the addictive personality of the addict who is unable to control their use of it. The way to recovery for Julie therefore is to take the focus off food and put it on her behaviour patterns.

To help residents like Julie, The Rehab devised an eating plan. It was not a diet and did not specify foods to be excluded or included. It was based on three moderate meals a day with a light snack at specified times, no purging, no weighing herself, and moderate exercise only. Julie, with guidance from her counsellor

131

and suggestions from her peer group, decided what she was going to eat and her abstinence was her sticking to eating as specified on her eating plan. She was responsible for eating and exercising as planned and her body weight and shape was left to her genetic inheritance (or 'power greater than herself' if you prefer) to decide. This simple plan was based on the premise that if Julie eats and exercises moderately she will end up the weight that is healthy for her. It may be thinner or fatter than anyone else but it is the weight and shape she is supposed to be; and if she does not like it she can be helped to change her attitude towards her body rather than trying to change her body itself. Even more important than this, she will be free from her obsessive thinking and compulsive behaviour which is making her life such a misery.

Julie sat down with a counsellor and decided what she was going to eat and when. Actually, she did not have unlimited choice in this because she was in a residential rehab where meals were cooked by a chef and the menus designed to provide a healthy balance of different food types. Also meals were served at set times in the dining room where residents ate together. As well as a choice of vegetarian or meat menu, the decisions left to Julie were what out of the available options she wanted to eat for breakfast, what she wanted to eat for the three snacks during the day, and whether or not she wanted to eat dessert at dinner time. She also had the opportunity to write on her plan particular foods she really hated (in her case fish and beetroot) which she would not be expected to eat if it turned up on the menu for that day. It was important to think carefully about what she wrote on her plan because she was going to eat like this every day until her counsellor and peers decided she may make an amendment. I have included a copy of The Rehab's full eating plan and contract in Appendix 3.

A resident in the anorexic phase of food addiction would have an eating plan specifying small portions and would probably have cereal with milk or one slice of toast for breakfast, a piece of fruit for daytime snacks, no desserts and two crackers for evening snack. As that resident became more used to eating the amounts would gradually be increased to moderate. The conditions of the plan and the contract signed by the resident are the same for all food addicts.

It was important for Julie that she did not have a special menu but ate what was cooked for all the residents. For years she had been alone with her 'insane eating patterns' and, because she had never admitted to anyone how she was behaving, over time she came regard herself as unique. She did not know that she was a classic case of someone with food addiction and she did not know that other people acted as she did. It was a revelation to Julie that she was not alone and that other addicts identified with her out of control eating and with her feelings. At first she was fearful of sharing about her addiction as she thought her peers would be disgusted by what she said and not accept her. Instead she found that she was identified with, cared about, and supported as she took her first steps towards recovery. She worked the same Steps as her peers and she ate the same food as her peers. Every day she sat at the table and ate with them and gradually she came to believe that it was possible for her to eat like other people.

In The Rehab there was a small tuck shop where residents could buy themselves one treat a day. After she had eaten according to her original plan for a couple of weeks Julie asked if she too could buy from the tuck shop. Her eating plan was amended to accommodate this and some days she would opt for a bar of chocolate or a packet of crisps and eat it at a snack time. This approach is different from the abstinence plan of OA. The emphasis here is entirely on abstaining from the compulsive behaviour she did around food. This plan would go with Julie after she completed treatment and would become her habitual way of eating. If treats like chocolate or a piece of cake were not allowed for Julie she would have had to sit with her peers while they ate their treats, building up a resentment and a preoccupation with not being allowed to eat them. If there is one sure way to make addicts preoccupied and start craving something it is to tell them that they are never allowed to have it again.

It was not easy for Julie to abstain from her behaviours. When she felt anxious before group therapy she had the urge to vomit. After eating her meals she felt bloated and ugly and hated the thought that her body was building up layers of fat. She had strong urges to vomit after meals, which was why her plan required her to stay in the communal area with her peers for twenty minutes and share these thoughts and feelings. After twenty minutes she would consider it too late to vomit and the only action open to her to deal with her anxiety was to talk about it with people who would understand her and appreciate how brave she was to be so open and honest. Another difficulty Julie faced was that she did not know what a 'moderate' plateful looked like. This was defined by her counsellor as one layer of food covering the plate within the rim. The plates provided for residents were of a moderate size, which gave her a basis from which to work. Here the feedback from her peers was invaluable. Julie was responsible for serving herself and was expected to eat everything she put on her plate. If she took too much of one item or too less of another her peers told her that was not moderate and she adjusted her portions accordingly.

In eating this way Julie is working Steps 1, 2, and 3. She is admitting she is powerless over her addicted ways of eating and is abstaining from them. She is sharing the consequences of her food addiction and coming to realise how she has hurt other people as well as herself. She is working Step 2 by coming to believe that she can be restored to 'sane' eating, and she is working Step 3 by deciding to trust her peers to tell her what is moderate and what is not. Further, she is working Step 3 by deciding that she is not in control of her body weight and shape and trusts that if she eats healthily and exercises moderately her weight and shape will look after themselves. She may not have a 'god of her understanding' at this point, but she has put her trust in other people which is all that is required at this stage.

After a couple of months of following her eating plan Julie began to notice changes. The first thing she noticed was that she was experiencing hunger. For the first time in years her stomach was telling her when she needed to eat. By listening to her body Julie came to recognise when it was coming up to lunch time and dinner time, and she started to enjoy looking forward to a good meal. She experienced this as entirely different from the cravings she had had for bingeing and vomiting, and was happy that she could now start to trust her appetite to tell her when she needed nourishment. At the same time she noticed that as well as looking forward to meals she was enjoying the food she ate. She was so used to eating for effect it had been a long time since she had actually paid attention to the taste of what she was eating. Now

Julie is discovering the joys of eating food which tastes good. Food is no longer her enemy, a powerful demon determined to make her fat; it is becoming an ally and even at times a pleasure.

Other changes which Julie came to notice were an improvement in her physical health. Her hair, which had been thin and brittle, started to grow and became fuller and glossy. She went to the hairdresser's and got a new style which really suited her and made her feel great. She started menstruating again, and felt relieved as she had feared that maybe her food addiction had affected her fertility and she wanted to have children at some time in the future. Her energy returned and she enjoyed being able to go for walks in the countryside instead of having to exercise until she was exhausted. Her body clock re-set itself and she felt tired at bedtime and refreshed in the morning. She did also gain some weight. She was abstaining from weighing herself but knew she had put on some weight when her jeans got a bit tight. This caused her some anxiety but she did not panic; she re-affirmed her decision to trust her healthy eating plan and accepted that if it was healthy for her to be a few pounds heavier than she had been, well so be it. She bought some bigger jeans.

The day came when Julie announced in group therapy that she had just realised that she had not been preoccupied with food and eating for some time. Because she had whole-heartedly accepted her eating plan she knew what she was going to eat and when, so she did not need to think about it all the time. Such is the nature of preoccupation that that you don't consciously recognise it until it has gone. This was a huge relief to Julie and evidence that the programme was working for her. As well as just a hope that recovery was possible, Julie now had a real belief that it was. Boosted by this success Julie applied herself to her 12 Step programme with even greater commitment. At the start of treatment she had done what she was told whether or not she believed it would work; now she knew it did work she embraced the programme on a deeper level and made it her own.

When Julie came to Step 4 she found it hard to take personal inventory. She was all too ready to write at length about her blocks to recovery, which she referred to as 'defects'. This itself was a symptom of her biggest blocks which were shame and self-hate. Most residents when working Step 4 to some extent identified guilt and shame as blocks they needed to overcome but for Julie, who had hated her body so much for so long, even pre-dating her food addiction, shame which amounted to self-loathing was a deeply-rooted problem. It was not much help telling Julie she needed to love herself. Although this was true Julie had no idea how to do it and doubted that it would be possible.

To help her at least appreciate her body she was given an assignment to help her develop an attitude of gratitude. She realised she had much to be grateful for: she still had her own teeth, even if they did need a few fillings; her heart, lungs, kidneys, liver, and muscles were all in working order; she had two of everything she needed two of, and after all it was the only body she was ever going to have so she had better make friends with it instead of fighting it. In this sense Julie needed to make amends to her body for the way in which she had hated and punished it. When she came to Step 8 she put her body on her amends list, and in Step 9 she began to act in a loving way to her body by giving herself pampering relaxing baths and nourishing her skin with moisturisers. When she looked in a mirror she focused on the bits of her body she did like and ignored the bits she did not. It was a breakthrough for Julie the day she went for a massage. By revealing her body to another woman and allowing herself to be touched in a safe way Julie reached a new level of acceptance. She discovered that the way to self-acceptance came through acting in a self-respecting way, and the way to self-love came through acting in a self-loving way.

When we first met Julie she was ill and alone, lost in a nightmare from which she could see no way out. Working the 12 Steps has transformed her life. By admitting her powerlessness over her addiction she has found freedom. By deciding to trust other people she has found that she is no longer alone. By taking her inventory she has come to see that she is not perfect and she does not need to be; she has many assets and is valued and cared about by many people. As she abstains from her addict behaviour she experiences physical recovery. As she shares her feelings and other people share their feelings with her she experiences emotional recovery. As her preoccupation leaves her she experiences cognitive recovery. And as part of a group of peers she starts on a journey of spiritual recovery which will take her as far as she wishes to go.

Recovery is not quick and does not end at the completion of treatment. Julie lays the foundations of her recovery in The Rehab but develops and enriches it in the meeting rooms of her 12 Step group. Before treatment Julie's particular sense of uniqueness came from her addictive behaviour. She felt special when she over or under ate and worthless when she did not. She always had a deep down fear that if she did not behave this way she would lose her sense of being special. Without her identity as an anorexic or bulimic who would she be? What if she did all this hard work of changing and becoming her 'real self' and people did not like her? By facing her fear head on and recovering anyway, Julie is discovering that recovery is making her more special, not less. Maybe not everyone will like her, but she need not let that bother her. She knows she is likeable and that the people who matter to her love her. On the foundation of Step 1 Julie builds her recovery, clean, precious, and free.

Chapter Five

Behavioural Addictions

In this chapter I will consider various self-defeating behaviour patterns and aim to reinforce the theory that all 'addictions' are basically the same and the 12 Step programme offers a route to recovery from all of them. In previous chapters we have seen how there are certain people who are predisposed to become addicted to chemicals. These people are also predisposed to become addicted to behaviours. These are people who find that certain behaviours make them feel euphoric or soothe painful emotions and who over time come to think obsessively about these behaviours and act on them compulsively in spite of serious unwanted consequences.

During my years at The Rehab I have worked with residents who exemplify these behavioural addictions and I will refer to these people in this chapter. To protect their anonymity I have changed their names and any descriptions which may identify them. The behavioural addictions I will consider are perhaps the most commonly found and are, in no particular order, gambling, self-harming, spending, working, cleaning, and eating disorders. Eating disorders or food addiction has been given a chapter to itself. This of course is not an exhaustive list as addicts can become addicted to anything. If you think about it obsessively, act on it compulsively, can't consistently predict when you will stop once you start, and continue to do it even when experiencing serious unwanted consequences, you are addicted to it whether it's injecting heroin, eating ice-cream, posting on Facebook, or washing your hands.

The Rehab was registered as a treatment centre for 'younger adults suffering from chemical dependency', which means people aged between eighteen and sixty-five who are addicted to alcohol or drugs; so all our residents were chemically dependent and some in addition were dependent on certain behaviours. Whatever their dependencies they all followed the same 12 Step treatment programme, the only significant difference being the wording of Step 1. Alcoholics who were also gamblers admitted they were powerless over alcohol and over gambling; alcoholics who were also co-dependent admitted they were powerless over alcohol and over other people; drug addicts who were also self-harmers admitted they were powerless over chemicals and over self-harming, and so on. Some residents were powerless over four or five behaviours as well as chemicals. Introduction in group therapy could have become long and tedious if every person present listed all their dependencies: 'My name is John and I am powerless over alcohol, drugs, online poker, computer games, and self-harming.' 'My name is Janet and I am powerless over alcohol, dieting, relationships, exercising, and cleaning.' In our group therapy everyone used the same introduction: 'My name is ..., I have an addictive illness.' Another way of saying this is 'My name is ..., I am powerless over my addiction' or, if you prefer, 'My name is..., my addiction is more powerful than I am.'

Robert, alcoholic and gambler

Let me introduce you to Robert. Robert is in his forties, the only son of affluent parents, public school educated, a professor in a British university. He has a large home, a loving wife, and two delightful children. He is also an alcoholic and a compulsive gambler. He started drinking socially in his late teens and drank heavily throughout his years as a student. It was while he was an undergraduate that he met Ann, his wife-to-be. They both enjoyed a full social life and both often drank to excess. On completion of his postgraduate studies Robert got married and was appointed as a lecturer in a university near his home town. With a generous wedding gift from his parents plus his and his wife's incomes Robert was able to buy a beautiful home in a pleasant part of the country. By the time he was thirty Robert was the father of two healthy babies and everything was set fair for a happy ever after.

Before she was married Ann had enjoyed drinking with Robert. He had been spontaneous and fun. She had found it exciting when he swept her off for a summer driving through Europe in a camper van, touring the vineyards, sampling the wines. She thought it was romantic and glamorous when he bought her an evening gown and took her to a casino in Monte Carlo for her twenty-first birthday. As she got older, however, Ann matured. When her children were born she gladly embraced the responsibilities of parenthood. She did not want to go to parties so often and did not want to drink until she was drunk. She still enjoyed a good bottle of wine with a meal and often invited friends to dinner parties, but she drank moderately and for pleasure and when she had had enough she said so. She started to see Robert in a new light.

Robert had said he wanted children but after the pride and joy of the babies' births he did little to involve himself with their care. He didn't change nappies and he didn't read bedtime stories. He said he was too busy earning a living to keep the family in the manner to which they had become accustomed and did not have the time or energy to cater for the needs of little children. Anyway Ann was such a good mother, she was much better at all that than he was, and the children were perfectly happy and wanted for nothing, so that was all right then. Robert continued to enjoy university life. He was surrounded by bright young students who drank a lot and members of the intelligentsia who also drank a lot. Robert had been drinking heavily as a student and continued to do so as a parent. The qualities of spontaneity and fun which Ann had found so attractive in her twenties looked more like irresponsibility and selfishness now she was older. Sometimes Ann thought she did not have two children, she had three. Robert was behaving as if he had never left university, which in a sense was true.

As time went on Ann became more and more resentful of the way Robert was behaving. He came home from work late saying he had been working on an important research project. He saw very little of the children because they were usually in bed when he got home. He smelled of alcohol when he came home from work, saying he had had a glass of wine with colleagues, and drank a bottle of wine in the evening to relax after a hard day's work. He started having to go away at weekends to attend conferences or talk about his research findings with academics at other universities. He was sure Ann would understand as she was always so supportive of his career, and she knew he only did all this for the sake of her and the children, didn't she? And the day would come when they had enough money to finance the children's education and take early retirement in comfort, so she really had nothing to complain about, did she?

As Robert's absences became more frequent Ann started to fear that he was having an affair. Eventually she asked him outright and he swore by all that was holy that he was not. She found no evidence to justify her suspicions and her friends could find out nothing about another woman so Ann came to accept that Robert was just being Robert, selfish, inconsiderate, immature, and unreliable. She decided that as she was to all intents and purposes a single parent she had better start behaving like one. She stopped expecting Robert to pull his weight as a husband and father and got on with raising her children practically by herself with help from her parents and in-laws. As the children got older she got on with her own career and gradually became more independent and self-reliant.

Ann's world fell apart the day her bank card got refused in the supermarket. When she went to the bank to ask why, she was told that the joint account she had with Robert was empty. The next day she received a letter from a company she did not recognise telling her that the debt on her credit card now stood at ten thousand pounds and if she did not start to make payments within seven days legal proceedings would be commenced. Ann was astounded. She did not have a credit card from the bank in question and had certainly not run up a ten-thousand pound debt. She rang Robert, who was staying in a hotel attending a week-long academic conference. His voice sounded rather strained on the phone but he assured her it must be a mistake, a case of identity theft, you heard a lot about that these days, and he would sort it all out when he got back in a few days' time. Ann made a few more phone calls and what she discovered shocked her to the core. Robert was not at a conference. He had been suspended from work because complaints had been made by his students that he was often drunk during tutorials. He had not been attending academic meetings, indeed he had been forced to give up his research project some time ago as his work had been well below the required standard and he had been accused of plagiarism, which brought the university into disrepute. Ann searched everything in Robert's wardrobe, looking for clues as to what he had been doing and especially what he had spent the money on. She was expecting to find receipts for luxury holidays for two or expensive pieces of jewellery. She did not find any of these. What she did find was a betting slip, and in Robert's locked and private desk along with half a dozen other credit cards she found a little book in which was recorded a list of all his winnings and losses and all the people to whom he owed money.

Worse was to come. Robert came home in a pathetic state. He was horribly hung over, tearful, afraid and ashamed. He begged Ann's forgiveness and promised to tell her the truth, the whole truth, and nothing but the truth. He told her that he had borrowed money from his parents, saying it was to buy things for the children, and spent it in casinos. He told her he had borrowed money from all their friends and lost it on roulette. He told her he had somehow, she did not completely understand how, managed to apply for a credit card in her name and had destroyed the bank statements when they arrived. He did not tell her that he had emptied the children's savings accounts and failed to make mortgage payments on the house. She was to find that out later.

Robert appeared a broken man. He told Ann he loved her and begged her to help him. He said he would do anything, anything, if only she would give him one chance. Ann said she would give him one chance and one only: if he went into rehab and committed himself to recovery from both alcohol and gambling addiction she would put on hold the divorce proceedings she had already started. One week later Robert was admitted to The Rehab.

Robert's parents were church-goers and he had been brought up to believe in God. He had not practised his religion or attended church since his childhood but he retained the faith of his upbringing and had no resistance to the use of 'God' in the 12 Steps. What he did have resistance to was everything else in the Steps. Within a week the broken, ashamed, and fearful Robert had pieced himself together again and become the witty raconteur, telling his fellow residents amusing stories of his escapades, how he won huge amounts of money in glamorous casinos, and kept a well-stocked cellar of fine wines in his country house. His group of assorted alcoholics, drug addicts, gamblers, criminals, and fraudsters smiled grimly and said 'Welcome to The Rehab, Robert. You're in the right place.'

In common with all the other residents Robert spent his first six weeks working on Step 1. By writing down and sharing in group therapy specific examples of how he had experienced a loss of control after taking his first drink or placing his first bet Robert came to admit that he was indeed addicted to alcohol and gambling. By receiving feedback from his peers and staff Robert came to realise that his addicted behaviour had caused grievous damage to his family. As his denial was eroded he came to see that his amusing stories were nothing more than the deluded bragging of an immature self-centred man. Robert started to feel very uncomfortable. He wasn't James Bond any more, suave in his tuxedo, king of the casino, and his stories did not seem so glamorous now.

As well as the financial damage he had done to his wife, children, parents, and friends, Robert had to face up to the reality of the emotional damage he had done to them. His wife had grown away from him, developing her own friendships, interests, and career. She was becoming ever more independent both emotionally and financially and, truth be told, she had been managing her life and her family without his support for so long that she really did not need him any more. He had become a liability, one more person she had to take responsibility for, and she was not sure whether she had the energy or the will to do it. She had grown to become strong and capable and sensible because she had had to, but that did not mean she was not emotionally vulnerable. She was deeply hurt and extremely angry because of the way he had lied to her and stolen from her, and, even worse in her eyes, the way he had neglected and stolen from their children.

When Ann and the children came to visit Robert in The Rehab it was immediately clear that none of them found the visit easy. The children were very good. They greeted their father politely. They sat quietly one each side of their mother and answered any questions he asked them. Yes thank you I am doing well at school. Yes I do enjoy playing football. Some children when visiting their father would run down the steps and fling themselves into his arms. They would sit on his knee and chatter away about anything and everything. It was sad to see this little family where no one knew what to say and no one hugged and no one wanted to sit on Daddy's knee. Robert was very quiet after they left. He was just waking up to the fact that he did not know his children and they were wary of him. He wasn't the loved and respected head of the household; he was the one who made Mummy cry.

Robert pressed on with his Steps. In Step 2 he saw other addicts getting well by working the Steps and came to think he could too. In Step 3 he wrote a handover prayer which he addressed to the God of his understanding and asked for knowledge of God's will for him and the power to carry that out. He had a hard time in Step 4, writing down examples of his self-defeating character traits which stood blocking his path to recovery. With help from his group Robert peeled back the layers of denial, the masks and the poses, and had a look at his imperfect self. He identified immaturity, self-centredness, and dishonesty as major blocks. He saw how he blamed others, carried resentments, and indulged in self-pity. He saw how he covered his fear and sense of inadequacy with grandiosity. He saw how he had valued the outward signs of success, the huge house, the expensive clothes, more than the love of his family. He saw how lonely he had been for so long.

It was equally hard having to own his good qualities. He did have the qualities of honesty, courage, and a willingness to work hard. He did have a faith, he could make a decision to trust, and he did have some hope that he could change. He did manage to find the humility to admit his mistakes and resolve to make amends for the harm he had done. To what extent he would act on these assets when he left treatment remained to be seen. Robert completed his Steps 4 and 5 and moved into the second-stage house where he would work the Steps of change, build a relapse prevention plan, and prepare to rejoin the outside world.

As he worked on his Steps 6 and 7, staff and peers started to suspect that all was not well with Robert. He said all the right things. He did all his reading and written assignments on time and had a good understanding of the Steps. He often affirmed that from now on he would not drink again and would devote himself to becoming a good husband and father. The sense of unease felt by peers and staff sprang from the way Robert approached his Steps assignments: he did them in the way that students read books and write essays. He agreed with the Steps on a cognitive level but had not wholeheartedly embraced them and made them his own. As time went on it became clear to everyone, except Robert, what was happening. Robert had admitted he was powerless over his addiction but he did not fully accept it. Hundreds of his own examples had testified to the fact that he could not have just one drink or just one bet, and that whenever he did drink or gamble bad consequences followed, but after he had got over the first shock of reality his old denial had started to creep back in. At the back of his mind he held on to the thought that a fine wine shared with academics couldn't hurt that much, and it was an overreaction to say that one drink could cause him to lose everything.

There is a phenomenon often seen in rehabs which we referred to as 'the Return of the Ego'. One day an addict will be sitting in your office, begging you for help because their life is in ruins, their health is wrecked, their sanity is hanging by a thread, and they can't go on. They will do anything if only you will agree to help them and offer them a place in your rehab. So you do. Within days of being admitted they are acting as if they run the place, don't see why they have to follow all these stupid rules, and no one's going to tell them what to do, understood? From rock bottom to ego inflation as fast as blowing up a balloon; and, like a balloon, fragile and full of hot air – and just as fast to deflate, if you keep a pin handy in your box of treatment tools.

Robert's time in treatment did not end well. He went into town one day to buy groceries for the second-stage house and came back hideously drunk. He was given a disciplinary discharge for breaking one of the core unit expectations and was put on a train home. When he got in touch with us again later he had no memory of this at all. It was with only hindsight that we were able to piece together what had happened to lead to such an unhappy conclusion.

Robert's denial had started to return when Ann told him that in spite of everything she did still love him and did want to give their marriage another try. She said she had never really wanted a house that was too big and clothes that were too expensive; what she wanted was a loving and secure family with a husband she could trust. They could sell the house, downsize, enrol the children in state schools, pay the debts, and make a fresh start. Somewhere at the back of Robert's mind a secret little voice breathed a sigh of relief and said 'So I haven't lost everything then.' From this small seed a tree of denial grew. Before long Robert had convinced himself that the damage he had done was not so bad, after all Ann was not divorcing him, he could make it right with the children, his parents would forgive him of course, and his friends would understand, he would pay everybody back ... and there really was no need to sell the house, he had worked hard for that house and he deserved a big house, he didn't want to live in a three-bedroom house with a little garden, that wouldn't do at all for someone of his standing ...

Robert had identified his blocks to recovery in Step 4 but he had not put in the effort to change them required by Step 6. He was sorry for himself that he had been forced to spend six months rehab; he was resentful that Ann thought he was selfish and immature; he resented his parents for finding out about his debts and being disappointed with him. Robert was constructing for himself a false world view which did not fit with reality. While he was being well fed in Hotel Rehab Ann was out in the real world trying desperately to keep her children fed and housed. His peers tried to challenge Robert's thinking but while he outwardly complied he inwardly dismissed their feedback. He was urged to open up and talk about his fears and feelings but he kept his feelings to himself and said he was fine. Ann noticed this change in him and sensibly said that it would take her some time before she could trust him again, so she thought it a good idea if when he completed treatment he live somewhere else for a while to prove he really could stay sober and not gamble. Robert complied again. He agreed Ann was right but secretly he seethed with anger.

If Robert had been honest and trusted his group he could have prevented the relapse which was coming ever closer. If he had believed that he was allowed to feel angry he could have talked it through with peers who understood, and eventually processed and let it go. If he had shared his fears he could have found identification and support. As it was, he chose not to. The day came when he thought to himself 'I bet I could have one drink and not lose anything'. He walked into a pub at 11 a.m. and ordered one drink, just to prove that he was in control and could beat addiction, and didn't come out until 7 p.m.

What we did not know at that time, because Robert had been very careful to keep it hidden from everyone, was that he had never really been committed to stopping gambling. Because his alcohol addiction had become so obvious it was easy for him to keep the focus on that. Gambling became seen as somehow secondary to the alcoholism: he only gambled in casinos where champagne flowed, he didn't frequent seedy betting shops or play the slot machines in arcades. Denial told Robert that if he didn't drink he wouldn't be in casinos so he wouldn't gamble any more. The truth was that Robert had never stopped gambling throughout his time in treatment. He bet against himself and did it all in his head. He bet on who would be the first person to say the word 'powerless' in group therapy, whose visitors would be first to arrive, how long a new resident would last before saying he wanted to go home. Because he had gone through the days betting on mundane events Robert had not been abstinent from gambling. It did not matter that he was not in a gambling environment, or that no money was involved, or that the bets were unknown to anyone else; his mindset was unchanged. Whenever he had won at roulette he had to keep trying to win more. Whenever he had lost he had to keep trying to win back his losses. It didn't really matter whether he won or lost, it was the gamble he desired. He took risks like a gambler and he played for high stakes. Robert had never accepted that the bank always wins. He hadn't accepted that addiction always wins either. He staked his recovery and his family against a gin and tonic, and lost.

I have mentioned Robert not because his is a heart-warming story of recovery against the odds but because it illustrates some very important points I wish to make about addiction and recovery.

1. If you are addicted to behaviours as well as chemicals it is no use thinking you will give up one but not the others. No addiction is less damaging than another in the long term. While it may be true that the consequences of some addictions may appear to be less destructive than others, an obsessive-compulsive relationship with anything is going to do damage to your emotional, cognitive, and spiritual health and have a damaging effect on people who care about you. It's no good thinking that if you stop drinking your gambling will take care of itself, because it won't. It's no good thinking that you can abstain from heroin and still drink alcohol, because sooner or later you will find that you are now drinking alcoholically and from there it is an easy step to use heroin too. If you want to recover from addiction you need to abstain from everything you can't control, not just your drug of choice.

2. If you want to recover from addiction you have got to be open, honest, and willing. You may not start out this way but you have got to become so, otherwise your chances of making a sound and long-lasting recovery are very small indeed. In early recovery you cannot trust your own thinking. Denial is such a powerful state of mind it is almost impossible to know you are in it unless other people point out reality to you. Denial is rather like dreaming – you only know you have been dreaming when you wake up. If you do not share your thoughts and feelings honestly with recovering peers you are vulnerable to all the habitual addict ways of thinking: justifying, minimising, blaming others, ignoring the obvious, and convincing yourself you are right and everyone else is wrong.

3. If you want to follow a 12 Step programme to recovery it is no use just reading about it, thinking about it, or talking about it. You do actually have to do it. If you don't do what the Steps suggest, you will not change. If you do not change there is no reason why you should not relapse. Furthermore, it is a 12 Step programme, not a 2 Step programme. Recovery is not just admitting you are an addict and have caused dreadful damage to yourself and others, and relating this every week for years in meetings. Steps 1 and 12 may keep you alcohol-free but if you still carry all your blocks to recovery you are not recovering cognitively, emotionally, and spiritually and are what is known as a 'dry drunk'.[11]

4. 12 Step rehab is an intensive kick-start into 12 Step recovery, not the whole of it. Recovery is a way of living in which certain principles are acted upon every day. The Rehab provided an intensive introduction to the Steps, rather like an intensive course in a foreign language – by the end of it you can hold a conversation well enough but to become really fluent you need to carry on speaking the language until it becomes a natural part of your daily life. Like recovery, the longer you do it the better you get. Do not think that six weeks or three months or six months or two years in rehab is going to fix you. Rehab does not make you

---

[11] The wife of a non-drinking alcoholic once said to me, "He used to be a lying, selfish, drunk bastard – and now he's not drunk," just before she divorced him for adultery.

well, all it can do is show you how you can get well yourself and keep you in a safe place for a time while you practise. Meetings are the place where you go to develop your recovery, to learn from others, to give back to others, to be part of a recovering community. Rehabs come and go. Meetings, thanks to their 12 Traditions, are always there and available to anyone with a sincere desire to get well.

5. Recovery from addiction is not a straight line upwards. It is a pathway which twists and turns and sometimes goes backwards. The journey of recovery sometimes includes relapses. When relapse happens all is not lost provided that the person gets back to meetings and looks again at Step 1 with the experience gained from the relapse. Addiction runs deep, and lapsing into complacency and neglecting to stay aware of one's thinking and behaving opens a door for old patterns to return. Relapse happens when the warning signs are missed, usually because one has been apart from one's recovery community and relying on oneself alone for too long.

6. No matter what you personally believe about the 12 Step programme, it is proven by a substantial body of validated objective research[12] that this is an effective intervention in the treatment of addiction. The Steps work if you work them. If you do what they suggest you will get well. If you don't do what they suggest and don't get well, don't blame the Steps for 'not working'.

Before leaving Robert I will add a postscript to his story. After his relapse he found his way to another treatment centre where he did well until he went home, whereupon he relapsed again. Robert will not find recovery in treatment centres but he can find it if he wholeheartedly embraces the 12 Steps and becomes part of a recovering community.

Jessica, drug addict and self-harmer

---

[12] Kelly J F, Yeterian J D, The Role of Mutual-Help Groups in Extending the Framework of Treatment, *Alcohol Research & Health*, Vol.33, Issue 4.

I will introduce you now to Jessica, who is addicted to chemicals and self-harming. Jessica is in her twenties. The daughter of an addicted mother and an absent father, she spent her childhood in care. She started drinking at the age of ten and self-harming at fifteen. At the age of sixteen she ran away to the city where she lived on the streets until being 'befriended' by a drug dealer, introduced to drugs, and installed in his crack house. When Jessica was twenty-four she gave birth to a son, the child of her 'protector'. The baby was born prematurely and addicted but after hospital detoxification and months in a special baby care unit slowly started to thrive. His father was pleased to have a son and set up Jessica and the baby in a flat of their own. It was because the child was on the at-risk register that Jessica was assessed as a high priority case for residential rehabilitation, and services worked together to find her a suitable placement. There are very few rehabs in Britain which are registered as parent and baby units and there was no bed available when Jessica and her baby needed one. Jessica urgently needed treatment as her baby was being considered for adoption, so she made the difficult decision to leave her baby in temporary foster care and go into rehab without him.

Jessica was ready to stop using alcohol and drugs. Any enjoyment she once had from using had gone long ago and she was sick to death of feeling ill and wretched every day, compelled to do whatever she was told to get the drugs she hated but needed, being dependent both on the drugs and on those who supplied them. She had no belief in God and no faith in anything or anyone. Her rules for living had become simple: Don't trust anyone, and Do whatever you have to do to survive. If Jessica had not had her son she might have remained stuck in her addiction hell until it killed her. As it was she found herself given a chance and she grabbed it with both hands.

Jessica had no difficulty with accepting Step 1. She knew without a doubt that she could not control her use of chemicals and needed to abstain. Indeed she had had enough of chemicals of all kinds and sincerely wanted to never to take another drink or drug as long as she lived, she just did not believe it was possible. It was a huge relief to Jessica to accept that she had an addictive illness and to be part of group of peers who identified with her, accepted her, and did not judge her. She met other mothers who had used throughout their pregnancies, other parents who had had children removed from their care, other young adults who had never had a childhood: other survivors, who didn't trust and didn't have faith, just like her. Slowly, slowly Jessica came to see these others not just surviving but changing. Those who had been there the longest were even laughing, enjoying waking up in the mornings, being kind to one another with no ulterior motive. They sounded, looked, and behaved healthy. They didn't crave chemicals all the time. Cautiously Jessica moved into Step 2 and began the process of coming to believe that she could recover.

The word 'God' had no real meaning for Jessica. She certainly could not hand over her life and her will into God's care. She had only just escaped from virtual slavery and she wasn't about to hand over her will to anyone. She did, however, see the sense in not acting on impulse and allowing herself to be guided by other people who were working the Steps and knew how to do it. She had been dreading Step 3 but when it came to it she found it quite simple. She made the decision to ask for help and act on the advice she was given.

It was in Step 4 that Jessica was hit with a tsunami of grief, anger, and self-hate, and in Step 4 that she had an overwhelming urge to self-harm. There is no room in Step 4 for secrets. A truly searching and fearless moral inventory of oneself is going to uncover whatever is buried and bring it into the light. Jessica had been sexually abused from a very young age. Over time she had learned how to dissociate herself from her body. Men would do things to her body while she was elsewhere, shut away in a small private space that no one else knew existed or would ever be allowed to enter. She could not save her physical self from the abuse but she protected her emotional, cognitive, and spiritual self as best she could by locking it away and trying to ignore it. Jessica defended her safe space with high walls without windows and it became a prison. Her memories, her pain, her outrage, her despair, her hatred, were locked away in the dark for so long that, when the heroin flowed through her veins, she almost forgot they were there.

It was all very well locking the most precious part of herself away somewhere out of reach, but there were times in her life when Jessica wanted to feel real. Numb was for the most part comfortable but sometimes she felt a need to check if she was actually still alive. She achieved this by cutting her arms with a razor blade. She felt the cut. She watched the blood. This is my body; this is my blood; I did this. I am not a piece of meat; I can feel; I am alive. She felt euphoric. After this first experience with self-harming Jessica found that she could use cutting to alleviate all sorts of problems, not just to get high. When she had to agree to have sex for money she could rid herself of the disgust she felt by cutting herself. When she felt dirty and ashamed she could feel clean again when she made herself bleed. When she felt anxious and afraid she could cut herself and feel relief. When she felt helpless she could feel she had some control over her life when she set out her cutting paraphernalia in an ordered line and cut herself with precision. When she felt desperate she could pick up a knife and slash. When she felt angry and hated herself she could cut her arms and legs. When she hated the body that men defiled she could cut her breasts and her belly. She wore long sleeves and jeans. She had sex in the dark and remained as clothed as possible. Cutting was her secret, her survival weapon, and she wasn't going to let anyone take that away from her.

In Step 4 Jessica shone a light into all these dark and hidden places and the full horror of her life overwhelmed her. She went through all the stages of grieving for the childhood she had never had. As denial fell away she became angry, then blaming, then depressed. As do most victims, she blamed herself. It was her fault her parents did not want her. It was her fault nobody had ever really loved her. She was weak and dirty and toxic. She was a bad mother who had abandoned her baby. She hated her body, her behaviour, and her violation of her moral principles. She hated herself, body and soul. At the same time, she was without drugs or alcohol and had no access to pain relief. Jessica did the only thing she could do in the circumstances. She shut herself in her bedroom and slashed her arms with a knife she took from the kitchen.

Now her secret was out Jessica had the opportunity to address her self-harming addiction for the first time in her life. The first thing she had to do was take herself back to Step 1 and consider whether she was powerless over her self-harming. As she already had a good understanding of Step 1 in relation to chemicals it was not hard for Jessica to apply the concept of powerlessness to her mood-altering by cutting. By sharing with her peers examples of how she had been compulsively cutting in an attempt to avoid painful reality, she came to see that this behaviour had all the characteristics of addiction: she was preoccupied with it, she did it alone and kept it a secret, she did it for the effect it produced and had to cut more deeply and more often to get the same relief; once she started she could not be sure that she would not go too far, and she could not stop doing it even though she risked infection and her body was covered with scars. The question now for Jessica was whether she was willing to recover from self-harming as well as drug addiction, because if she did she was going to have to make a commitment to abstain.

It was relatively easy for Jessica to abstain from chemicals while she was in rehab as none were available. It was more difficult to abstain from self-harming because there were knives in the kitchen, and scissors, glass, and sundry sharp objects were not hard to find if she searched. Although some steps were taken by staff to protect Jessica in the early days – she was asked to hand in her razor and scissors and was barred from going into the kitchen – the decision to abstain from cutting had to be made by Jessica of her own will. The thought of never again being allowed to use self-harming as a way of coping was frightening for Jessica, so she adjusted her thinking in the way all her peers had done in relation to their drugs of choice. It is unreasonable to expect any addict to say with certainty 'I will never use again'. The best that one can say with certainty is 'Just for today I will not use'. At the beginning a whole day was too much for Jessica to commit to, so she made her decision an hour at a time. 'All you have to do,' said her peers, 'is hold on for an hour. You can manage that. Then you can make a new decision. All you ever have to do is an hour.'

Jessica found that she could go an hour without cutting herself, especially as she had people she could talk to if she did have urges to cut. Before long the hours added up and she could go a day. She also found that, contrary to what she had always feared, one did not die of feelings. They certainly hurt but they did not kill her. Another thing which she was surprised to discover was that if she held on long enough her feelings started to change or fade away. Jessica had always used something to medicate her painful feelings and had not learnt that it is the nature of feelings not to last for ever. Armed with this revelation she started for the first time in her life to allow herself to have feelings and manage them.

While it is possible that Jessica could have worked the Steps for drug and self-harming addiction in the appropriate meetings, I think it would have been difficult and dangerous for her to do so. Jessica's needs were deep and complex and best met in the safety of a residential unit where she could receive counselling as well as peer support in a 12 Step environment. In The Rehab Jessica began her long journey to recovery. She did not just need to recover physically and take care of her body. She needed to become able to think of herself in a new way, as a strong and capable survivor with many assets and talents. She needed to come to believe that she deserved to get well and to be happy, that even if her parents had not been available to show her love she was nevertheless essentially precious and loveable. Just because she had been treated as worthless did not mean that she was.

It would take Jessica time to let go of her self-hate and come to appreciate and love herself, to accept her past and let go of the rage that hurt only herself, but during her months at The Rehab she made a good start. After leaving rehab she continued her recovery in meetings where she found a sponsor who helped her work all 12 Steps until they became internalised as a way of life. Jessica's dreadful experiences in childhood were not wasted. By sharing her experiences, strength, and hope in meetings Jessica showed many newcomers that recovery is possible if you all walk the Steps together, and anyone can do it if you take one small step at a time. Bit by bit Jessica built a new life for herself in recovery and eventually was reunited with her baby. She proved to be a very good mother.

Three important points arising from Jessica's story are:

1. It does not matter if you don't believe in, or don't trust, God. You can still work a 12 Step programme using a form of words which is simple and practical. If you do this for long enough you will experience emotional, cognitive, and spiritual growth. You may or may not come to believe in the God of your childhood but you will come to your own understanding of a power greater than yourself which will help you in your ongoing recovery.

2. No matter how far down the scale you have gone in addiction, recovery is possible.

3. No matter how dreadful your experiences in addiction have been, you can use them to help other people recover.

Pam, alcoholic and compulsive spender

Pam is in her late fifties and is addicted to alcohol and shopping. She has been married to Bill for thirty-five years and they have three adult children and two grandchildren. Bill has always been the family breadwinner and Pam has only ever worked part-time for a bit of 'spending money' of her own. Pam does not like socialising or drinking in pubs, she likes to buy alcohol in supermarkets and drink in her own home. In Pam's eyes she likes a little drink to relax in the evenings and she does no harm to anyone. This is not how Bill and her children see her.

The family decided that Pam needed to go into rehab when Bill had to go away for a weekend and came home to find her unconscious on the sofa surrounded by empty wine bottles and lying in her own vomit. She was taken into hospital where she had a withdrawal fit and blood tests showed she was in the early stage of liver disease. She was detoxed in hospital and sent home with the warning that unless she drastically cut down her drinking she was going to damage her liver beyond repair. Pam took this as a frightening tactic on the doctor's behalf and did not take it seriously. She did not want to go into rehab, saying that she could not leave the family for so long, and she promised faithfully she would limit her drinking to the evenings when Bill would be there to keep an eye on how much she drank.

After a few of months of taking days off work, watching Pam like a hawk, searching the house for bottles, checking the supermarket receipts, and still finding her drunk in the middle of the afternoons, Bill was exhausted and suffering from hypertension. The children were worried and angry. Pam was secretly rather smug because Bill could never work out how she got her alcohol into the house or where she hid it. She blatantly lied to her children, saying Bill was exaggerating: he had no proof, did he? She had a system for getting rid of the bottles. Matters really came to a head one day when Pam's daughter left her two small children in Pam's care while she went to the hairdresser's. She returned two hours later to find the children sitting on the kitchen floor surrounded by the contents of the cupboards and trying to open a bottle of bleach, and Pam drunk and snoring on the sofa. Pam was given an ultimatum: get help to cut down your drinking or you will not see your grandchildren again.

Pam contacted her local alcohol service and started to attend weekly sessions with a key worker who explained to Pam about units of alcohol and told her to keep a diary of everything she drank. Her family members were pleased that Pam was making an effort and for a time she did manage to drink less. She wasn't entirely honest in her units diary and she didn't tell her key worker quite all the days she drank, but she turned up for her appointments on time and always kept a packet of mints handy so everyone was happy.

Now she was drinking less she had more money in her purse and more time to fill during the day. One fine day she woke up feeling more energetic than she had done for some time and decided to catch a bus into town and go for a look around the shops. She came home at tea time with two new dresses for herself plus a pair of shoes and a handbag, a new shirt for Bill, and two very cute outfits for the grandchildren. When Bill got home he found her bright-eyed and happy, delighted with her purchases, and he was pleasantly surprised when she announced that she had not even thought about having a drink all day. Bill was so pleased with Pam's progress that he treated her to a week's holiday in Paris. Pam loved every minute of it, especially as the shopping opportunities were so exciting, and she came home laden with presents for everyone.

Pam kept on with her controlled drinking classes and managed to restrict her drinking to a couple of glasses in the evenings. At the same time her shopping was increasing. It got to the point where she felt the shops had become boring and she was no longer excited by the thought of walking round them. She started to feel restless but she didn't know why. She felt as if she was missing something but she didn't know what. One day her daughter mentioned that she was having her groceries delivered as she had ordered them online, and a whole new world of internet shopping opened up for Pam. The time came when Pam had so many new clothes that she needed a new wardrobe to hang them in, which she put in one of the spare bedrooms. She had new storage shelves fitted to accommodate her new shoes. Many of her purchases remained on the hangers on which they were delivered and were never actually worn. It was the thrill of buying them and waiting for them to arrive that Pam loved, not the clothes themselves. She tried on her new shoes in her bedroom and looked at herself in the mirror, then put them back in their boxes and stacked them with the others.

Bill started to question whether Pam really needed more new clothes but he was so relieved about her drinking less that he did not want to rock the boat and paid the bills with a fairly good grace. Pam started to look beyond clothing for her shopping thrills. 'What we really need', she convinced Bill, 'is to have the house decorated.' Pam chose new colour schemes and got the decorators in. The rooms looked so nice when they were done that the furniture looked shabby in comparison and obviously needed replacing. So did the curtains and carpets. So did the kitchen units and the bathroom suite. 'Wouldn't it be lovely,' Pam said, 'if we had a conservatory?' 'Anything to keep you happy,' thought Bill with one eye on his bank balance. Eventually the house was done. Everything was clean and new and perfectly gorgeous. Pam sat in her dream home and felt nothing at all. Two weeks later Bill came home from work and found her out cold drunk on their lovely new sofa.

Pam was shipped off to The Rehab in disgrace. She was terrified at the thought of being away from her family and having to associate with drug addicts and criminals, and she begged Bill not to abandon her there. Bill and the children stood firm and gave Pam a choice: stay in rehab and stop drinking, or be divorced. Pam spent her first week in The Rehab crying, making tearful phone calls to her family to come and take her home, but they refused. Once she came round to the idea that her family meant business this time, Pam stopped trying to manipulate them and resigned herself to getting on with her treatment. To her surprise she found that the drug addicts and criminals were people just like her, who had feelings just hers, and who needed some kind of mood-alterer to make their empty lives bearable just like she did.

In Step 1 Pam learned that her compulsive shopping was just as much an addiction as her drinking. It had taken over her life and become more important to her than her family. She needed to know she had a husband as she craved a sense of security, and she relied on Bill to finance her spending, but over the many years of their marriage she had become so used to his being there that she had forgotten how she felt about him. Of course she 'loved' him, but she was not sure what this meant any more. She was in a relationship with addiction which excluded relationships with real people and she looked to addiction to get her emotional needs met, without success.

Pam also came to see that counting units and trying to drink moderately was not going to work for her. There was always the risk that once she opened a bottle of wine she would carry on drinking until she passed out. She had never been really honest about how much she drank and when she finally admitted it she was surprised to find that instead of shame she felt a huge relief, and that instead of being judged she was congratulated for being honest. She was among people who knew she had been lying and had only been waiting for her to get honest so that they could include her completely as an important part of their group of recovering addicts.

From this point on Pam's recovery went from strength to strength. She had been brought up in a Christian tradition and described her religion as 'C of E'. She did not worry about what 'god' meant or what 'handing over her life and her will' might mean for her. She got to Step 3 and she simply did what it said. She said her prayers every night as she had done in her childhood, asking for blessings on the people she cared about, and she decided that after completing treatment she would start going to church again and get involved with the social activities which centred on her local church. Every morning she started her day with a simple prayer, 'Please God, help me stay clean today' and every night she was grateful, 'Thank you, God, for helping me stay clean today.' She abstained from alcohol and from shopping one day at a time and as the weeks went by she thought about them less and less.

When Pam came to taking personal inventory it hit her that that at age fifty-seven she did not know who she was. She had had a role as a wife and then as a mother, but after her children had grown and moved away she felt as if they had taken her identity with them. Her contact with her children was mostly limited to telephone calls and her grandchildren were not brought to visit often. She and Bill lived in a beautiful empty house and he was out at work most of the time. Her drinking had come between her and the friends she once had and she had become almost fearful of leaving her house, much preferring to drink at home and shop online in the place she felt most secure.

Not only did she not know who she was, Pam did not know how she felt or what was the point of anything. She had everything she wanted but had no idea what she needed. Whatever she got was not enough. She felt as if she had an empty hole of meaninglessness inside her that no amount of alcohol or things could fill. Bill and her children's love and concern disappeared into this empty hole without even touching the sides. She didn't feel it and it disappeared like snowflakes down a well. Pam was not robbing post offices or causing chaos in the community but her addictive illness was every bit as destructive and life-threatening as anyone else's. She was suffering from what addicts refer to as 'a hole in the soul' and was in urgent need of spiritual recovery.

Pam worked her way through the 12 Steps and made a relapse prevention plan in preparation for leaving The Rehab and going home. The Step 12 wording Pam used begins 'Having had a spiritual awakening as a result of these steps ...' Unlike many of her peers Pam had not worried and attempted to analyse what 'a spiritual awakening' might mean. What she did know was that when she arrived at Step 12 she felt like a different person from the Pam who had come into rehab. As well as feeling physically well she was experiencing a full range of emotions, many of which were enjoyable. Her thinking was much clearer and she saw how deluded she had been when she was drinking and compulsively shopping. She had shared openly and honestly with her group how she felt about her relationships with her husband and children and once she had admitted that things were not perfect, and it was safe to say so, she had felt her feelings change. She felt a fondness for Bill she had not felt for some time and gradually she remembered what it is to love.

Back at home Pam put her relapse prevention plan into action. She attended AA regularly and volunteered to do service in her home group by washing up the cups after the meetings. She asked a woman whose recovery she admired to be her sponsor and with her help she continued to develop her understanding and practice of the 12 Step programme. Every day she followed her recovery routine of handing over her day to God in the morning, and at night saying thank you for another clean day. Pam stuck to her plan to attend church and join in its social activities, where she made some good friends and had fun being involved in fundraising activities. In addition to this she decided to spend a few hours a week doing voluntary work. She applied for and got a job in a charity shop which she enjoyed because she got to meet lots of people and she had a sense of satisfaction knowing that she was making a contribution to a good cause. She did once or twice feel a small temptation to buy all the good quality items that came into the shop but donated most of her unworn new clothes to the shop and sold them instead.

It was about a year later that Pam realised what a spiritual awakening was, and that she had had one. She was sitting in the church garden eating her sandwiches after a morning spent arranging flowers for a wedding. There was a break in the clouds and the sun came out. Pam was filled with a feeling of calm and warmth and safety. It filled her up from her toes to the top of her head and was very pleasant indeed. In that moment she knew that life was precious beyond words and that she was a part of it. Her life had meaning. She loved and was loved. She did not need to drink or shop today. That hole had filled up from the inside. She wasn't empty any more.

From Pam's story we learn:

1. If you have a spiritual illness you need a spiritual recovery. If you have a hole inside, you cannot fill it with things.

2. The more you give, the more you gain. By engaging with others in recovery and by making a contribution to the community at large you bring meaning into your life. With meaning comes value. With value comes self-esteem, gratitude, and even sometimes happiness.

Peter, alcoholic and compulsive over-worker

Peter is forty-two. He is the middle one of three brothers, married, and the father of three children. He has been dependent on alcohol for more than ten years but because he is a binge drinker and does not drink every day he does not believe his doctor or his wife when they tell him he is an alcoholic and his health is at risk. He works as an investment banker and recently has been bringing home a very large salary. His aim is to make enough money to retire in comfort at the age of fifty. In Peter's eyes he is a responsible father working hard to provide a high standard lifestyle for his family. He may have to work long hours now but after another eight years he will be free to spend much more time with his wife and children, they will have a good life and want for nothing, and it will all be worth it. Because he works hard he is entitled to play hard. He doesn't let drinking interfere with his work, he just takes a week off every now and then and gets hammered.

In Peter's wife's eyes he is a cold and unloving husband who has no time for her and is hardly ever home. In Peter's children's eyes he is 'Daddy' but that is about all they know of him. In his brothers' eyes he is a driven competitor who will not be satisfied until he has beaten them at anything from Monopoly to money-making. In his doctor's eyes he is a man who is overweight, has dangerously high blood pressure, has had one heart attack already, and will be lucky to make it to age fifty if he does not make some radical alterations to his life style.

Peter was admitted to The Rehab after his body made the decision for him. He had another heart attack and spent time in intensive care. After having heart surgery he was told in no uncertain terms that if he wanted to live he had to address his drinking and his over-working and the best place for him to do that was in a rehab in the middle of nowhere where mobile phones and laptops were not permitted and he would be eating three healthy meals a day and no junk food. Peter was too weak to object.

If you have read the previous addicts' stories you will be familiar with Peter's path through The Rehab. The main problems Peter faced were admitting he was an alcoholic and seeing how much his compulsive over-working had damaged other people. Like many people Peter had no understanding of what an alcoholic is: he envisioned the stereotype of an old tramp on a park bench, swigging cheap cider and sleeping in a cardboard box. Peter was young and rich, he wasn't unemployed, never drank anything cheap, and could go weeks without drinking at all, so how could anyone possibly call him an alcoholic? He saw himself as different from the members of his group and doubted his need for treatment. He thought rehab was going to be a kind of rest home in the countryside where he could relax and recuperate after his heart surgery. It was something of a shock to find himself in group therapy every morning and expected to participate.

It was in group therapy one day that Peter had his first experience of tough love. 'Tough love' is what one resident gives to another when he tells him directly and honestly the truth as he sees it: it is 'tough' because it challenges denial and is often hard or unpleasant to accept, and 'love' because to give it is risky and the giver has to care enough about the recipient in order to give it. It is not love in the sense of sympathy, in fact it usually appears unsympathetic in the extreme. The last thing an addict in denial needs is sympathy. All sympathy will do is reinforce an addict's self pity and blaming of others: 'Poor Peter, everyone having a go at you about your drinking, and after you working so hard you've put your health at risk, you've had a hard time of it, mate, I sympathise with you ...' An addict in denial needs tough love which challenges his thinking, exposes his justifications and excuses, and tells him like it is.

Peter had been sharing with his group how he did not drink every day and, compared to some of his colleagues, his drinking was not that bad at all, it had never interfered with his work, and he only did it for a bit of a reward after he had been working especially hard. So there had been no really damaging consequences to other people. So he wasn't really as bad as the other people in the group. Peter was avoiding eye contact so was unaware of the effect this share was having on his group. When he had finished Barry spoke up, 'You sit there with your posh voice and your piles of money and you think that makes you different from me? You're an alcoholic, mate, just like I am. The only difference between you and me is that you haven't lost anything yet. I have – I've lost my wife and my kids and my home. I've lost my job and I get food from the bins outside supermarkets. You think that isn't going to happen to you? Why not? What makes you so different? Do you think I started out like this? Do you think I chose this? I had a home and family just like you. I lost everything because of my drinking. Wake up to reality, mate!' Barry got his second wind, 'How long do you think it's going to be before your missus says she's had enough? How are you going to feel when she gets another bloke and he's bringing up your kids? Drinking for a reward?! Who are you trying to kid?' Peter's face, which had started red, was now white.

Barry's feedback may sound harsh but it provided the shock of reality that helped to chip away at Peter's denial. It is one thing for professional people like doctors and counsellors to tell you that you have a progressive illness which is well on the way to having devastating consequences, and quite another for a person who has stood in your shoes to say 'I recognise you as being just like me. This is what happened to me. Don't let it happen to you.' Also it is also much easier to fool an addictions professional than it is to fool a recovering addict, which is another reason why a peer's feedback is so important. As has been said frequently in group therapy by peers who don't buy into justifications, 'You can't kid a kidder.'

Peter had never been to an AA meeting before coming to The Rehab. This was his first encounter with the 12 Step programme and it took him several weeks before he started to make any sense of it. This was frustrating for Peter because as a compulsive over-worker he put a great deal of time and effort into his reading and written assignments. When Peter was asked to read a brief pamphlet and write half a page on what he learnt from it, he wrote a critical analysis of the pamphlet which covered six pages. When asked to write specific examples of his powerlessness and consequences and write three examples to a page, Peter's examples were three pages each. Peter spent so much time on his written work that his peers complained he always had his head in a book and was not interacting with them. He wrote down all his insights but did not share with his peers who felt they did not know him. Consequently they were wary of him and did not embrace him fully into the group.

Over-working was Peter's way of coping with stress. He could spend hours immersed in his work and 'not have time' to make relationships with people. On a fundamental level Peter was afraid of intimacy and work was a socially acceptable way of avoiding it. Society might criticise a man for neglecting his family by spending too much time with his friends, but surely not for working too hard? As The Rehab was an abstinence-based unit, all a resident's dependencies were stripped away, leaving him nowhere to hide and nowhere to look but at himself. Peter's alcohol had been removed and now it was time for his over-work to be removed. Peter's next assignment was to spend one week without reading or writing anything and sharing every day with every member of his group. If you are not sure if you are addicted to something, try not doing it for a week and see what happens. After half a day Peter was in the office begging to be given some work to do. He was intensely uncomfortable having to talk to his peers and having to manage his time to be able to talk to everyone.

By the end of the week Peter's peers agreed that although he had found it hard at first he had stuck to his assignment and as a result they felt they knew him better and trusted him more. Peter was pleasantly surprised to hear that his peers felt closer to him and actually liked him. He had always been afraid of revealing too much of himself in case people rejected him. Work had been his way of avoiding the anxieties of relationships, and alcohol had been his way of avoiding everything when working was causing him more stress than the relationships he was working to avoid. As well as working Step 1 with regard to alcohol Peter needed to admit he was obsessive-compulsive about working and that this addiction was doing just as much damage to his health and his family as his alcoholism. He was shocked to tears when his wife sent to The Rehab the family members' questionnaire she had filled in, saying honestly how hurt and unloved she felt as a result of his being obsessed with work and hardly ever spending time at home and the effect this was having on their children. Peter's denial fell away and he started to get an understanding of how his life had been ruled by addiction and how different it could be if he were to become free from it. Peter completed his treatment at The Rehab and as he changed his attitudes and behaviour he became more emotionally healed and he and his wife entered a new and closer stage of their relationship.

Three important points I wish to draw from Peter's story are:
1. It is very difficult to wake up from denial and face reality

without honest feedback from other recovering addicts. If you are lost in the dark you need someone to switch on the lights for you so you can see where you are.

2. Sympathy is no great help to an addict in denial but empathy is invaluable. Sympathy tends to enable an addict to stay in denial. Its message is 'You have suffered enough, I am on your side, I will not let anyone hurt you with painful confrontation, I will defend you. It is us against them.' In this situation sympathy is enabling addict thinking to remain unchallenged. Empathy is entirely different. Its message is 'I feel your pain when you do. I will not try to take your pain away because this is the pain of growing awareness and you need to have it. I will, however, stand by your side while you are in pain and hold you if you fall. We are all in this together.'

3. If you are a professional working with an addicted client, involve the client's family. The family members are the ones most affected by your client's addiction, who know more about the addict's behaviour than he is telling you, and whose honest feedback can prove to be your most effective tool for challenging your client's denial. Ask them to write down how the addict's addiction has affected them. Read this out in group therapy and invite peers to identify and give feedback. From my years at The Rehab I can say without doubt that the reading of a parent's, spouse's or child's questionnaire is one of the most powerful interventions you can use.

Hayley, drug addict and compulsive cleaner

Hayley is in her thirties, separated from her husband, the mother of two children who live part of the week with her and part of the week with their father. Hayley has never considered herself to be a drug addict, although she has been dependent on prescribed tranquillisers for years. She has had what might be described as an 'average' kind of life. She was one of three children, lived in an averagely well-off family, did averagely well at school, and works part-time for an average salary. She has suffered no particular traumas, has never used illegal drugs, and never broken the law apart from a couple of minor motoring offences. She has never liked drinking alcohol and only drinks occasionally and then only moderately.

Hayley married young and had her two babies before she was twenty-one. After the birth of her second child she suffered severe post-natal depression and started taking prescribed anti-depressant medication. It was two years before her depression started to lift. During this time she started to fear that her husband would become bored with her being so depressed and unable to run the home and care properly for the children, and she began to suffer from anxiety. She continued to take her anti-depressants and in addition was prescribed medication to calm her anxiety and help her sleep at night. Hayley had never wanted anything from life other than a nice home and loving family of her own. She had married her childhood sweetheart and assumed they would spend all their lives together. When she became aware that her husband was not happy in the marriage Hayley believed that she was not good enough as a home maker and she determined to do better. The first thing that needed doing, she thought, was to give the house a good clean.

Hayley was no longer in the depths of depression but she was still pretty well medicated. Her energy had started to return and she noticed her surroundings more than she had done. Her home did look rather dingy. Her husband worked all day and spent a great deal of his time caring for the children. By the time he had done the shopping, cooking, laundry, playing with, reading to, and putting to bed there was not always time for much cleaning. Hayley did not blame him, she just felt guilty that he had had to do it all for so long. Hayley made a start in the kitchen. She emptied all the cupboards, threw out all the unused junk that had been gathering dust in there for ages, relined the shelves and drawers, and gave everything a good scrub. At the end of the day she felt a sense of achievement and slept better that night than she had done for ages.

After her cleaning blitz on the kitchen Hayley deep cleaned the house room by room. She found she enjoyed it. The physical activity lifted her spirits and the finished results made her feel proud. The thing about housework is that no sooner have you cleaned a floor than someone walks on it. No sooner have you polished all the glasses and lined them up in the right place on their shelf than someone comes and says they want a drink of water. 'A woman's work is never done,' quoted Hayley, who started cleaning all over again.

Hayley is dependent on her medication and does not always take it as prescribed. When she was feeling particularly anxious she was prescribed benzodiazepine drugs which she was told to take 'when needed'. Hayley needs to take them more and more. She doesn't take them to get high or to get numb, she takes them when she feels anxious and she feels anxious more and more often. Hayley does not know it but she is addicted to benzodiazepines and will suffer dangerous withdrawal symptoms if she ever stops taking them suddenly. Hayley is also developing an obsessive-compulsive relationship with cleaning. She cleans every day. If she does not clean she feels restless and anxious. She is not enjoying cleaning as much as she did at first but she cannot relax until she has cleaned the house thoroughly.

Compulsive cleaning, like any addiction, is progressive. Hayley cleaned the house for hours and became resentful if anyone dirtied it again. She couldn't bear it when the children came home from school and dropped shoes, coats, bags, and sundry bits and pieces all over the rooms she had just tidied. She hated it when her husband came in from work with wet shoes and made marks on the carpet. She was proud of her home but she did not want visitors coming round now, walking on her carpets with their dirty shoes, eating off her plates with their dirty hands, and making crumbs on her sofa. Gradually Hayley's obsession with cleaning spread from things to people. The children were bathed every day and their clothes washed every night. Hayley showered twice a day and expected her husband to do the same. No one was allowed to wear outdoor shoes in the house. Food was not allowed in the living room and the children were not allowed to help themselves from the kitchen because they made a mess. Hayley's husband had put up with all this for years because he loved her and their children and hoped that one day the tablets would work and once again she would be the Hayley he had married. After ten unhappy years he became friendly with a woman he met at work who did not mind if he ate a sandwich while watching TV with his shoes on, and told Hayley that he was moving out. He was not far away and was still generally supportive to Hayley; he saw the children frequently, and they stayed with him from after school on Fridays until he took them to school on Mondays.

As you would expect, Hayley was unable to cope with her feelings about this and her addiction went up a gear. Because she was not causing a social nuisance or breaking the law, Hayley's addictive illness was not widely known. Her local GP surgery was a large practice and she usually saw whichever doctor was free so she had not built up a relationship with any one doctor. She applied for repeat prescriptions and rarely saw a doctor. When she had a medication review she said she felt better taking the tablets and did not feel ready to stop, so the prescriptions continued. The only people who knew about her escalating cleaning addiction were her children because they still lived with her. The children's teacher noticed a change in their behaviour. They had become quiet and withdrawn. They appeared nervous, as if afraid of doing something wrong. They did not join in outdoor games at break times and got very upset if they ever spilled anything on their clothes or their shoes got muddy. Their hands often looked red and sore. They avoided eye contact as much as possible. Alarm bells started ringing for the teacher who asked their father if she might have a word when he collected them from school one Friday.

The children were reluctant to tell their father what had been happening at home. They knew their mother had a problem and they did not want to be disloyal or cause any trouble. They had already lost one parent from the family home and they were afraid of losing another. They may not be happy with the way their mother was behaving but she was the only security they had. Gently he encouraged them to talk to him and bit by bit the truth emerged. Hayley's cleaning addiction had become completely irrational and she was unable to control it. As soon as the children came in from school they were made to stand in the hall and take off all their clothes. Their mother made them stand in a bowl of water containing disinfectant and washed them before they were allowed to put on clean clothes and slippers. They were then made to stay in their bedrooms until tea time. In their rooms they were allowed only to sit or lie on the bed. They were allowed to play with one thing at a time and after using it they had to put it back in its right place. They ate their meal in the kitchen. They had to wash their hands before and after eating. They were allowed in the sitting room in the evening to watch television for a while but they were not allowed to sit on the furniture and had to sit on the floor and not touch anything. Before bed they had a bath and changed into clean pyjamas. Hayley gathered up all the day's clothes and put them in the washing machine. Every day when they were at school she disinfected their toys and changed their bedding.

There are many, many children of using addicts who suffer appalling abuse or neglect in their family home, and being over-cleaned may not sound to be so very damaging, but Hayley's behaviour was deeply damaging to her children's emotional health, and although their bodies did not show outward scars, the damage to their sense of self-esteem would take a long time to heal. These children believed they were dirty, in fact they were so dirty that it would not just wash off, it had to be scrubbed with disinfectant. Everything they touched got dirty too, so they must be very dirty indeed. If they came home with dirt on their shoes or clothes their mother would be angry with them, or cry, so clearly they were bad as well as dirty. They did not know what was wrong with them, or what they should be doing, or not doing, but there was surely something very wrong with them. Not knowing what it was made them anxious and afraid. They thought they had better sit quietly on their beds and contaminate the house as little as possible.

When their father found out what was happening he took decisive action. He told Hayley that he knew what she was doing and told her she must get help. He went with her to the doctor's and asked for an urgent review of her medication. The doctor agreed that she should be detoxified from benzodiazepines and maintained on a non-sedating anti-depressant. Hayley was admitted to a psychiatric hospital where she was detoxed, and the children went to stay with their father. With social services' involvement funding was made available for Hayley to receive residential rehabilitation. When she was well enough Hayley was admitted to The Rehab to work a 12 Step programme for chemical dependency and while there she also addressed her addiction to cleaning. After six months in treatment Hayley continued her recovery in NA. In her second year of recovery she discussed with her doctor whether she might stop taking anti-depressants. With a very gradual reduction regime and support from her recovering friends in NA she managed to reduce her dose to zero and found that, with the tools she had acquired to manage her emotions, she did not need them any more. With help Hayley managed to repair her relationship with her children. They understood that she had been ill and they still loved her; in time they also came to trust her. They regarded themselves as having two homes and they divided their time between both parents. The arrangement worked well for all concerned.

Hayley's story illustrates the following important points:

1. There are some people who suffer from both an addictive illness and clinical depression. Although these may be closely interrelated I believe these are two separate illnesses. Doctors and addiction professionals working with these people face two difficulties: it is sometimes hard to make a sound diagnosis of either when both conditions appear to be present, and if both illnesses are present, which one do you treat first? Many people who are diagnosed as suffering from depression are actually deeply unhappy people leading unfulfilling solitary lives as a result of having been addicted for many years. If your life is ruled by an obsessive-compulsive condition as a result of which you have lost everything you held dear, then you can reasonably be expected to experience the same symptoms as clinical depression. The question is, do you abstain from all chemicals, work a 12 Step recovery programme for your addiction, and see if the 'depression' clears up over time? Or do you take anti-depressants to enable you to face the challenges of working a 12 Step programme to deal with your addiction?

It is not my intention in this book to enter into this ongoing and often heated debate. I will say only this. In The Rehab we had the following policy: If a resident had been diagnosed as suffering from depression prior to the onset of addiction, and if that resident had been taking anti-depressants as prescribed for a long period of time to good effect, then that resident could continue to take those anti-depressants in as low a dose as needed for the duration of their time in The Rehab. If, however, a resident in active addiction had gone to a GP, described symptoms of depression, and been prescribed anti-depressants which had made no significant difference to their mental or emotional health, then that resident was not allowed to take anti-depressants while in The Rehab.

Addicts don't like handing over their drugs, even if they are medication which is having no beneficial effect. We often encountered resistance from potential residents when told they would have to be drug free. They protested their human rights. Who were we to say they were not allowed to have medication? We reassured them that if after a while they noticed a deterioration in their mental health we would arrange for a medication review and if it became evident that they did need anti-depressants they could have them. When we further pointed out that no one was denying their right to take medication, they were being given a choice – carry on with your chemicals, or be admitted into The Rehab – they chose to stop taking the anti-depressants. After a couple of weeks they cheerfully admitted that they did not miss them, they had never worked anyway, but free drugs were free drugs and it was worth a try, wasn't it?

Hayley was one person who did have a sound diagnosis made of clinical depression. Her anti-depressant medication was not properly effective because of her untreated addiction to Valium and compulsive cleaning which was in itself adding to her feelings of worthlessness and hopelessness. In her case she continued with her anti-depressants while in The Rehab. As she progressed in her recovery from addiction, her mental health also improved to the point where she no longer needed to take anti-depressants.

The point I am making here is that addictions workers should be aware that while some of their clients may be suffering from clinical depression, others may not. Wrong self-diagnosing was happening for the majority of addicts asking for admission to The Rehab because, for an addict, any drugs are better than none. Most addicts will be perfectly able to work a 12 Step programme without any anti-depressant medication. A thorough assessment of an individual's treatment needs is necessary.

2. There is no hierarchy of addiction. This point is explicitly made in the Basic Text of NA. Whether a person is addicted to heroin or to over-the-counter painkillers is not important. One chemical is not worse than another, one addict is not worse than another, and all addicts are equally deserving of help. In times of economic recession when social services funding for residential rehabilitation is scarce, it is the addicts who are causing the most damage to the

community who tend to get the funding. For the many addicts who cannot be funded nor pay the fees themselves, rehab may not be an option. This is a sad and unfair state of affairs. Fortunately the 12 Step programme is freely available to every addict with a genuine desire to stop using and millions of people all over the world are finding recovery in the meeting rooms.

3. The damage done to children of addict families is vast and largely unknown. Only the tip of the iceberg comes to light. There are usually some indications in the children's behaviour that something is wrong but if no one notices and no one takes action the harm will continue. Hayley's children were fortunate that their teacher noticed and talked to their father. They were fortunate that their father talked to Hayley and to her doctor. If these people had taken no action Hayley's addiction would have continued unchecked. The point is that we cannot leave it all to social workers. If we as members of the community believe children are at risk we are all responsible for doing something about it. It may be risky, embarrassing, scary, or a bother, but someone needs to be told.

Other behavioural addictions

As I have said before, an addict can become dependent on anything. It is not necessary to study more examples of behavioural addiction or combinations of addictions as I hope by now it will be clear that any kind of addiction unfolds in the same way and the Steps provide an antidote for any kind of addiction in the same way. Jayne is another multi-addicted ex-resident who knows this to be true.

The first 12 step meeting I went to and is my homing meeting is OA. Before I went to my first OA 12 step meeting I did not know what to expect but it did not surprise me that the members shared their stories and I was able to identify with them. I then thought AA to be for people with a disease I did not have, until I learnt different.

As an OCD sufferer who is getting well with the help of the 12 Steps I would like attention given to the fact that a washing

---

> /cleaning disorder and intrusive thoughts can be overcome with the help of the 12 Steps just as alcoholism, drug addiction, and eating disorders are.
>
> *Jayne A.*

Before I end this chapter I will mention some behaviours which have caused problems for addicts after they have completed treatment at The Rehab.

Exercise addiction has become a problem for food addicts. We saw in Julie's case that when she was in a dieting phase one way she tried to burn calories and lose weight was to exercise. Moderate exercise is healthy and enjoyable, you feel energised and experience a moderate level of mood enhancement. Exercise becomes addiction when you feel compelled to over-exercise even when you are physically damaged by it, when you are losing things and relationships you do not want to lose because you are so obsessed with it, when you feel anxious agitated or miserable when you don't do it, and when once you start doing it you could go on until you drop rather than when you choose to stop. People recovering from chemical dependency often take up sports or exercise as they start to enjoy life again. As with any new activity in recovery, moderation is advised.

Sex addiction is commonly misunderstood, largely I believe because of the salacious way the term is bandied about in the media. A sex addict is not someone who enjoys sex and has a lot of it. A sex addict, male or female, is a person who is filled with shame and guilt, who hates themselves because of the way they feel compelled to behave, and who may crave real intimacy but is denied it by their addiction to fake intimacy. Sex addiction is not what might be described as mutually enjoyable promiscuity; it is addiction to sex that is in some way degrading. Because of this it is usually a closely guarded secret and not disclosed even when in treatment for chemical dependency. A recovering addict who suffers from sex addiction and is too afraid or ashamed to admit it is at high risk of relapsing into chemical dependency, as sooner or later accumulated shame guilt or fear is going to become unbearable and only deadened by the original drug of choice.

Co-dependency is sometimes referred to as relationship addiction. It manifests itself as thinking obsessively about another person and compulsively trying to control them. Co-dependents use people as drug addicts use drugs: they depend on a particular person for their good feelings and even their sense of self, they are obsessive and possessive, they may lose their friends, family, home, health, and sanity in order to maintain a relationship which they think is love but is in fact addiction. If the object of their obsession manages to leave, co-dependents are likely to enter into one obsessive-compulsive relationship after another. The emotional pain of co-dependency is intense and is a high risk factor for relapse into drug and alcohol dependency.

Use of internet Just as new drugs are being invented, new technology is providing more behaviours on which people who are predisposed to becoming addicted can become dependent. Social networking sites are a phenomenon of the present age and are used by millions of people worldwide who have verbal relationships with vast numbers of people they have never met. People who fit the addict profile tend to have difficulty maintaining healthy relationships with people and, for them, use of the internet can be dangerous. In the same way as drinking alcoholics share a false sense of intimacy with each other, and drug users feel affiliation with other drug users, online relationships can provide a false sense of connectedness and intimacy. Take away the chemicals and what do these people really share? How well do they truly know and connect with each other? Similarly, take away the technology and what degree of genuine intimacy is left for people with hundreds of Facebook friends? If all your blogs and tweets suddenly stopped functioning, who would really care about what you think and how you feel? Some people recovering from chemical dependency feel lost and lonely if for some reason they cannot access social networking sites. An addict feeling lost and lonely is vulnerable to relapse and needs to engage with a group of real people whom he can meet, share with, drink coffee with, and hug. There is nothing intrinsically wrong with moderate use of the internet, but for real healing spiritual intimacy you can't beat really present people.

Important points arising from these examples are:

1. Behavioural addictions start off slowly. You don't wake up one day and find you are obsessively thinking about it and compulsively acting out. It is most usually something you do occasionally, you have a reason for doing it which seems quite logical at the time, and you get some kind of enjoyment out of it. Joining a gym, going on a shopping spree, cleaning the house, having a bet on the Grand National, going on a diet, starting a new relationship, joining Facebook, working overtime – these are all perfectly reasonable things to do and there is nothing wrong with doing them in moderation. The simple point I am making is that recovering addicts have to be careful. Pay attention to what you do, what you think, and how you feel. If you start to feel uneasy about anything you do frequently, check it out. If your friends make jokes about or comment on the frequency with which you do it, check it out. If you are an addict, you need to be vigilant. Addiction does not go away, it may lie dormant and it can take many forms. If you deliberately harm yourself or indulge in sex that degrades don't wait until you do it frequently, get some help from other recovering addicts without delay.

2. If you are dependent on certain behaviours as well as chemicals and you have the opportunity to be admitted into a 12 Step rehab, do not let fear or shame prevent you from disclosing it. The 12 Steps can be applied to any addiction and recovery is possible, but first you have to acknowledge it. If you are not sure if your behaviour is an addiction or not, check it out with the experts, other recovering peers.

3. There are thirty-six different 12 Step fellowships currently holding meetings in Britain. Whatever your particular chemical or behavioural addiction, there is likely to be an adaptation of the Steps relevant to you. You can attend as many different groups as you like and focus on your various dependencies in any order you want to. I would suggest, however, that if you are chemically dependent you work the AA or NA Steps first. Until you are drug

and alcohol free you will not have clear thinking and a full range of feelings, and you are unlikely to be able to work the Steps of other fellowships with much success until you do. Also it is easier to understand the concept of powerlessness when applied to chemicals than when applied to behaviour. With an acceptance of powerlessness over chemicals it becomes the next logical step to accept one's powerlessness over behaviour in the same way. Finally, don't let your focus on your behavioural addiction lead you to forget that your primary addiction is to chemicals. Some recovering drug and alcohol addicts become so keen on identifying themselves as co-dependents and working those Steps that they miss the warning signs of impending relapse into chemical dependency.

4. The 12 Steps programme is a wonderful thing, but some people need extra help. If you have suffered sexual abuse, working a 12 Step programme can show you the way to addiction recovery, but you may well need specialist counselling as well. If you suffer from post-traumatic stress, phobias, or bereavement you may need other kinds of therapy in addition to the Steps. I have heard it said that if you are working a 12 Step programme well enough you do not need extra therapy. I disagree. Sometimes professional therapy is required. A caring group of recovering addicts can provide invaluable support for the duration of the therapy, but does not eliminate the need for professional help. The implication that if you need extra help you are failing to work the Steps well enough is not helpful and can lead a person to feel shamed and hopeless. Abused and traumatised people carry enough shame as it is; they do not need to be given any more.

5. It is interesting to wonder why people get addicted to the particular chemicals or behaviours they do. While I believe that addiction itself is not caused by social or environmental factors, I do believe that an addict's 'drug of choice' may be influenced by his circumstances. If illegal drugs are scarce in your neighbourhood and if because of your upbringing and lifestyle you have never come across them in your daily life, you are more likely to become dependent on alcohol first. If you grew up in a family where dieting, exercising, or cleaning were important family activities you may give them equal importance in your adult

life, and in times of stress you may turn to them when seeking comfort or relief.

6. Are all these different compulsive ways of behaving desperate and unsuccessful attempts to get a basic human need met? Is it the need for love? The need for meaning? Is it the need for a 'spiritual awakening'? What this means will be discussed elsewhere in this book.

Chapter Six

The 12 Steps for Family Members

We have seen in a previous chapter that it is not only addicts who suffer from addiction. People who are closest to addicts, their family members and friends, suffer as much if not more. Addicts may not realise this, for admitting the pain they are causing to people who love them is something they would prefer to avoid. Denial is a powerful factor in enabling addiction to continue. A using addict is faced with two conflicting beliefs: on one hand he believes that his addiction is causing pain to his loved ones; on the other hand he believes that the only thing he needs in life right now is to feed his addiction. Two conflicting beliefs cannot be held at the same time so one of them has to go. The using addict does not have the power to resist the urgent demands of his addiction, so the belief that he is hurting his loved ones has to go. Denial in this sense is not lying; it is the inability to face up to an unbearable truth. If he really knew the pain he was causing and empathised with his loved ones he would not be able to continue using. Anything which threatens his using has to go. This is what is meant by being powerless over your addiction, or your addiction being more powerful than you are. Addiction alters the way you think. You stop seeing the reality that is staring you in the face.

Family members usually do not understand this. They do not know the power of denial. They are living in the real world, experiencing the heartbreak and the fear, and they take their addict's using behaviour as evidence of lack of love. 'How could you do this to me? See how much I am suffering. If you loved me you could not do this.' Addicts whose denial starts to be eroded by a weeping loved one usually go out and use more in an attempt to numb their internal conflict between love and addiction, a conflict that addiction has to win.

During my years at The Rehab I talked with many family

members of addicts. I met many mothers and fathers, many husbands, wives, and partners of using addicts who came with their addicted sons and daughters and loved ones for an assessment prior to admission for treatment. I met many children who came to visit Mummy or Daddy during their treatment. Almost without exception all these family members feared that they were responsible in some way for the addiction of their loved one. Most of them had been suffering the pain of living with a using addict for many years, had sought and pleaded for help for their loved one, had their hopes raised and then dashed when their loved one could not stop using, were stressed and exhausted and running out of hope. They stayed with their loved one out of love, and fear and guilt. 'He is my son. I can't turn my back on him.' 'If I throw her out she might die. I can't do that.' 'Where did I go wrong?'

I would see parents come to the assessment. They looked pale and scared, in their smart clothes, having made an effort. 'We are good people. You will judge us because our child is an addict, but we are good people. We are the people who are always in the background. Our child is at the forefront, the one who needs help, the one the doctors and care workers and counsellors talk to. We are the ones who cry at night, who pay the debts, who visit at the hospital bed. We are the ones who drive to appointments. No one asks us if we need any help. We are the ones who cope'. I would invite these people into my office. 'And how are you? How have you been managing to cope with their addiction?' Silence was usually followed by tears. 'You do know that none of this is your fault, don't you?' Tears turned to sobs, maybe of relief, 'No one has ever asked us that before ...'

Be in no doubt, the family members of addicts need help just as much as their addicts, and they need it for their own sake, for their own personal healing from the effects of addiction. They also need it because their recovery will significantly increase the addict's prospect of recovery and lessen his chance of relapse. Recovery is all about change. If an addict in treatment changes and returns to a family whose members have not changed, he is going to find it hard to maintain the changes he has made and easy to slip back into old patterns of behaving. The best way for family members to help their addict recover is actually to recover from the effects of addiction themselves.

Although family members are often grateful for being shown kindness and concern they are at the same time reluctant to follow advice. Once the tears stop and they are told about the 12 Step programme for family members and the meetings of Al-Anon where they can find identification and support from other family members, they can be just as resistant to going to meetings as their addicts can. Some of their excuses are the same as their addict's: 'I'm not a groups kind of person', 'I don't think I could talk about this to anyone', 'I have all the support I need from my family'. In their case the clincher is 'Oh no, I'm not the one who needs help ...' even though their family is being torn apart behind the 'fine' facade. If you reading this are a family member of a using addict I say to you: give it up. Whatever you try, you will not be able to stop your loved one using. They are powerless over their addiction and so are you. If and when they want to stop using they can find recovery with the help of the 12 Steps and the recovering community. You do not have to wait for them to get well before you do something to improve your life. You can recover from the effects of his addiction in the same way as they can, and you can start any time you like. The sooner you start the better – for you and for them.

To reinforce the point that family members need to change just as addicts need to change, let us look at what typically happens in an addict family. Welcome to the theatre. You are about to see a play in three acts. At the end of Act 3 the curtain rises again and the play continues with Act 1.

Act 1 Using addict

The curtain rises and Addict is alone on stage, drinking. He is over-sensitive, lonely, guilty, and anxious and hides this behind a facade of bravado. He is independent. He needs nobody. He does as he likes. He is as immature and needy as a baby, and as demanding and autocratic as a king.

Because of his drinking, problems arise. He drinks at work and is suspended. He spends his money on alcohol and fails to pay the rent and bills. He drives while drunk and is banned from driving. He starts a fight in the street and is arrested. Act 1 closes with Addict in trouble, facing a term of probation.

Act 2 Addict in crisis

The curtain rises and other characters enter the scene. Addict is passive and watches while others take action. Enter Victims, Addict's employer and colleagues. These are the people who have covered for Addict in the workplace, told lies for him, made excuses for him, done his work for him, and given him more chances. They like him and want to help him. They will give him one more chance.

Enter Professional Enablers, Addict's probation officer and social worker. They like their work. They get a sense of satisfaction when they help people in trouble. They are kind and understanding people and do not want to distress Addict any more as he is having difficulty coping as it is. They go out of their way to help Addict and end up doing for him what he could take responsibility for doing himself. They help with his housing and his debts and write favourable reports to Court. They send him on a controlled drinking course and teach him how to count units so he can get his driving licence back early.

Addict's wife steps centre stage. She has been present all along but in the background. She is the most powerful character on stage and goes by many names: Enabler, Provoker, Compensator. As Provoker she attempts to make Addict stop drinking. She nags, complains, argues, fights with, shouts at, pleads with, bribes, weeps, threatens, and temporarily leaves Addict, to no avail. As Compensator she adjusts her life to fit with whatever Addict does. He stops working, she gets a second job. He gets a driving ban, she drives everyone where they need to go. He ignores the children, she reads the bedtime stories, helps with homework, pushes them on the swings, gets them to school and home on time. He runs up debts, she negotiates repayment schemes. He brings shame on the family, she holds everything together. As Enabler she does everything she can think of to keep her family together and restore some order to the chaos caused by Addict. Everything she does is intended to help Addict stop using or reduce the harm being done. As Enabler she believes that she is helping to keep Addict alive.

Act 2 ends with passive Addict being rescued from crisis by others, who pick up the pieces and shield Addict from the consequences of his actions.

Act 3 Re-inflation of the Ego

The curtain rises on Addict centre stage. Rescued from crisis and restored to family, Addict starts to feel better. He starts to think, 'Well, nothing too bad has happened. I haven't lost everything. They were exaggerating.' Before long Addict starts to feel resentful. 'What a drama they made. Humiliating me like that. Who do they think they are?' It is not long before Addict concludes 'They are the ones with the problem. I don't need help. I don't need any of them. No one is going to tell me what to do.'

Act 3 ends with Addict leaving the stage and going to buy alcohol.

Act 1 Using addict repeat from the top ...

Among recovering families this dynamic is known as the merry-go-round named denial[13]. With each turn of the merry-go-round the crises become worse. The dynamic is not so much a circle as a downward spiral. For family members it can end in breakdown, homelessness, divorce, removal of children into care, or any of the other horrors awaiting addicts who don't get into recovery. If we look at the three Acts we can see that best place for change to have a chance of happening is in Act 2. In Acts 1 and 3 Addict is using and in denial. Nothing anyone says is going to have much effect on him in this state. Act 2 provides a brief window of opportunity when the consequences of his addiction are all around him and no longer possible to ignore, his denial and defences are as low as they are ever going to be, and he is being introduced to treatment services. At this point intervention is possible; for it to be successful all the players in the drama have to jump off the merry-go-round. Addict needs people to push the merry-go-round for him. It is very hard work indeed if he has to push it round all by himself.

By 'jumping off the merry-go-round' I mean changing the way

---

[13] This description of this dynamic is derived from the pamphlet *Merry-go-round named Denial*, published by Hazelden, which is conference approved literature and available to buy online from the Al-Anon website http://www.al-anonuk.org.uk/

you respond when he is in crisis. When a person is ill you do all you can to make them better. When a person is burdened by problems you do all you can to relieve him of them. Unfortunately this does not work with addiction because using addicts are in denial. The more you make an addict feel better, the more he thinks he doesn't have a problem. You more you fix his problems for him, the more he can use with impunity. He does not need to be rescued. He does not need to be given one more chance. He needs to be smacked in the face with reality until he wakes up.

We saw in Chapter 2 how addicts in The Rehab worked Step 1 and how their denial was eroded as a result. Now we will look at the Steps from a family member's point of view and see how they can transform the life of someone who is not an addict but is adversely affected by the addiction of someone else. Because all the other fellowships have adapted AA's Steps to suit the membership of their particular group, I have made similar changes to the wording of the Al-Anon Steps, replacing 'alcoholics' and 'addicts' with 'family members'. To illustrate my points I will let Elizabeth share her experiences of working the Steps. She is the wife of an alcoholic but her experiences are shared by men and women, husbands, wives, partners, and parents of alcoholics and drug addicts irrespective of their drug of choice. Her husband's name is John.

Elizabeth's story

A friend of mine gave me the phone number of a lady whose husband was an alcoholic and suggested I ring her. When things finally got unbearable I did ring. This lady told me about Al-Anon and said it was run by family members for family members, and that she had found it really helped her survive the nightmare of living with an alcoholic. We met for coffee and I found I could talk to her about what was happening in my life and she totally understood. She suggested I came to an Al-Anon meeting with her. I wasn't keen at first because I didn't want to talk to lots of people about my problems but I was so desperate I agreed. The meeting was held in a church. This put me off a bit as I am suspicious of people trying to convert me to their religion but she said it was just a place to meet and you didn't have to be religious. The first thing

I saw when I walked through the door was a huge effigy of crucified Christ dying in agony. I thought it was utterly repulsive and nearly went back home straight away. The people in the meeting were very kind. They shared their stories with me and I heard how they had 'worked the steps' and how their alcoholics had got well. I thought it was all right for them, my alcoholic was still drinking, but I did hear a lot of kindness in the room and good humour and when they asked me to come back next week I said I would.

In the meeting I noticed that everyone had a little blue book and sometimes someone would refer to it. I like books. If ever I am faced with a new experience I want to read a book about it. I saw how precious these blue books were, the way people carried them with them, and I asked where I could get one. The lady chairing the meeting said I could buy one, but not until I had been to six meetings. I was rather cross about this as I thought that if I could read all about it first I would be able to get my life sorted out faster. I wasn't even allowed to have a flick through one to see what it was all about. I eyed their books enviously and decided I wanted one very much. After the end of my sixth meeting I got my book. I was thrilled. I found it was a book of daily reflections, called *One Day at a Time*[14]. After six meetings I felt more comfortable in the group and had decided to go regularly. It started to sink in that these people were not there looking for tips on how to make their alcoholics stop drinking. They were there for themselves. They had given up trying to fix their alcoholic and were taking charge over their own lives for once. The thought of that started to appeal to me.

Once a month the group had a 'step meeting'. Over the course of a year I listened to people sharing their understanding of all twelve Steps. The message I heard repeated frequently was 'Keep coming back. It works if you work it.' I had kept coming back, and was starting to feel less unhappy, but I had not started 'working it', whatever that meant. It was time for me learn about the Steps and doing what they said. I was quite looking forward to it and thought

---

[14] Conference approved Al-Anon literature. Later updated and titled *Courage to change*. Available to buy online from the Al-Anon website http://www.al-anonuk.org.uk/

it would be like some kind of college course. Maybe I'd get a reading list. Maybe I'd graduate at the end.

It took me a long time to work my way through the 12 Steps, and at the end I realised I was still at the start of my recovery. The Steps themselves were simple. In fact they were so simple I couldn't understand half of them and had a hostile reaction to the other half. I stuck at it because I was desperate. In the depth of my despair even something which appeared so ridiculous was worth a try. I say ridiculous because I could not for the life of me see how talking to these nice people and putting everything in the hands of God was going to do anything at all to improve my situation, apart from getting out of the house for an hour and a half once a week. I really struggled with the God words. Handing everything over to God sounded like sitting there doing nothing and blithely saying 'Nothing to worry about, God will make everything OK'. What if God didn't, though? That was my worry. When someone showed me the version of the Steps without the religious words most of my resistance disappeared at a stroke. The two version were shown side by side, like a translation, which it was for me. If that is what the Step means I can understand that, so there's no reason why I can't do it. So here are the Steps I used and this is how I worked them.

Step 1

We admitted we were powerless over alcohol – that our lives had become unmanageable.	We admitted our addiction was more powerful than we were, and that we had become unable to manage our own lives.

I didn't get this at all. I wasn't the one who was an alcoholic. I wasn't powerless over alcohol. I could take it or leave it, and I could take some and leave it which is something John could never do. My life may be 'unmanageable' but I'd like to see you manage to bring up three kids and do two jobs and still get to parents' evening on time. I was angry with Step 1. It sounded like a criticism I didn't deserve.

When I looked at the translation it made immediate sense to me. This may be because I read it wrong. I saw it as 'We admitted addiction was more powerful than we were, and that we had become unable to manage our own lives'. Of course addiction is more powerful than me. I have been waging war against John's addiction for over ten years and it has beaten me every time. Because I have been so preoccupied with his addiction for so long I am so stressed and tired that I have become unable to manage my own life. How simple is that. How undeniably true.

I know I misread it but if I had seen the 'our' I would have got all hung up on whether I am an addict or not, and whether trying to stop an alcoholic drinking is itself and addiction, and my brain would have missed the simply obvious. Addiction is more powerful than I am. Like a light coming on, this realisation made everything look different. If addiction is more powerful than I am, why am I wasting my energy trying and trying and trying to beat it? Why don't I put my energy to better use, like managing my own life, maybe?

Step 2

Came to believe that a Power greater than ourselves could restore us to sanity.	Seeing other family members in recovery we came to believe that with help we too could recover.

I didn't have a problem with being called 'insane' because most of the time that is how I felt. I did have a problem with a 'Power' taking over my brain though. The translation summed up what was happening for me in the meetings. I kept going to meetings and listened to what other family members were sharing. I saw how they were changing, even in the few months I had been going. They were more positive, taking more action, solving their own problems, having a life outside of the alcoholic madness. They called that 'recovery'. Although I was still feeling low and my self-confidence had been worn down over the years I was coming to believe that if they could change then maybe I could change too.

They were willing to help me so why not try doing whatever it was that they were doing and see what happened? I heard people calling Step 2 'the Step of Hope'. Hope was something I hadn't felt for a long time and wasn't sure any more how realistic it was. Someone in a meeting shared what it meant for him, and I liked this very much.

Hearing others with the same problem gave me hope.
Hearing Other People's Experiences = HOPE

Step 3

Made a decision to turn our will and our lives over to the care of God *as we understood Him*.	We made a decision to stop acting on impulse and instead to be guided by the principles of the 12-Step programme.

Straight to the translation for this step. I did not like the sound of putting my will (my free will!) into the hands of God, and I would have liked to trust my life into the care of God but couldn't. I could make a decision, though, because I have free will (I couldn't make a decision without it, could I?). It was a tough decision to make, to trust something other than my own impulse, but I could see the sense in allowing myself to be guided by principles. Better to be guided by principles than just react to individual events. Better to have some idea of a bigger picture if you want to make sense of life.

Step 4

Made a searching and fearless moral inventory of ourselves.	Made a searching and fearless moral inventory of ourselves.

This didn't need a translation as it told me very simply what to do. There are various guides to making an inventory and you can use whichever one you prefer. I used the guide reproduced at the back of this book, mentally changing 'your addiction' to 'your husband's addiction' where required.

Writing my personal inventory was a revelation and very uncomfortable to do. I was quite familiar with the list of blocks to recovery itemised in the guide as I had been taking John's inventory since I first heard about AA. Having to see how these same character traits applied to me was a humbling experience because the deeper I dug the more I identified with them. I felt even worse then. John had these traits but at least he was an alcoholic – I didn't even have that excuse. That thought got me down for a while until I recalled that being over-hard on myself was one of the items on the list. Feeling bad because of having these traits was not going to achieve much. I had to view them as emotionally neutral, a list of things which needed changing, not something to despair about. The first time I wrote an inventory I only did half. I missed out the assets altogether. I was told by my sponsor to do it properly and found it just as uncomfortable having to write down my good qualities. I still don't know why this should be so very uncomfortable, but it was. Step 4 was bad enough but I was completely dreading Step 5.

Step 5

Admitted to God, to ourselves, and to another human being the exact nature of our wrongs.	Admitted to ourselves and another person the exact nature of our blocks to recovery.

I didn't fancy baring my soul to another person and would have much preferred to admit all this to myself in the secrecy of my own head, but the Step was plain enough and had to be done if I wanted to continue to do all twelve. I shared it with my sponsor. She provided me with coffee and tissues and gave me a big hug when I had done it. She did not hate me. The sky did not fall in.

Step 6

Were entirely ready to have God remove all these defects of character.	By acting always on our strengths and assets we saw our blocks to recovery diminish.

Now I knew the parts of me I wanted to get rid of and the parts of me I wanted to develop. I wasn't sure how I was going to make these changes but at least I had a set of aims. I was starting to see where I wanted to get to even if I was not exactly sure of the route. In my Step 4 I identified resentment, fear, envy, and self-pity as things which caused me a lot of pain. These were traits I had even before I met John so I couldn't blame them on his alcoholism. This was a shock in itself as lately I had been blaming John for everything that was wrong with me, thinking 'I wouldn't be like this if he wasn't so horrible to me'. Now I had to face up to the fact that I was responsible for me and I needed to change myself whether he stopped drinking or not. For once I became the priority in my own eyes and his drinking became irrelevant. The translation told me how to make the changes: act on your good qualities and not on your blocks. The ones that grow are the ones you feed.

Step 7

Humbly asked Him to remove our shortcomings.	We asked for help, to accomplish what we could not achieve alone.

Being without shortcomings sounded like being perfect and I couldn't see that happening. I didn't want to be perfect anyway as that sounded like being more holy than the angels. I was just discovering that it was OK to be human and I didn't want to be totally transformed even if it was possible. I could ask for help though, and I asked it of people in the meetings. I asked how they dealt with fear and self-pity and all the other things on my list, and was given sound advice on what to do about them. One of my favourites was:

FEAR

Face Everything And Recover
Or
Forget Everything And Run

So I did things I was afraid of doing and as a result my confidence grew. As my confidence grew I became more assertive. As I became more assertive I became less manipulative. As I became less manipulative I became more open, honest, direct, and easier to trust. Not everybody liked me but at least they knew that what they saw was what they got. Of course I still have fears and as the years go by new fears are added, but I have also developed my courage so am not afraid to ask for help when I need it.

Step 8

Made a list of all persons we had harmed, and became willing to make amends to them all.	Made a list of all persons we had harmed, and became willing to make amends to them all.

I didn't mind making a list of the people I had harmed while unsuccessfully trying to make John stop drinking. I knew I had been impatient and snappy with the children and had rows with my parents about whether to leave him or not. My brother and sister got fed up of me crying to them about John but not doing anything they suggested, so our relationship had suffered. My work colleagues had suffered when I was too stressed or preoccupied to do my work properly. I was quite prepared to admit all this and make amends by sincerely apologising and behaving better from now on. What stuck in my throat was putting John's name on the list and becoming willing to make amends to him. Me make amends to him? What about him making amends to me!

This needed a lot of attitude-adjusting on my part. I asked my group members how they saw it. How did they think my behaviour had harmed John? Like the true friends they were, they told me straight. For a start, no one enjoys living with a nagging, weeping, manipulative, needy person who is depressed most of the time. No one enjoys having all their faults broadcast to family and friends, and being blamed for everything that is wrong in the family home, even if they are a drinking alcoholic. I had to admit they had a point. They next bit of feedback they gave me took me by surprise. 'All your attempts to pick up the pieces after him were just enabling him to carry on drinking. Every time you cleared up his mess you gave him the message that he could drink without consequences. You weren't saving his life. You were enabling him to drink himself to death.' I was stunned. Maybe if I had allowed my brother to 'have a word' John would have taken it seriously? Maybe if I had done as my sister suggested and taken the children and left him he would have tried to do something about his drinking? Maybe if I had ejected him from the family home he would have gone and got the help he needed, and not died in a gutter at all?

Step 9

Made direct amends to such people wherever possible, except when to do so would injure them or others.	Made direct amends to such people wherever possible, except when to do so would injure them or others.

Making direct amends was easier than I had feared. Everyone was pleased to see how I was changing by working the Steps and were willing to accept my apologies for the way I had treated them. As well as apologising they needed to see a change in my behaviour and I took this seriously. I don't feel as if I have to keep on making amends for ever but I do like behaving better and being more considerate and loving towards them, so I continue to behave like that even though it is no longer an obligation. There weren't any amends that would have resulted in injuries so that was not a problem for me. The problem that arose was that I owed John amends but was not sure how to make them or when.

I had become willing in Step 8 to admit the things I had done wrong and apologise for them, but I was not going to apologise to John for things that were not my fault and I was not going to make amends while he was still drinking. If I had been 'enabling him to carry on drinking' by letting him get away with drinking without consequences, I wasn't going to enable him to carry on drinking by starting to apologise and giving him the message that it was all my fault and he was not responsible for anything.

Another problem I faced was that someone in my group had pointed out that one of the people most hurt by my behaviour was myself, therefore I needed to make amends to myself. This involved being kind and compassionate to myself, putting my own wellbeing before John's, and doing what I could to get my own needs met. The difficulty with this was that I knew now that I could not carry on living with a drinking alcoholic. I was becoming more crazy, ill, and badly behaved the longer it continued, and John showed no inclination to stop drinking or even try to cut down. He was isolated in his own world with alcohol and had shut me out of it a long time ago. At this stage in working my own programme I came to realise that I had to make a choice. I knew I couldn't change him, so did I want to live with him as he was, or not live with him at all? Many of my group members had reached this point in their recovery and decided that they did want to stay with their partners, drinking or not. They reckoned that by following the Steps and acting on their assets they could learn to tolerate the drinking and not let it destroy them. In time a lot of their partners had joined AA and stopped drinking. I didn't think that was going to work for me. If John wanted to be in an exclusive relationship with alcohol, I didn't want to be with him any more.

Step 9 said I had to make amends, but not if it caused injury to others. Was divorcing John going to cause him injury? Not if staying with him meant enabling him to drink himself to death. Was staying with him going to cause me injury? That was definitely true, but how should I weigh up injury to one against injury to another – and then what about injury to the children? How could I accurately foresee the consequences and whether they would turn out to be injurious or not? It was not an easy decision but one I made eventually by thinking carefully, considering advice, and applying principles and not just acting on emotion and impulse.

Step 10

Continued to take personal inventory and when we were wrong promptly admitted it.	Continued to take personal inventory and when we were wrong promptly admitted it.

I carried on taking personal inventory by having a little review of my day every night when I went to bed. How have I got on today? Did I act on any of my old blocks today? Did I use opportunities to practise acting on my assets? Some days I did better than others. I used the meetings to share my progress and my setbacks. On the whole I was going in the right direction. When I wasn't, someone would tell me. I didn't usually like being told but accepted it with the best grace I could and made any amends that were necessary.

Step 11

Sought through prayer and meditation to improve our conscious contact with God *as we understood Him*, praying only for knowledge of His will for us and the power to carry that out.	Sought through mindfulness and meditation to develop our spiritual and ethical selves.

Here was another one of those Steps that needed translating for me. I took this to mean I should carry on behaving well, in an ethical manner, and develop my attitude of acceptance and care for the world around me and everything in it. I paid attention to what I was doing. I made time to sit quietly and just be aware. I started to see the world in a different way. Some things that had been important to me became less important, and some things I had not even noticed before became very important. There were moments when I was filled with a feeling of peace. In the meetings I still heard the word 'God' but now I didn't automatically close my ears. I took 'God' to be shorthand for whatever it was that filled me with peace and made me glad to be a part of the universe. I even started to use the word myself. I didn't mean the crucified Christ. I couldn't really define what the word did mean to me but it meant something now.

Step 12

Having had a spiritual awakening as a result of these steps, we tried to carry this message to alcoholics, and to practice these principles in all our affairs.	Recovering from the effects of addiction as a result of these steps, we shared our experience with others seeking recovery and continued to practice these principles in all our affairs.

I didn't know if it was a 'spiritual awakening' but something was certainly happening to me as a result of working these Steps. I was recovering from the effects of living with addiction, I knew that was true. I kept on going to Al-Anon and shared my experience with anyone who came to the meetings. Sometimes family members of drug addicts turned up, desperate for help. I saw them as exactly the same as family members of alcoholics and shared with them too. I took on service positions and went on 12 Step calls. My life got better and better and it all began when I gave up trying to beat addiction and started working on my own recovery. It is a nasty illness and it doesn't just affect addicts. I didn't even know how ill it had made me until I jumped off the merry-go-round and like the hero in the children's stories 'with one bound he was free'.

My recovery does not end with completing Step 12. It has become a way of life, a journey, a process of deepening awareness. I didn't get a reading list and I didn't get a graduation, but I got me back – oh, and a key ring.

Chapter Seven

About Meetings

Many addicts suffering from a spiritual emptiness are lonely and lost. They have a vague unspecified yearning for meaning and purpose and a sense of belonging. This makes them vulnerable to exploitation by charismatic 'spiritual leaders' who offer them what they need in exchange for their devotion and their money. It is not surprising that these addicts become cynical and suspicious. If all they hear about AA is talk about God and 'the programme' their initial thoughts are likely to be along these lines: 'It's all very well saying I can recover from addiction if I go to meetings and trust the members of AA with my life, but I am going to want to know a bit more about AA before I take such a huge risk. What if it is some kind of cult, as so many people seem to believe? What if I'm going to get brainwashed by some religious fanatics, or have to hand over my life savings, or have to go round recruiting new members? What if once I join they'll never let me get away? And who runs it? Who are these people? For all I know it could be one big scam with some people at the top getting very rich and powerful.'

In the first part of this chapter I shall explain how AA is structured, who runs it, and the safeguards that are built into its constitution which exclude the possibility of exploitation, and in the second part I shall outline what you can expect when you go to a meeting.

How AA is structured

Meetings of addicts are like individual addicts in that they all have certain fundamental similarities and yet each one is different. If you come across one you don't like, don't assume that you will dislike all the others.

One thing individual addicts have in common is their 12 Step programme which defines recovery and tells them how to do it. One thing meetings have in common is their 12 Traditions, which define what it is to be a 12 Step meeting and tells members how to run it. As the 12 Steps are fundamental to an individual's recovery, so the 12 Traditions are fundamental to the existence of the meeting. The 12 Traditions are just as important as the 12 Steps, for without them every group of addicts would be entirely different from any other group and the sense of a world-wide recovering community based on the same governing principles would not exist. It is due to the existence of the 12 Traditions that you can walk into any 12 Step meeting anywhere in the world and have a good idea of what to expect.

These are the 12 Traditions of Alcoholics Anonymous, drawn up by the founders of AA and authors of the 12 Steps. In having the wisdom to define these Traditions they ensured the continuation of AA throughout economic recessions, wars, political and social changes, and fashions in state-funded drug and alcohol treatments. The Traditions may not be as much studied as the Steps but they are equally important.

The Twelve Traditions of Alcoholics Anonymous

1. Our common welfare should come first; personal recovery depends upon A.A. unity.

2. For our group purpose there is but one ultimate authority – a loving God as He may express Himself in our group conscience. Our leaders are but trusted servants; they do not govern.

3. The only requirement for A.A. membership is a desire to stop drinking.

4. Each group should be autonomous except in matters affecting other groups or A.A. as a whole.

5. Each group has but one primary purpose – to carry its message to the alcoholic who still suffers.

6. An A.A. group ought never endorse, finance, or lend the A.A. name to any related facility or outside enterprise, lest problems of money, property, and prestige divert us from our primary purpose.

7. Every A.A. group ought to be fully self-supporting, declining

---

outside contributions.

8. Alcoholics Anonymous should remain forever non-professional, but our service centres may employ special workers.

9. A.A., as such, ought never be organized; but we may create service boards or committees directly responsible to those they serve.

10. Alcoholics Anonymous has no opinion on outside issues; hence the A.A. name ought never be drawn into public controversy.

11. Our public relations policy is based on attraction rather than promotion; we need always maintain personal anonymity at the level of press, radio, and films.

12. Anonymity is the spiritual foundation of all our traditions, ever reminding us to place principles before personalities.

These Traditions were first published in the April 1946 edition of *AA Grapevine* under the title 'Twelve Points to Assure Our Future' and were formally adopted at AA's First International Convention in 1950. All 12 Step fellowships, AA, Al-Anon, NA, ABA, CA, GA and all the rest, are governed by the same 12 Traditions with minor changes being made to refer to the specific addiction of its members.

On the face of it, this should not work. How can a movement, which consists of thousands of autonomous groups, which has no leaders, is not professional, has no external funding, charges no fees, does not promote itself, and whose members are anonymous, ever manage to last one year, let alone eighty? How can something which must never be organised maintain unity world-wide? How on earth can a bunch of alcoholics, some of whom are still drinking, get it together to turn up in the same place at the same time, let alone run 4400[15] weekly groups in Britain alone? Maybe its very simplicity is what makes it work. Maybe it works because it has one primary aim and everything else is immaterial. Maybe it works because it embodies a genuine democracy you are unlikely to come across anywhere else. I don't know why it works, but I know it does.

Reading through the Traditions I am struck by their single-mindedness of purpose. By stripping away every unnecessary

---

[15] Figure provided by Alcoholics Anonymous (Great Britain) website, 2014.

distraction or complication they endow this purpose with a singular power. The common welfare of AA comes before anything, because the personal recovery of individual alcoholics depends upon it. Anything which threatens the continuing existence of AA in its pure and simple form is specifically excluded by the Traditions. People can do whatever they like, but if they are not following the Traditions they can't call themselves an AA group.

I am also struck by the fact that the existence of the group is more important than, and does not depend upon, any individual. No matter who you are, how long you have been in recovery, how rich, famous, or influential you are, how intelligent or how spiritually awakened you are, the AA group is paramount and you are just another member of it. You may be the chairperson of a meeting, but it is not your meeting. You may know a great deal about the Steps and recovery, but you alone can't make decisions about how the meeting operates. You may be eloquent and persuasive, but you alone can't speak for AA. You may have transformed your self and your life as a result of working the 12 Steps and feel a burning desire to shout your message from the rooftops but, if you do, you have to remain anonymous.

The wise founders of AA knew all about human frailty. They knew how individuals, sometimes with the best of motives, can destroy something by imposing their will on it, or by leading it onto financial ruin, or by becoming seen as its representative or figurehead and bringing it into disrepute when their personal failings become known. That is why they made sure in the Traditions that no one has more power than anyone else, that each meeting has to be financially self-supporting via donations by its members, and membership grows by attraction and not by individuals promoting it. If a particular meeting does not attract new members and dwindles to the point where it cannot afford to cover the cost of renting a meeting room, then that meeting will close. On the other hand if a meeting has only one or two members and together they pay the room rent and follow the Traditions, they are still an AA meeting and can meet for as long as they like, providing a place where alcoholics seeking help can find it.

Of course there is some structure in AA. The important point is that 'our leaders are but trusted servants; they do not govern'. Alcoholics who are abstinent from alcohol and working a 12 Step programme are encouraged to do 'service' in the meetings. This means they volunteer to take on responsibility for some activity necessary for the smooth running of the group in particular or AA as a whole. Service positions within a group include collecting members' donations and paying the room rent, bringing tea, coffee, and milk for refreshments, chairing the meeting, washing up afterwards, ordering AA literature from AA suppliers if members request it, answering the telephone enquiries line, and accompanying newcomers to meetings. The people who take on these responsibilities do so as volunteers, on a temporary basis, because doing service is good for their recovery as well as necessary for the group. Recovering people who feel they want to make a positive contribution to the community can make a real and valuable start by washing up after meetings, or turning up every week with a bottle of milk. It is not a small thing. It marks a radical shift in attitude on the part of a self-centred alcoholic and is evidence of the beginning of the 'spiritual awakening' referred to in Step 12.

Individual groups are the front line of AA. They form the base of a pyramid made up of four tiers: Groups, Inter-groups, Regions, and General Service Board. Each group chooses one member to act as their Group Service Representative (GSR). This person coordinates service activity on behalf of the group and meets with neighbouring GSRs a few times a year in an Inter-group meeting. Inter-groups can coordinate activities within their area, and connect and consult with each other at regional level. There are fifteen Regions in Britain which provide a forum for discussion and an exchange of information concerning best practice. At the top of the pyramid is the General Service Board (Great Britain) which is a registered charity. Groups, Inter-groups, and Regions are recognised by the Charity Commissioners as informal, autonomous affiliated groups which have no independent constitution. There are twenty-one members of the GSB and they are all elected to serve for a fixed term only.

This goes some way to answering two questions which will probably have occurred to you by now: If AA has no leaders, how does anything ever get done? And if the only ultimate authority is a loving God, how are people going to know how to resolve conflicts of opinion among the serving leaders? The answer is that decisions are made by group consensus and based on set principles rather than the opinions of whoever holds a particular service position at the time. Christians may call the ultimate authority 'a loving God as He may express Himself in our group conscience'; non-religious members may call it principle-based democracy. When considering any proposal, at any level, the questions to ask are: Will this jeopardise the welfare of AA in any way? Is this in accordance with the 12 Traditions?

This is copied from the Alcoholics Anonymous (GB) website and explains how 'the collective conscience' works: 'The General Service Conference is held annually in York where delegates from all regions gather. In a series of committees (comprising a representative from each region and GSB members) questions which have been submitted from members, groups, intergroups, and regions earlier in the previous year are considered and responses drafted to reflect the collective conscience of AA-GB. Thus, guidelines are drafted, amended, ratified, and then published throughout the Fellowship on an annual basis.'

So no, it's not a cult, it's not a conspiracy, and there is no leader. No one is getting rich and no one is more powerful than anyone else. It is totally free and totally optional. There is no small print, no hidden costs, and no exclusions – which in my eyes makes it quite extraordinary.

What to expect in meetings

In a previous chapter we looked at some reasons why people seeking recovery from addiction are reluctant to go to meetings. As well as the reasons already discussed I will propose another: embarrassment, because people don't know what to expect and how to behave. This is not a frivolous reason, it is a genuine concern. If you are addicted, stigmatised, maybe destitute, maybe in withdrawal, over-sensitive, paranoid, and jumpy, the last thing you want to expose yourself to is the risk of being smirked at because you don't know where to sit, or what to say. If you are one such person, the next bit is for you; forewarned is forearmed.

Perhaps the best way to arrive at your first meeting is to go with someone who is already a member. This could quite easily be arranged as follows. There are meetings all over the country. If you want to find out if there is one where you live you can go to the AA (GB) website, enter your location, and you will see the all meetings in your area. Alternatively you can look in your local newspaper, library, or health centre where there is likely to be an AA poster. Posters often include the name and contact number of a local member who has volunteered to be a first point of contact for newcomers and will go with you to your first meeting if you would like that. If you cannot find a first point of contact number you will have to be brave and go on your own. This far less difficult than you think.

Meetings are often held in church halls. This is not because of any religious connection but because church premises are often cheap to rent and sometimes free. Do not let the fact that the meeting takes place in a church hall deter you from going. You have been in far worse places in the course of your addiction. Meetings start at the time advertised. Some members arrive early because they have volunteered to prepare the room or set out the teacups, or simply to say hello to other members and have a cup of tea. After the meeting is closed some members like to stay on for a while to chat or drink tea. The meeting itself starts when the chairperson opens it and ends when the chairperson closes it. It is up to you when you arrive and leave but it is good manners to be present for the duration of the meeting itself unless you have a good reason for excusing yourself and leaving prematurely.

There are large meetings and small meetings and chairs are usually arranged accordingly. A large meeting may be held in a hall where rows of chairs are arranged to face a 'top table' where there are a few chairs reserved for the chairperson and members who have been invited to share their stories in this particular meeting. You can sit anywhere you like in the audience. A small meeting may be held in an office with chairs arranged around a table. If there is no obvious place reserved for the chairperson you can sit where you like. In a meeting every member is equal, the chairperson is a member volunteering to undertake the role, and no members have a right to certain seats, even if they have been attending that meeting for decades. You may hear it said that 'the most important person in any meeting is the newcomer'. That means you. You are welcome. The meeting is there for your benefit.

Other points to bear in mind are that everyone there is an alcoholic, just like you. Everyone is entitled to their opinions, just like you. Everyone has the right to be treated with respect, just like you. Treating someone with respect involves following certain codes of conduct. These are some of the behaviours which are expected of you, and everyone else, in the meetings. If someone is sharing, wait until they finish before you start to speak. Do not argue or disagree with anything they say, nor give feedback or advice in response. Meetings are a place where members can say anything they please provided it will be helpful to their recovery. If a member wants to share about the problems they are facing at home, or express their feelings of joy, anger, grief, or whatever, they can make use of meeting time to do that. Your job is not to judge nor come up with solutions. Your contribution to that person's recovery is to give them the gift of good listening. You can, if you want to, say that you identify with them, which helps them know they are not alone in having this problem, but meetings are not a conversation – they are a special time in which people can be open and honest and share things they feel they cannot safely say elsewhere.

Meetings are the one place I can go where I don't have to be ashamed of being an alcoholic. *Linda*

It is customary at some small meetings for every person present to introduce themselves. The form of words used is 'My name is [first name only], I am an alcoholic.' The chairperson is usually the one who starts and if you are seated in a circle you introduce yourself when your turn comes. This may be the only thing you say at your first meeting and if that suits you then it is enough. Sometimes a meeting will have a theme. It is the chairperson's job to tell you what the theme for the day is and introduce the topic by sharing or introducing someone else who will share first on that theme. If members are aware that this is your first meeting they may hold a 'newcomer's meeting' for you. People will share what their lives were like while they were using and how working the 12 Steps has helped them achieve abstinence. You can share if you want to; even if it is your first meeting you may say something that is just what another member needs to hear at this time. Sometimes a chairperson will ask if anyone else has anything they want to share. If there is an uncomfortable silence and you feel all eyes are on you because you haven't said anything yet, you can always say something along the lines of 'I prefer not to share anything today.' Saying anything at all is making a start to your process of learning to trust, identify, share, and get well in a group of peers.

Perhaps the biggest block which stops newcomers sharing in meetings is fear of saying something inappropriate or 'not good enough'. Some alcoholics who have been going to meetings for ages can make it look so simple – they open their mouths and out come words of wisdom and inspiration which leave you feeling totally inadequate. How can you ever get to be so eloquent, so knowledgeable, so confident? What use is your contribution going to be to this meeting? What can anybody learn from you? You would be surprised. Your story is unique and no one has heard it before. Your struggles and doubts may be exactly what the people there today need to hear. I would suggest that you do not think too carefully about exactly what you are going to say. If you spend too much time planning it you will miss what other people are sharing and you will be so preoccupied with when to say it that you will be a mass of nerves when you do get the chance. A share is not a prepared speech. A share comes from the heart. It does not have to be perfect, and often spontaneous is best. Most important of all, you share it because you want to share it, not for anyone else's benefit but for your own.

Be aware of what kind of meeting you are attending. Most meetings are 'closed' in the sense that the only people there are alcoholics. Some meetings are 'open' in the sense that anyone wanting to know about AA or learn about the 12 Steps or hear the experiences of alcoholics in recovery may attend. Non-alcoholics in open meetings may be addictions professionals, family members of alcoholics, teachers, social workers, or anyone else who is interested. If you don't want non-alcoholics to hear your shares or want to keep your membership of AA hidden from the general public, make sure you are going to a closed meeting. Whether a meeting is open or closed is stated on the list of meetings available on the AA website.

Another thing to bear in mind is that some people in a closed meeting may still be drinking. Membership of AA is self-selecting. You don't have to be referred or introduced by anyone, and you don't have to have reached any level of recovery before you can join. A person 'becomes a member' simply by attending a meeting. There is only one requirement for membership – the desire to stop drinking. This means that even if you are still drinking you may attend meetings provided that you do want to stop. If you attend a meeting and are no longer drinking, you may have to be tolerant of other alcoholics in the meeting who have not been able to work Step 1 yet. If you are attending your first meeting while still drinking, you may be advised simply to listen until you start to make some sense of it. If you have been abstinent and relapse, get yourself back to a meeting as soon as you possibly can, drinking or not. If you attend a meeting while drinking it is obviously a good idea to drink as little as possible before going. The chairperson has the right and the responsibility to ensure the safety of the meeting by asking a drunk member who is being disruptive to leave the room.

When you walk in the meeting room you will probably see on the wall a poster showing the 12 Steps. These will contain the word 'God' and members will be eager to tell you that 'God' can mean whatever you like and the 12 Steps are not religious but are spiritual. You probably won't believe them. Do not let this prevent you from coming back again. At the end of the meeting you may find that everyone stands up in a circle, holds hands, and says the serenity prayer together. Do not be alarmed. This is a traditional way of marking the end of a meeting. It is not religious unless you want it to be. After the serenity prayer sometimes members hug each other. You can stand there feeling horrified, or join in, or try to escape by offering to put the chairs away.

Many alcoholics emerge from their first meeting with a strong desire to have a drink. If this happens to you, don't worry; it is not at all unusual, and you don't have to act on it. Your addiction is under threat and will not want to let you go without putting up a fight. You may experience all manner of doubts, cravings, and general resistance, but reassure yourself that this is normal and keep going back to the meetings. It will help if you talk to a fellow member about it. The chances are that person will have felt the same at some time, and will be able to reassure you that these feelings will become less as time goes on. People often go together for a coffee somewhere after the meeting place has closed. This is a perfect time to get to know your fellow members, learn how to socialise without a drink in your hand, and stay in the protection of the group when you feel vulnerable to cravings. If you are invited to join them say yes.

Of course not all meetings are like this. Every meeting is autonomous and can decide for itself how it opens and closes meetings, whether hugs are included or not, if or where smoking is allowed, and other such matters. If you are not comfortable with any particular group practices you may ask for the matter to be reviewed in a group conscience meeting. In a group conscience meeting your voice will carry as much weight as anyone else's. A group conscience meeting may come to a decision you personally do not like but you always have the right, and indeed the responsibility if you think a decision is wrong, to question it.

Any literature you see for sale in a meeting and any readings you hear are 'conference approved' and you can trust that they are a true expression of the beliefs of AA. The preamble and readings will probably be the same whichever meetings you attend, and the expectations regarding not giving feedback or advice in the meeting. Two other things which are universal are some mention of Tradition 7 and the rule of confidentiality. Tradition 7 says that every group must be fully self-supporting, declining outside contributions. This means that money needed to rent the meeting room and provide any refreshments has to be raised by the members of the meeting. A hat may be passed around. If you have very little money and have only pennies to spare, put in pennies. If you can afford more, give more. There is no set amount expected. Members give what they can afford to cover the cost of what the meeting needs. For some alcoholics putting money in a collecting hat may be a big change in attitude and behaviour. Some may have been more used to taking it out.

Perhaps the most important thing you will see in a meeting is a little card on the table which reminds everyone of the importance of confidentiality. Whatever you see or hear in a meeting stays in the meeting. If there is one thing that will ruin a group faster than anything else it is gossip. Everyone who attends a meeting is vulnerable to relapse. They need to feel safe in their group. They do not need to have their shares, doubts, fears, and secrets bandied about outside the meeting by members and members' friends. You certainly would not like it, so don't do it.

One other thing which damages a group and its members is something referred to as '13th stepping'. Sometimes in a group you may come across a member who seeks to charm you or impress you with his or her recovery with the aim of getting you into bed. This is deeply damaging to all concerned and should definitely be avoided. Meetings are there to save your life, not find a partner. It does not hurt to remember the simple fact that every person in a meeting has an addictive illness and some are less well than others. Yes you do have to learn to trust, but you don't have to be gullible.

When you have been to a few meetings you may be advised to 'get a sponsor'. A sponsor is a person who will be your guide and support as you work the 12 Steps. The sponsor/sponsee relationship will be explained to you by members or you can read about it in a conference-approved pamphlet. The best way to choose a sponsor is to listen and observe in meetings and when you come across someone whose recovery you like ask them if they will be your sponsor. Listen for someone who shares how they are working the Steps in their daily life, who is open and honest and shows that they trust their peers by sharing in the meetings, someone who does not take themselves too seriously, and who is kind but not a pushover. A good sponsor may already have a number of sponsees so don't take it personally if they say they can't be your sponsor at the moment. In an honest relationship between equals each person has the right to ask for what they want and each person has the right to say yes or no. Being direct may be uncomfortable if you are used to dishonest manipulative relationships, which you probably are if you have been in active addiction for any length of time, but get used to it. Honesty is one of the core values of recovery and like anything else it gets easier the more you do it.

A note to service providers

If you reading this are a professional working with alcoholic clients please arrange for them to go to AA. First you may want to find out more about it, and the best way to do this is to go to some open meetings. All meetings are autonomous and will have some procedural differences so go to as many different open meetings as you can. There is plenty of information about AA and all the other 12 Step fellowships available online and in conference approved literature, but the best way to find out is to experience it yourself and talk with members after the meetings. If you feel reluctant to go to a meeting because you fear you will be uncomfortable, not like it, or not fit in, this is exactly how your clients feel.

I'm afraid that giving your clients a leaflet and telling them to go to a meeting if they want to is not enough. A recent study found that referral by leaflet-giving resulted in 0% attendance. Alcoholics need to be directed to go to meetings, preferably as part of their treatment contract with you, and they need to be taken to their first meeting by a member of that meeting. This 'assertive linkage' results in almost 100% attendance and enables faster integration into the group and better identification with other members. Identification with other addicts in recovery is a major factor in retention in treatment and predictor of successful long-term outcomes. For your clients regular attendance at AA will enhance the treatment you are providing, and at the end of treatment your clients will be established members of a peer support group which will nurture their continuing abstinent recovery.

The best way you can help your alcoholic clients is to go to some open meetings yourself, ask members of those meetings if they are willing to meet with and accompany new members to their first meeting, and get their phone numbers. When you next see a client, tell him he needs to go to AA and you will arrange a meeting between him and your contact. No matter how excellent your work with your clients, they will gain something extra from identification with other alcoholics in recovery. Your treatment plan and AA's programme do not have to conflict. If they work in partnership the long-term outcomes for your clients are far and away more successful than the outcomes of treatment alone.[16]

---

[16] Participation in Treatment and Alcoholics Anonymous: A 16-Year Follow-Up of Initially Untreated Individuals, Rudolph H. Moos and Bernice S. Moos, *Journal of Clinical Psychology*, Vol. 62(6), 735-750

This is a recommendation[17] from NICE, National Institute for Health and Care Excellence:

Supportive relationships among people on the journey to recovery from alcohol or drug addiction are a vital element in helping individuals build and sustain their own recovery.

NICE recommends that treatment staff should not only routinely provide service users with information about mutual aid groups but also encourage and facilitate all their clients to engage with mutual aid. There are significant gains to be had – as evidence shows that adding just one abstinent person to a drinker's social network increases the probability of abstinence in the next year by 27%.

... And to service users

In conclusion, to all addicts: Go to meetings. You have nothing whatsoever to lose. They are a free gift and have no strings attached. You do not have to pay anything, sign up to anything, or let Jesus into your life. There you will find people just like you. They are doing what the 12 Steps suggest and are discovering that they work. If you don't like it, don't want to be abstinent, and don't want to go again you don't have to; in that case 'your misery will be refunded'.[18]

I will close this chapter with Sharon's story to illustrate how one alcoholic who didn't 'get' AA kept going back until she did. She is one of the people who combined residential treatment in The Rehab with regular attendance at AA and who is now enjoying life happy, fulfilled, and alcohol free.

(2006). Published online in Wiley InterScience (www.interscience.wiley.com)

[17] Published by National Treatment Agency, Public Health England, 2014.

[18] Overheard in an Al-Anon meeting.

I can't remember when I stopped 'wanting' a drink and started 'needing' one, but it was a nightmare that was to consume me for many years. I worked as a psychiatric nurse, and at one stage was the senior nurse on the Detox Unit for three years. I assessed people coming in for treatment and was very aware that I was drinking far more than lots of them and shared the same secretive patterns, so the alarm bells were ringing loud and clear. My workmates knew I was having problems but were scared to approach me about it. Whilst working on detox we encouraged those on the ward to attend AA, though I didn't really know what it entailed, other than it lasted about an hour.

I started attending a Day Centre for treatment using the 12 step programme, and had to attend three meetings a week as part of my contract. One of the volunteers told me which meetings she attended. She'd been dry for nine years, and I can still remember my amazement that she still went to AA ...

Why?? If she wasn't drinking?? So obviously I assumed it was a quick fix to get you sober and then you didn't need it any more.

I remember my first meeting well. It was on a Monday afternoon in one of the 'posher' parts of Swansea, so hopefully it would be quiet and nobody would know me. I was terrified of being recognised by one of the people I'd seen through Detox. (I was special and different ...) It turned out to be quite a busy meeting, and they gave me a warm welcome and did a 'newcomers meeting' for me. They all sang the praises of 'the programme' and God was mentioned several times. I came away feeling very uncomfortable with the whole scenario if I'm honest.

In the Day Centre, we worked with the 12 Step Programme. I struggled badly, and was discharged for relapsing several times (you were asked to leave for a month). I just couldn't grasp the concept of a Higher Power whatsoever, and eventually gave up. I went back to the Day Centre one driving ban and job dismissal later and tried all over again. Once more, I couldn't grasp the Steps at all. My counsellor tried his hardest, I was given various handouts and tapes to listen to, but yet again never got past Step 1. Things spiralled out of control, and I realised I needed to go away for help. I'd always dismissed the thought of rehab as 'my family wouldn't manage without me', despite the reality being I was causing no end of problems. It was a huge relief when I got the funding for The Rehab. My key worker explained to me that they used a different version of the 12 Steps there, and it was indeed a place of sanctuary where I needed to go.

I remember reading my welcome pack on admission, and looking at the 12 Steps, written alongside the original AA Steps I was used to. I can only describe it as being 'comfortable' reading, written in a way which seemed more modern and made sense to me. Even though I was brought up in a church-going family, and have been christened and confirmed, I'm not a particularly religious person any more, and the word 'God' in the Steps can be quite distracting if you're new to recovery.

I was able to get past Step 1 for the first time, and actually cried when I was given my Step 2 booklet.

My time away in The Rehab gave me the peace and space I needed to focus on the programme, and I'm finding it easier to work the Steps in my daily life. I feel my understanding of the spiritual nature of the Steps is getting easier with time. My biggest achievement was approaching an old friend, who had reported me in work on three occasions, and as a result 'she got me sacked' (it wasn't my fault, or my drinking ... it was her ...) I saw her in January and made direct amends to her, explained how I'd put her in an impossible position, and had turned my family and a lot of our mutual friends against her. We spoke for an hour, had a big hug, and are now in frequent contact. The relief I got after making this amend was a feeling like I haven't had for many years, literally like the weight off my shoulders and an incredibly spiritual experience. I told all my family and they thought I'd lost the plot, but shared it in my home group and they were all thrilled for me.

I am eternally grateful for my new way of living with no alcohol, and have the guidance I had in The Rehab to thank for that, as everything else I tried failed quite spectacularly. I continue to use AA regularly, and have a wonderful home group. The word God is used a lot but I am able to understand it in my way. I do, however, find myself explaining to newcomers that they might hear the word God, but that it's not in a religious context. We say in the Steps about God 'as we understand him', but you can be so nervous/scared/ill in your early stages of recovery that it's only the word God that you hear. I watched a daytime TV programme recently and a woman with drink problems was being interviewed, and she dismissed AA, saying she found it of little use 'because I'm not religious', and this went out to millions of viewers without being challenged.

I have listened to shares from people with many years of sobriety who work the programme, who struggle with various issues that many people without addiction would not see as a problem. I think the complex way of thinking that addiction brings is still very much there, but they have the tools to deal with them now.

Chapter Eight

Spiritual Recovery

In previous chapters we have seen how many newcomers to AA and other anonymous fellowships have been put off by seeing the word 'God' in the 12 Steps and been deterred from going because they fear that attempts will be made to convert them to Christianity, or that the 12 Step programme will not work for them unless they believe in God and are willing to hand over their life and their will into His care. We have seen how my re-wording of the Steps came about as a response to their needs and offers a translation more readily acceptable to non-religious addicts and provides a simple, practical set of Steps with achievable goals which anyone can attain irrespective of their beliefs. We also saw that the 12 Step programme is not a modular educational course with a certificate of completion at the end of Module 12, but describes an ongoing process of personal change which in time becomes a way of life. In this chapter I would like to explore what happens to people who work the 12 step programme over a period of years, in particular the notion of 'spiritual recovery' or the process of healing from the spiritual damage done by addiction.

In annual reunions I meet ex-residents of The Rehab who have been abstinent from mood-altering chemicals and compulsive behaviour for a long time, some for two years, some for more than twenty years. No matter how long they have been abstinent they still see themselves as 'in recovery'. They do not see themselves as cured, or as no longer addicts. Even when they have lost the desire to use drugs and alcohol they know that addiction is still more powerful than they are and if they let it back into their lives they know what the consequences will be. If the occasion arises when they think they might fancy a drink or a drug the question they ask themselves is not 'Do I want a drink?' but 'Do I want those consequences again?' Put like this, the decision is easily made:

'There is no way on earth I want to go through all that horror again, or lose the life I have now.' In recovery addicts are building a new life for themselves and now they have something of value they do not want to lose. Quite simply, using is just not worth the risk.

> Every time I got back in the ring with addiction it knocked me out. After years of thinking 'This time will be different' I finally decided not to get back in the ring. *Terry*

When these recovering addicts talk about their lives since they stopped using they describe their efforts and achievements. They are making decisions about what they want and setting themselves goals. Sometimes they attain their goals and sometimes they don't, but they are resilient and adaptable and have the ability to re-think and re-direct themselves when necessary. Their old life in active addiction is gone, the structure demolished, and the site cleared. They are creating for themselves a new life founded on the principles of the 12 Step programme and are finding that, with help, they are achieving things they once could not even hope for.

> Having things you didn't feel were possible is much more satisfying than achieving what was merely expected of you. *Lowri*

They enrol at college and learn about things that interest and inspire them. They train for and find work which they find satisfying and rewarding. They enter with an open heart into their relationships and enjoy feelings of intimacy, affection, and love. They leave behind the company of using addicts and make a new social circle for themselves. They have friends who are in recovery and friends who never were addicts, and as their life changes their identification and sense of belonging transfers from people who are ill to people who are well. They do not forget the still-suffering addict, they have understanding and compassion and will help anyone who wants to recover, but their lives are no longer filled only with addicts and they see themselves as valuable members of the community at large.

For these people recovery is bringing profound changes in attitude and thinking, and over time changes in belief. Where once they believed that change was not possible, they now have tangible, undeniable proof that change is happening. Where once they believed that the only person you could really rely on was yourself, they are experiencing the undeniable truth that some people are trustworthy and will help you achieve things you cannot achieve alone. Where once they dismissed any idea of a god or Higher Power, they are having experiences which lead them to believe that maybe there is 'something' in addition to other people which, if they are open to it, adds to their wellbeing.

> My spirit was awoken when I first made a decision to begin letting go of my old way of thinking. *Ben*

Sometimes they will hear in a meeting, or in a supermarket, or in a bus queue, exactly what they need to hear to resolve a problem they are having. Sometimes they will bump into someone they haven't seen for ages who will be just the right person to give them the help they need that day. Sometimes someone will make a suggestion which, if they act on it, will lead to a new career or a whole new phase in their life opening up for them. Sometimes an invitation, if accepted, will lead to them meeting the person they have been hoping to meet for years. Some people call happenings like this coincidence, some call it serendipity. Some call it Fate, or Destiny. Whatever it is, people in recovery start to notice it happening to them more and more often.

You can't see anything if your eyes are closed, and you can't learn anything if your mind is closed. You can't feel love if your heart is closed. In the same way, you can't grow spiritually if your spirit has been reduced to a tiny flicker and shut away in a dark prison of addiction. You have to open your eyes, open your mind, open your heart, and rejoin the human race. Then see what happens to your spirituality.

Here are some experiences of addicts who were resident at The Rehab and continue their recovery in 12 Step meetings. These are people who thought they would not be able to benefit from the 12 Steps because they were deterred by the word 'God' and had no useable concept of 'God of your understanding'. They show how working the 12 Step programme over time opens the way to a growing belief in a benign 'something' which works for their good. Furthermore this belief is based on and springing from personal experience and not on any previously held doctrine or belief.

The first is one person's experience of addiction. While in The Rehab he discovered his ability to express himself in writing. This is the first piece he wrote:

...........suicide   to   spiritual   ride...........

Sometimes the things i want are just out of reach,
in god's time i'll break through like a submarine on its breach,
it's a good lesson to learn to teach myself,
to keep me growing in spiritual wealth, an keep me from acting out wrapped up in self,
an that's a shit place to be, trust me,

i've been working hard on that to set myself free,
by doing the things i don't want to do and working on me,
it's stopped me being mental, riding around in self pity central,
that dark lonely place, depressed, self obsessed,
suicide do i go through with it, that's the test,

do not take this in jest,
many times i thought about plunging a knife straight through my chest,
wow scratching and spinning the blade on my left breast,
to get away from the insanity and lay myself to rest,
emotional pain is a bitch and i'd had enough,
tease me, please me, i pierced the skin call my bluff,
that was the extent of my head war,

---

i just thought i was rotten to the core, deranged and above the law,
in my head that shit's still pretty raw,
what i saw and did was an illusion and cataclysmic,
off key causing mayhem like a nuclear ballistic,
head and soul fucking twisted, too much bad shit to be listed,

i've always done what i want,
incredible, Billy the kid, the rebel, whacked out crazy and fucking terrible,
a Tasmanian devil, whipping up chaos and carnage,
so low not even a name to tarnish,
but will let off with a barrage of abuse, no power to choose,
chemical nut job on the loose, walking a tight rope with his neck in a noose,
nothing left but a head on code red,

emergency, red alert, red alert.
intentional overdose, that fucking hurt,
a bottle of tequila 50 blues and a hand full of codeine,
an i still woke up thinking is this a dream,

that went on for months believe,
just slip away into the night i'm begging please,
that was the state of my mental health,
i'd get fucked off cos i couldn't even kill myself,
waking up thinking no not another day, how can i face it when i'm this way,
and that's a sad thing to say,

through all this i still thought i was o.k.,
the one man show who can't see the state of play, still doing it my way,

fucked up from the neck up, smashed to pieces from the neck down,
isolated, alone, fucking raging,
someone save me i beg you i need containing,
come and get me i need saving,

have you ever heard your insides complaining, mine were raving,
you're no good, you're worthless you're a piece of shit,
i listened that's why i tried to end it,
you will never be anything, you have nothing to offer, you're nothing on this planet,
i believed that, i'd really had it,
it was like acid being poured on my brain,
or being hit in the face by a suicidal steam train,
it was a force like no other,
i'm running on fumes, i'm empty, nothing left to give, why do i bother,
lover, grandma, cousin, brothers, no one could pull me out
 not even my mother,

i had one more go at suicide,
this time i really tried, closer closer,
it very nearly complied, but i woke up 36 hours later with my head fried,
everything i owned smashed to pieces, me sat in the middle
i broke and cried,

that moment was the beginning of my spiritual ride,
i could no longer hide, living a lie,
so decide, time to try and bring myself back to life,
that's the first time i ever honestly prayed,
the next morning it was like darkness had been stripped by a wave,
it left me with a crave to go and ask for help,
which is exactly what i had prayed for,
god just touched me with a bit of his wealth,
there my journey to where i am began,

i went to the doctors got into rehab and laid out a plan,
the detox kicked my arse no shit,
i tell you this i'll never forget it,
my entire body hurt for two months,
opiates have a subtle way of masking the bumps, scars, wounds,

breaks emotions and feelings,
but after a while i began seeing, the hurt an pain began to slip,
12 step program baby this is it,

slowly growing into the person i am today,
with the help of others what can i say, i'm impressed,
to have these people in my life i am truly blessed,
they help me lay my demons to rest,
they even got through my impenetrable defensive and denial proof vest,
i bet that was a serious test,
but no less, they stuck at it, and that's the power of this program,

you're all worth something good just as i am,
we all help each other however we can,
i never realised i'd get this much at the beginning of my plan,
that's because it's god's plan that's got me where i am,
early days was just about staying away from the toot, pipe and can,

everything i have today is a result of this program,
as on day one i had nothing a completely broken man,
i owe my life to it and the people within it,
that's why i give everything i can to it,
but i ain't perfect and i definitely ain't a saint,
i can still complain and still be a bit of a pain,
but i tell you this the acid has left my brain,
i'm still left with a few stains,
but working the steps removes them and the goodness remains,

i haven't got where i am or the things i have by going and grabbing them,
believe me that's the one thing that will stop you having them,
i love my family more than anything in the world,
to get back with them in god's time has took 3 years and a third,
the day that happened i floated off, free bird,
that blew me away,

do the right things the right things will come your way, it's fate,

good things come to those who wait,
do not contemplate, get on this program before it's too late,
an if something is right and meant to be, you know what i mean,
it will happen in god's time you will see,

we have an illness we are infected,
so get connected, self respected,
surrounded by the right people feel protected,
your problems detected, your head inspected,
your troubles dissected, breathe new life resurrected,
higher power and sponsor elected,
let go be directed, from all that a new way of life selected,

trust the program and work it for you,
a life beyond your wildest dreams can come true,
you will start to feel new,
a few problems but that's life what can you do,

i hope what i've just written in some way has helped you,
all good things in time,
here's my experience of suicide to spiritual ride............

Drew H.

I finally hit rock bottom in 2009, and had started a process of engaging with my service provider who had been helping me for nearly twenty-seven years. I'd been on a script of methadone since the age of sixteen, and finally after a hospital visit with deep vein thrombosis and in a coma I came to that decision that it talks about in Step 3 – that I was going to make a commitment and do whatever it takes to get clean.

When I came out of hospital after 8 weeks I started to drink more and still continued to use heroin, but I knew that I had to do something different. I went to see my drug worker at my local community drug team and for the first time I finally got honest in the way that I really felt. While having a deep meaningful conversation it was suggested that I should go to rehab. I'd never heard of rehab, I'd thought that it was only the rich and famous that went to rehab, and my key worker showed me some leaflets. When she showed me The Rehab's leaflet I knew that was the one for me because I knew that I needed somewhere that was away from all the temptations of a city life. My key worker set me a date so that I could have a face to face assessment with the treatment centre, which later that month I attended. I didn't know what to expect, I kept hearing the words of the 12 Steps and had no clue what they meant.

When going on my face to face assessment I met some lovely friendly people. For the first time in a long time I felt that these people cared. I was taken to meet the residents and shown into the lounge of the treatment centre where I met all the residents who shared their experience of their journey in the centre. I can remember seeing a poster on the wall and seeing writing, and what stood out for me was I could see the word god! They might as well be talking a different language as I hadn't a clue. I went away from there with a bit of hope. Later on in my recovery I found this to be a massive part of Step 2 and how important Step 2 was going to be for my ongoing journey.

The first part of my journey was to do a detox, and I knew I was ready because I had hit my rock bottom. I was then picked up and taken to The Rehab where I was to be introduced to the 12 steps. When I came to The Rehab I had envisaged that I was going to be brainwashed and that all these people were going abduct me into a cult of a god squad. As I started to settle, I started to question why the word god was written in so many books that I started to read. I went to see my counsellor and shared my experience of when I was a small child that I'd been abused by a nun and that's why I found it difficult to put my trust into something that had failed me when I was a child. My counsellor showed me a version of the 12 Steps that was re-written without using the word god, and I was advised to follow that if I found it difficult. As I started to work the Steps I got more comfortable with working with this new version.

I suppose for me when I first came into treatment I was totally confused about my higher power. Speaking to my counsellors, it was suggested that I used my peers. As my confidence and my trust in my peers grew I started to understand what a power greater was. I suppose over the last four years that I've been in the rooms of Narcotics Anonymous my higher power has changed. I couldn't exactly tell you what it is right now, but while being in recovery I have these moments of clarity where I have an overwhelming feeling of content and I feel that is when my higher power is working its magic. I have faced a lot of adversity while being in recovery but I've always known from the first steps that I took into The Rehab that my using was over and that my higher power was going to take care of me.

Today my life is truly amazing and my higher power has given me many gifts in my recovery. Sometimes those moments of clarity show me that the decision I made in 2009 to get clean was the best decision I've ever made.

It teaches us in the 12 Steps that by helping others and showing acts of kindness, love, and compassion for others that we can only keep what we have by giving it away.

Dez

I had a very poor opinion of AA before I went into treatment for addiction. I think it's called 'contempt prior to investigation' in the *Big Book*. From hearsay, I believed that AA was religious claptrap. I could not understand how sitting in a room full of drunks talking about drinking could possibly help me to get and stay sober. My secret fear was that I was 'too alcoholic' – that I must drink far more than these people who profess to be alcoholics. I had reached a point where the only time I wasn't drinking was when I was unconscious. When I was awake I had to have alcohol, I believed it was blotting out the paralysing fear of being alive.

When I finally asked for help, I was lucky enough to get the funding for residential rehabilitation. I was incredibly grateful and relieved. It was like crossing the finishing line of a long, long race. I didn't care what they did at the rehabilitation centre, they were going to get me well. I remember seeing 12 Step program mentioned in the information pack sent out prior to being admitted, but that did not register with me.

So, I arrived at the centre and, after dropping my suitcase off to be searched, I was shown into the communal living area. I spotted the bookcase and my heart lifted – I was told no books were allowed. I will never forget that moment when I stood in front of the books. They were all AA and NA literature and Hazelden publications. I had a complete meltdown in my head. I panicked. I thought 'If I've got to get religion, I'm doomed. I may as well get my suitcase now and go home.' But something happened in that moment, because I heard myself reply ...' Go where, Sue? Back home? You've left the fear and nightmares and isolation at home to come here and get well. You're really going to go back to that?' I don't know why but the panic seemed to subside. I suppose I had my first experience of fundamental acceptance. If this is what it takes then I was prepared to try. I had been granted the gift of desperation and I was truly ready to try anything to recover. Although I didn't realise it at the time this gift gave me willingness to accept, the open mindedness to consider new ideas, and the honesty to confront the truth about myself.

So, I got with the rehabilitation program. It was suggested that instead of using the word God, that I used the term Higher Power if it helped to come understand that I was indeed powerless over people, places, and events in my life. Of course I had the power to make decisions and I still do today, but I have no control over the outcome. That has always been out of my hands. I learned how to accept this fundamental truth. I was shown the secular version of the 12 Steps and the simplicity and wisdom contained within was revealed to me.

First, I realised that the God of my understanding wasn't the white man with a big beard and sandals sitting on a cloud firing thunder bolts whenever he felt like it. It was understanding what a power greater than myself was, what it felt like, and how it showed itself to me on a daily basis. A power that alcohol had blinded me to. I had singlehandedly run my life into the ground because I believed I had control over people, places, and things, and tried to mould life to meet my needs. The truth was that all my great decisions had got me sitting in a rehab with an obsession and compulsion to drink that overshadowed everything – my beautiful children, my work, my daily life … me. I had to surrender the belief that I had control and develop faith that someone or something else would help me.

My Higher Power has changed in my two and a half years of recovery. At first, it was the people at the rehabilitation centre. I knew I couldn't recover alone, but I could do it by questioning and listening to the people who had been through this process. I listened to their experiences, their individual 'dark nights of the soul' where they were brought to their knees by addiction. I took note of the strength they showed in surrender. These people gave me hope, and I gained the courage to take my own leap of faith in the 12 Steps. Today, my higher power is the cycle of life. It is the world around me … the sun rising and setting, the eternal cycle of waves on the shore. It was happening long, long before I came into existence and it will continue long, long after I am gone.

Today, I hand my will and my life over to the care of a 'God of my understanding' (my Higher Power) and I am happy with that. I use the 12 Steps daily, guiding me to do the right thing. I use the Serenity Prayer. I accept the things I cannot change … people, places, situations. I ask for the courage to change the things I can … my reaction and attitude – me. I ask for the wisdom to know the difference. And I think ultimately, my higher power is the act of giving unconditional love, love that was shown and given daily to me during treatment.

I came across an explanation that sums up what spirituality means to me. 'Spirituality is not the same thing as religion. It's about realising that you don't exist alone, and deciding what to do with that realisation.' (*Facebook page, RightFromTheRooms*).

Sue B.

The Twelve Steps and Buddhism – A Personal Account.

'Spiritual not religious'

When I first encountered the 12 Steps, the word GOD mentioned in Steps 3, 5, 6, and 11, and indirectly in Steps 2 and 7, was a definite barrier to my sense that the program could work for me. My rationale was that if GOD could help me, why hadn't he done so already? And that the religions of the world in my eyes were the cause of much suffering in the forms of sectarianism, persecution, and fundamentalism and they seemed to divide people not unite them, to promote disharmony and conflict rather than harmony and peace.

One approach that helped me in those early days was the idea expressed to me by another recovering addict that the 12 Steps was a spiritual, not religious programme, and the difference was that religion was for people who didn't want to go to hell and spirituality was for people who had already been there. I could relate to this, as thirty years of addiction had certainly become a living hell of loneliness and despair that I had become imprisoned by without hope of release.

If I were to define spirituality it would be as a felt sense of being connected to the world and other people, a feeling of belonging and having a place and a contribution to make towards the overall sum of human happiness. In fact the complete opposite of my experience in active addiction where I felt separate and 'other' from the perceived normal human experience, and my actions were negative towards myself and contributed towards the total sum of human misery.

From my current perspective, to my mind the central question is one of trust. There are many theories addressing the question of how we become what we are. From theories of child development, and of the effects of childhood trauma, to Buddhist ideas about ego and the root of suffering, there is a common theme. The central unifying factor is that trust in something is a necessary prerequisite for change in the self-structure. Only with trust in something can there be a permanent change in behaviour, thinking, and emotional well-being.

That trust can facilitate the necessary change from heavily defended individuals, who will do anything to avoid the pain at the centre of their being to the point of self-destruction through alcohol or drugs and other addictive behaviours, to congruent useful human beings with a lot to offer society in many and varied ways.

By the time I got into recovery I could not even trust any more that my drugs would protect me from my pain. I felt like my pain was so great that without my defences I could not survive it. So how do we come from a place of not trusting anything to being able to trust enough to go to that place inside of us that is so wounded? Well in my case little by little. I could not just suddenly trust God. But I could start to trust some of the people I met in the programme and gain some hope.

From those small beginnings my trust has grown and with it my ability to process my early traumas and make changes at the foundation of my self-structure. I have an increasing ability to self-regulate emotionally, and an increased compassion for myself and all sentient beings. The 12 Steps and programme associated with them has led me to a god of my own understanding. I now believe that all beings are basically good, as is the world and all that is contained within it. I sometimes forget this for a while and go a little askew, however these times now remind me of the basic abundance and goodness of life rather than lead me to hopelessness and despair.

I would like to thank all the people, too many to mention, inside and outside of the programme, for your help along the way. May we aspire to heal ourselves and the world.

Richard

I was brought up as a staunch atheist, although when I was younger I remember having a longing for something like God to comfort my woes. At the mere sight of the word God I became wrapped with fear and contempt and did not see past it to 'as we understand Him' or 'Higher Power'. As such I did not engage and continued to punish myself and my family by drinking.

After being a hopeless alcoholic, drunk, and trying everything to stop, including AA, I found myself with nowhere to turn and for the first time it was suggested I pray, and from the moment I began including the idea of God into my life I have gotten better. When I have short periods of forgetting to include God, I get worse and I become sick and my life becomes unmanageable.

I have seen what I have seen and it has influenced my concept of a Higher Power. As an intellectual type, I felt the need for my Higher Power to be tangible and so my initial connection with God was rooted in my feeling of awe at the magnitude of life on Earth. I knew that there was a power greater than myself that gives life, and for me that was evidential by what I could see. Whether it is science or God, it is a power greater than me.

My need for tangibility has lessened but not gone and I have found it unnecessary to relieve myself of this logic, because my concept of God has developed as I have experienced my life, and the lives of those around me, improve so dramatically and without prejudice of where I have come from or who I have been.

My feeling of a connection with God has grown – from *faith*, in the process of recovery found from the example of others before me – to *belief*, from my self-evident recovery – to *knowledge* of God's presence, due to my intellectual, evidence-based experience which has given me that ability to completely accept God's presence.

I do not know God and I do not understand God but I strongly believe that She is the reason I am graced with a sober life today. I describe God in the feminine because my concept of 'life giver' is exclusively purported to the feminine of all species I know of. Whether that is correct for God I do not know but it helps me to perceive Her in this way. Maybe the ancient Grecian Deity Gaia is my God.

Without striving for a conscious contact with God and listening for guidance, I am left with the same negativity, unreasonable thinking, and unruly behaviours that got me to the place I was in when I became ready to accept my own concept of God into my life in order to get better from my spiritual (or lack of spiritual) illness. I believe that God offers me guidance through my prayers and meditation but also through other people and some situations and circumstances. As such I can reveal myself to others and accept guidance to help me become a better person.

My spirit was awoken when I first made a decision to begin letting go of my old way of thinking. I know that God has always been with me but I have been ignorant to Her presence. My spiritual awakening is one of both revelation and education. It seems to come suddenly and has continued to enlighten me and my spirit.

Ben[19]

Before my first meeting I wasn't entirely sure what AA was like. I'd only ever heard it mentioned in a joking sense. I suppose I just thought it's somewhere people go when they're in a mess and need to talk about it. I was mortified to be at an AA meeting. A family member came with me to support me. I was the youngest in the room by a couple of decades. This made it difficult for me to take a lot in. I remember being particularly embarrassed by the serenity prayer – especially the holding hands and the 'Keep coming back, it works if you work it' part, I think I must have seen it on TV somewhere (probably being mocked for some comedic value) and I felt really ashamed that I had ended up there.

I was put off by the 'God' talk. I took the mention of 'God' as being synonymous with 'doesn't work'. I was relieved to be in the company of people who seemed to have the same problems as me, and I enjoyed listening, with relief, to their own accounts of the effect that addiction had had on their lives but I shut off to any talk of 'the programme' and 'God' – I found it cringe-worthy to be honest. It was definitely the power in

---

[19] Ben's contribution is copied with permission of the Higher Power Project, University of Chester, who interviewed Ben originally. Further information about the Higher Power Project can be found online: www.**chester**.ac.uk/higherpowerproject

identification that meant more to me and kept me coming back.

I had dismissed God and religion from a young age – none of my family were religious. Some of my closest friends growing up were very adamantly anti-religion and anti-God. Many of the bands and musicians I listened to (and still listen to) shared this sentiment. It was difficult for me to consider what 'God' could mean to me, or anything of that nature, because I felt I was being untrue to myself, to my beliefs, which I had held for a long time and I believed formed a part of my identity which I did not want to let go of.

I think the version without 'God' words is a very useful tool for recovering addicts to have immediate access to the principles behind the Steps. I was told by people in the fellowship that my concept of God will change over time, and continue to change, which I have experienced. I think this in part was due to my mind becoming more open to the idea of God, considering it in less restrictive black-and-white terms but more of an abstract concept which reveals itself in my life when I am open to it. But in the immediate, I needed something to work with and a place to begin. The re-wording appealed to my logical mindset and allowed me to see what the step was really getting at. Because I had not been socialised into having a concept of God, I found it difficult to imagine how that would help me. It also made the step seem much less complicated – all it required of me was hope that I could recover with help, and that hope was evidenced by seeing other addicts around me recovering. It was not something my mind instantly closed off to because it was just a reality that I could accept.

There is a need for a version like this, especially as we are becoming more and more a secular society. I passionately believe that religion should play no part in an addict's need to go through the process of the 12 Steps, and if that means adapting a few words then so be it. I can understand the need to preserve the program, and this has its place, but there is a need also to make it inclusive. There is of course an argument that if an addict is desperate enough to recover, then the word God will not put them off. However, it should also be considered that addicts can have very different rock bottoms, and what is enough to cause one to seek recovery, may not be enough for another and vice-versa.

Personally, The Rehab's version was almost like a 'jargon buster' for me at first – it made it all sound far less complicated, was more direct, clear, and to the point.

I think the only opposition it will encounter is from fear of the Steps not being preserved. But it is made clear that this is just a guide to understanding the Steps for the modern day or those who have a genuine aversion to or no means to understand God for whatever reason. They are always printed alongside the original wording, as far as I have seen anyway. I see it as being almost like an atheist translation of the Steps, not a replacement to them.

Once powerlessness was explained to me I could understand the concept of Step One, because I found it logical and straightforward. I could identify that I was certainly powerless, and the same with unmanageability, but after that I remember reading the Steps and wondering what a power greater than myself would be. I always wondered what Step 3 meant. I could understand though that I had been impulsive in my life (no planning, no real direction, trying to solve things on my own, etc.). By using the revised version I have found that a better understanding of the 12 Steps comes with time.

Step 11 also – improving conscious contact was a very confusing wording for me and just threw open a whole load of other questions. I believe this Step in its original wording also has the potential to be misused – and I have done this myself – when I will pray around a self-seeking subject (usually something I want in my life and can't let go of). I communicate what I want to happen, with the proviso that the outcome is not down to me, and I will look for signs of what I am to do. Then, my mind has an excellent opportunity to delude me, and to become even more fixated on the situation and misinterpret information.

However, the wording which includes mindfulness/meditation as a means to develop my spiritual and ethical self – not to look for signs about what I should do in a situation, but to consider what the correct course of action to take would be from an ethical point of view – that makes more sense for me.

After treatment I decided that in order for me to recover I was going to need to engage more with life, so my policy for the first few months clean was to just say 'yes' to any new positive experience if I had that time free. That policy worked really well and all sorts of new things came into my life, my fear began to ease a bit, I met new people, made new connections, and began to discover aspects of myself I didn't know existed. I choose to understand this as a demonstration of Steps 6 and 7 – breaking out of my isolating patterns in order for change to take place. It was suggested to me that I try to live by the principles of Steps 10, 11, and 12 – consider my values in a situation and admit when I am in the wrong, develop spiritually as a human being (to me this is the feel-good factor that comes when I do the right thing for the right reasons), and helping other addicts to recover.

Over time my understanding of the spiritual nature of the Steps is changing. The Rehab was my first introduction to the Steps, and I needed something to work with as I have described above. I think I went into treatment with a set idea of what a 12 Step program was – I think I definitely over complicated it. The re-wording did help with this when I was in treatment. Treatment gave me an experience of life which I will never forget. I needed to draw upon this after a relapse. I had enough understanding of the disease and enough belief still in the program that I managed to seek help from someone in AA. I also knew I needed to go through the 12 Steps again, that they were my only hope because I really had no mental defence.

Learning about powerlessness and then experiencing it again first hand is a very frightening experience, because you are aware you have no control and that your mind is hijacked. I think the relapse really did show me that I had no choice in my disease – it taught me about the spiritual malady. I then understood why it was possible for people who had not drunk for 20+ years to relapse – before they picked up a drink they would not have triggered the allergy; they would have already lost the mental obsession to drink – which left the spiritual malady. I understood that I had a spiritual sickness which needed ongoing treatment with the Steps. I think I just understood the full implications of my disease. So I went through the process again,

I didn't question anything, we followed the directions in the *Big Book*, and I went through the Steps that way. I think the key is I was willing because I was genuinely frightened. I now do not take the need for spiritual healing lightly.

I do have a higher power now – in fact I have two. One is a Higher Power which I cannot describe, I just believe it is some force of good - but my own idea changes if I think about it. I found it easier, the more I prayed, to dismiss the questions in my mind – this is still largely a work in progress. The second is other addicts who I can seek advice and support from, because I find this always lifts my mood no matter how hopeless I think something is – I have seen my mood and outlook literally transform simply from sharing honestly with another addict. It still amazes me every time and I always wonder why I never act sooner to seek the support.

Lowri

I was sent to my first meeting whether I wanted to go or not as I was a patient in the Acute Assessment Unit in the Maudsley Hospital and attendance at meetings was compulsory. I didn't really know anything about it. At that point, I was saying yes to everything with no intention of following through. My reading about AA on the internet before I got to that point had been secretive and looking for reasons for it not to be right, so I saw it as 'religious'. (I associated it with the Salvation Army and the slightly strange people I avoided the gaze of on buses). I have never been anti-religious to be honest but not a great advocate either. I would sit on the fence and if there wasn't one I would try and build one to sit on. So the word 'God' didn't really put me off but I am naturally afraid of people who have overtly evangelical opinions about anything; it intimidates and annoys me. What I remember of the meeting, (I was heavily medicated) was that it was huge, there must have been sixty or seventy people in it and there was a much more charged atmosphere than in a church. It was powerful. While I don't remember a word of what was said, I remember that feeling. I took my *Daily Reflections* book that night, thinking it was free, and I still use it.

I think the version which does not use the God words is a massive help to anyone who wants to understand the Steps, regardless of whether they are religious or not. The Steps don't specifically tell you what to believe in, how to believe in it, or any of the specifics of how you would follow an orthodox religion, therefore there's no reason to learn them that way. I think it makes the concepts much easier to grasp, it makes them accessible to those whose haunches do go up at the word GOD. They also speed up the process, especially of opening the mind to further spiritual exploration and willingness. It's like, 'If that's what that means, maybe I can do it.'

In both my personal and professional experience, I think there is certainly a need for a version like this. From personal experience, pride would still stop me from admitting I didn't understand what the original Steps were asking of me. Everyone kept on saying 'It's a simple programme', well, not written like that it isn't. From a professional perspective, addicts' pre-engagements with the Steps are filled with other people's opinions, experiences, and biases. This way, when confronted with this 'scary/strict/religious/whatever your reason not to do it' programme, you may find yourself asking the question: 'I wonder why I was told that by so-and-so?' One of the first jobs in my work in a rehab was to get people to unlearn what they already had programmed in about 12 Step programmes. The revised version is simple, practical, achievable, and real. Each Step requires you to do something real so that you can develop a sense of the spiritual and understand or redefine the concept of FAITH as you go along. I have used these Steps personally, with clients and with a sponsee. I trust them.

My understanding of the spiritual nature of the Steps is continuing to change on a daily basis in step with my life. While the majority of what I do to maintain my sobriety is on a very practical level, actions like practising patience and love and tolerance and forgiveness serve to keep me away from the physical actions which may put me at risk, and the more 'religiously' I practise them the more they become a second nature to me. Practising opposites helps me to change the way I think as I see the results and the benefits of doing things differently. At a simple (and that's all I need to be happy me) level it's where someone is unpleasant to me: instead of writing them off or whatever I feel I want to do, punish, ignore, or mock, I do the opposite – try and understand, see if I can help, what could I be doing differently. These changes that come about through practising the Steps enhance the other side of my life which is synchronicity with my environment and the wider world. The spiritual side of the Steps has given me the capacity to step outside of most situations I find myself in and be more aware of the whole situation rather than just my part of it.

My understanding of a higher power is changing all the time very slightly and then, when I do any particularly intense period of work on myself or go through a difficult experience, I learn more about how it works for me and what it is. What's interesting and consistent and is one of the most powerful aspects of my higher power is that when I was desperate, on my arse, and a broken shell of a human being, I was asked ten characteristics of what I thought a god was. If you asked me what ten characteristics my higher power has they would be the same, as I see more evidence of those qualities being the ones that make me the happiest. Up there at No.1 is LOVE. My higher power, my god, is Love.

I think the Steps that came as a necessity to survive have allowed me to start living along these lines of new principles. My life feels utterly transformed in a spiritual capacity by the Steps. My first sponsor called it 'conscious living', some call it 'living in the now'. I can't imagine going backwards now.

Tim

In Chapter Three we saw how using addicts have more in common than they have differences. The stories in this chapter confirm my belief that addicts' experiences of recovery also have more in common than differences. Before starting to work a 12 Step programme not one of the people quoted above had a useable concept of 'God as you understand Him' or faith that such a power would help them recover from addiction and build a whole new life. As a result of working the 12 Steps, initially the re-worded version and later the original version, each one has found a power greater than they are which they can comfortably refer to as their Higher Power or 'god of my understanding'. Dez cannot say what his higher power is but he knows it takes care of him. Sue's higher power in treatment was her group of peers and now is the cycle of life. Richard has a Buddhist perspective and trusts the god of his understanding, a good world of which he and all beings are part. The god of Ben's understanding is a female life-giver whom he likens to Gaia. Lowri has two higher powers: one is a force of good which she cannot describe, the other is other addicts in recovery. Tim's understanding of his higher power continues to develop but the quality he most experiences it as is Love. These higher powers are all unique. Each is the product of a particular person's growing awareness, springing from his or her own experiences in recovery; they do, however, share certain fundamental attributes.

Tim refers to an assignment used in The Rehab for residents working on Step 3: 'Made a decision to turn our will and our lives over to the care of God *as we understood Him.*' The assignment was designed to get residents thinking about what 'God' meant for them, irrespective of whether they had faith in God or not. One of the questions was 'List ten characteristics of God as you understand Him.' The interesting thing is that everyone, non-believers included, came up with a list of characteristics which were remarkably similar. People who for their own reasons feared or were angry with god gave him the characteristics of a cruel father: harsh, punishing, unloving, distant, a tyrant. They did not want to believe in a god like that, and were surprised when told they did not have to. The question 'What do you think your life would be like if you believed in a god that was caring and helpful?' was shocking and gave them something to think about. For the people who were emotionally neutral about God, God was powerful, good, wise, loving, a creator, universal, and hard to define. They might not believe in him but they knew what he was supposed to be like.

After working a 12 Step programme for a couple of years, recovering addicts are developing an awareness of the existence of some kind of Higher Power. They may or may not feel comfortable calling this 'God' but they know for sure that there is something which is powerful, good, wise, loving, a creator, universal, and hard to define – in fact all the things that were generally seen as attributes of God. Furthermore, personal experience of this 'something' has a profoundly beneficial effect on the person's emotions and thoughts: they feel warm, secure, they worry less, they appreciate nature, and are in awe of the living world of which they are a part. The 'hole inside' is being filled.

> I have great inner peace, I am happy in my own skin, I love the garden, the birds. I believe in something. God – because that's the word I use – comes from within, inner peace, letting go of things. *Charlotte*

Although I have offered a revised version of Step 12, in keeping with the aim of simplifying and making inclusive the 12 Step programme, I see evidence all around me of the truth of the original wording of Step 12: '*Having had a spiritual awakening* as a result of these steps ...' People who work a 12 Step programme say they experience a spiritual change which develops and deepens over time. They also identify with the revised version: '*Recovering from addiction* as a result of these steps ...' I believe that these two versions are different ways of describing the same phenomenon.

> Addiction is a soul sickness we suffer from before we take a drink. *Nick*

Addiction is a spiritual illness and requires a spiritual recovery. Indeed some would say that the obsessive-compulsive use of mood-altering chemicals or behaviour is itself a person's attempt to medicate a soul sickness which is draining the sufferer of all joy, meaning, faith, hope, and love. Chemicals and behaviour work for a while to ease the pain of this 'soul sickness' but the sufferer becomes dependent and needs more and more to get less and less relief. Addiction causes spiritual damage, as we have seen, but maybe the spirit was in need of healing even before addiction took hold. Maybe there are some people whose DNA or brain chemistry makes them so sensitive, so easily hurt, so vulnerable, so fragile in their sense of self, that they seek something that will make them feel 'normal' and think they have found it in chemicals and behaviours. What happens next is that addiction compounds the symptoms they found so painful in the first place. What these people need is recovery from addiction and recovery from their spiritual malady. The 12 Step programme, however it is written, tells them what they can do to achieve it.

As we have seen, addiction damages not just the self but also the family circle and the wider community. I think it not an exaggeration to say that there are areas in Britain today where whole communities suffer from the spiritual malady of alienation and hopelessness, where the social rules are 'every man for himself and the devil take the hindmost', and individuals band together for safety in exclusive self-interest groups and deny the existence of 'society'. The good news is that, in the same way as the effects of addiction spread outward from the individual to the community, so recovery begins with the healing of the individual and spreads in ever-increasing circles through the community at large. If an addict's social circle includes even one person in recovery, that addict's chance of recovery increases by 27%[20]. If one recovering addict can make that much difference to a social network of using addicts, how much difference can hundreds of recovering addicts make to their communities?

There are hundreds, thousands, of recovering addicts living in accordance with moral principles, experiencing spiritual development, caring for themselves and other people, being responsible, active, creative, living with hope and the knowledge that goodness is a real power in the world. What a difference they could make to their communities if they put their mind to it. I know that anonymity is a fundamental principle of all the 12 Step

---

[20] Changing network support for drinking: Network Support Project 2-year follow-up. Litt, Mark D.; Kadden, Ronald M.; Kabela-Cormier, Elise; Petry, Nancy M. *Journal of Consulting and Clinical Psychology*, Vol 77(2), Apr 2009, 229-242.

meetings, and for good reason, for no individual personality must be allowed to overshadow the principles of AA. However there must be some way in which groups of recovering addicts can make life-enhancing contributions to their communities without becoming famous or identified with AA itself. There are countless individual recovering addicts quietly doing voluntary work, working for charities, in the care professions, in housing associations, bringing a bit of care into what is too often an uncaring society. There are football teams, choirs, bands, and drama groups made up of recovering addicts, all showing how valuable addicts can be to society. In the dark days of economic recession and political discontent maybe the time is right for groups of recovering people to get active in their communities and tell them 'We are recovering addicts' and say it with pride.

Post script

Recovering from addiction and being in a process of developing spirituality may bring serenity, wisdom and moments of joy, but it does not mean an end to problems and pain. Life unfolds as it will and for the most part there is nothing we can do to prevent it. We may be given great gifts but we also suffer losses, and there are times when we need to call upon all the wisdom of the 12 Step programme and the support of our recovering community if we are to bear these losses with courage and acceptance and not seek solace in addiction.

This is the story of one man who is using the 12 Step programme at one such time.

David's Story

David knew he had an addictive illness and asked for admission to The Rehab because he wanted to abstain completely from the alcohol which was ruining his life. Once in The Rehab and introduced to the 12 Steps he wondered if he had made the right choice. He saw the word 'God' and did not think he would be able to accept the programme as it was written. When he was shown the alternative version he found it logical and practical and had no problem accepting it. When he looked at both versions together and was told that they both meant the same, he easily overcame his resistance to the 'God' terminology and found that he could comfortably accept both versions. This open-mindedness allowed him to use the terminology of either version, which meant that when he attended meetings and listened to others talking about God or their Higher Power he listened and identified instead of mentally screening out what they were saying. David successfully completed treatment and continued to strengthen his recovery in AA meetings.

As David got well his life began to blossom. New opportunities opened up for him in ways he could not even have imagined. He got a university teaching job which he loved and was very good at. He was well liked and respected by his students and his colleagues and valued by his employer. He had

---

a circle of good friends in recovery. He fell in love with a beautiful woman who loved him too. The day came when he found out that his dearest wish was going to come true: he was to become a father.

Some years previously David had spent time doing voluntary work in Africa. He had loved the country and the people and enjoyed the work he did with them. He hoped to go back some day. He was not deterred by the scorching heat. When he was admitted to The Rehab David noticed a blemish had appeared on his forehead. It was quite small but was red and did not heal. When he finished treatment he went to his doctor and asked for it to be tested. While in the African sun David had not worn sunscreen and had not always worn a hat. The biopsy came back positive. David had skin cancer.

David had surgery to remove the tumour and chemotherapy to prevent a recurrence. He made a good recovery and was left with a little scar which did not even show as it was hidden by his hair. The doctors were happy with the outcome of this treatment and David was confident that the cancer was gone. It was a blow to discover, some time later, that it had not gone but spread into his parotid gland. More chemotherapy followed and more surgery. David coped well with all this treatment and bore it with a fortitude I found admirable. He said that he found strength in his 12 Step programme. In doing Step 3 he had 'handed over' and trusted a power greater than himself, and now he understood that he had to hand over and trust the doctors who had more power than he did in this situation. They would advise him on what to do, he would do the best that he was able and leave the rest to them. The outcome was not in his hands.

The treatment was successful, the surgery skilfully done, and David started to get well again. When at last tests showed that the cancer had gone, David and his partner celebrated his fortieth birthday and his clean bill of health. David had everything to live for. He watched his son's heartbeat on the ultrasound monitor and had never been happier.

Eighteen weeks into the pregnancy he went for a routine check up and was given the shattering news that the cancer had spread to his lung and was inoperable. More chemotherapy sessions followed. David's resistance to infection was low and he twice he caught pneumonia. He is in hospital again as I write this, which is why he is not able to write it himself. In a conversation we had recently he talked to me about how his 12 Step programme is helping him deal with his situation.

David talked about Step 1, Step 3, and the serenity prayer. He said that Step 1 told him that there were many things more powerful than him, and he had to admit that cancer was one of them. He had absolutely no choice in the matter and had to accept that he had it. There was no use in trying to avoid reality, or feeling self-pity and asking why; that would just be wasted energy. Acceptance did not mean however that he should just be passive and do nothing. First he had to accept what he could not change, and then he had to do everything within his power to recover. If the doctors told him a change of diet could help him build up strength to cope with the chemotherapy, then he would drink beetroot juice every day no matter how horrible it tasted. If visualisation could help boost his immune system, he would visualise his own internal white-hot sun burning away the cancer cells.

He reflected on The Rehab's motto 'Surrender to win' and how he was applying it to cancer as he had applied it to addiction. He had survived one terminal illness and had hope that he could survive another. If the recovery rate was even as low as 1% he was going to do everything he could to be in that 1%. He described it as a balancing act – having to surrender and also to fight. All he could do was act on the treatment plan and live in the hope that recovery was possible. The outcome, as with most of the big things in life, was in the hands of something more powerful than himself.

Today David is following his 12 Step programme. He has not fallen into despair and turned to alcohol to avoid reality. He may be powerless over his physical health but he does have power over his actions and his attitude. He is living in accordance with his moral principles. He has made his amends. He is choosing to live one day at a time, as he has learned to do as an addiction survivor. He is choosing to have trust and hope and love in his life. His baby son is due to be born in one month's time. He said "I just want to be the best father I can be, for as long as I can."

This is what spiritual recovery is. Had this happened to David

> while he was still in active addiction his response would have been to isolate himself and drink non-stop. As it is, he is choosing to live his life with courage, surrounded by love.

I think it is fitting that I end this book in the way that meetings traditionally end, with the serenity prayer. It is part of a longer prayer but these three lines contain enough wisdom to get you through many of life's most difficult times. On a first hearing the prayer may sound a bit glib, a bit too neat, a bit superficial, but the more you reflect on it and the more you act on it the more you come to value it. I have used it when I am hurting and don't know what to do, when I am faced with a reality I don't want to accept, and when it all seems too hopeless to go on. It starts with the word God, but you can address it to any life force you choose:

> God,
> Grant me the Serenity to accept the things I cannot change,
> Courage to change the things I can,
> And the Wisdom to know the difference.

I don't think I need to add anything to that.

Appendix 1

Diagnostic Criteria

Do I fit the profile of someone who is predisposed to develop a dependent relationship with a mood-altering chemical or behaviour? See Character Traits checklist. Is my use of a chemical dependent? Am I addicted? See Characteristics of Dependency checklist.

Character traits of dependent personality	Characteristics of chemical dependency
Weak ego	Preoccupation
Lack of openness	Using alone
Hyper-sensitivity	Using for effect (rapid intake)
Guilt proneness	Using as a medicine
Melancholia	Protection of supply
Emotionality	Using more than planned
	Increased tolerance
	Memory blackouts (alcohol only)
	Erosion of moral values
	Serious unwanted consequences

Diagnostic criteria for chemical dependency as used at The Rehab as part of the assessment process for potential residents.

Yes	In the past 6 months have you:
	Needed to use more [main drug] to get the desired effect, or has taking your usual amount had less of an effect than it used to?
	Felt sick or unwell when the effects of [main drug] have worn off, or have you taken more of it, or a similar drug, to relieve or avoid feeling unwell?
	Used [main drug] in larger amounts or for a longer period of time than you intended?
	Had a persistent or strong desire to take [main drug] or have you had problems cutting down, or controlling how often or how much you use?
	Spent a large amount of time obtaining, or using, or recovering from the effects of [main drug]?
	Given up work, recreational, or social activities as a result of your [main drug] use?
	Continued to use [main drug] despite having physical or psychological problems as a result?

If score is three or more, dependence is diagnosed.

Appendix 2

The Rehab Treatment Programme

Long Term Goals

1. Complete abstinence from all mood altering chemicals
2. Gain or return to full or part time employment, or voluntary work
3. No re-offending or returning to self-defeating behaviours
4. Build relapse prevention plan
5. Rehabilitation – ongoing meetings, housing needs, independent living

Short Term Goals First Stage

Step 1

1. Recognition of addiction as a problem
2. Gain insight into and confront denial
3. Own damage to self and others
4. Gain insight into attitudes and behaviour
5. Return and recognition of feelings
6. Improvement in self-honesty
7. Reduction in blaming and resenting others
8. Start of building relationships with peers

Step 2

1. Recognition of need and ability to change
2. Recognition of 12-Step programme as ongoing vehicle for change
3. Asking for help
4. Identifying and managing feelings appropriately
5. Identification of negative and self-defeating attitudes and behaviours
6. Choosing to develop new attitudes and behaviours
7. Establish hope
8. Begin self-worth building

Step 3

1. Commitment to change
2. Demonstration of trust
3. Willingness to risk and face fears
4. Acceptance of personal responsibility
5. Taking action on help given
6. Making decisions and plans for future
7. Growing assertiveness and self-esteem
8. Ability to defer gratification
9. Development of spirituality
10. Demonstration of acceptance of principles of 12-step programme

Step 4

1. Rigorous self-examination
2. Preparation for 'cleaning house' and letting go of 'baggage'

Step 5

1. In-depth interview with an objective listener exploring blocks and assets past and present
2. Courageous sharing of secrets
3. Reduction of shame
4. Start of letting go of the past

Completion of First Stage Treatment

Short Term Goals Second Stage

Integration- Self and community

1. Identify self as addict in recovering community
2. Continue to gain insight into and confront denial
3. Continue to gain insight into attitudes and behaviour
4. Acceptance of 12 step living

Change
(Steps 4,5,6,7)

1. Deepen awareness of current stage of personal development
2. Identify personal blocks, self-defeating behaviours / beliefs / feelings
3. Prioritise changes to be made
4. Commit to specific changes
5. Implement changes
6. Monitor changes

Restitution – Amends and Forgiveness
(Steps 8,9)

1. Identify persons who have been adversely affected by self while using
2. Take responsibility for own past behaviour
3. Become willing to make appropriate amends
4. Make specific amend-making plans
5. Implement plans
6. Forgiveness of self by self
7. Forgiveness of others by self
8. Freedom from past guilt
9. Re-affirmation of recovery values

Rehabilitation – Continuing development of relationship with self...
(Steps 10,11,12)

1. Monitor personal progress
2. Own mistakes and implement change
3. Continue to deepen awareness of personal assets
4. Set goals for personal development
5. Implement plan of action to fulfil personal potential

...with Higher Power

1. Incorporate into daily routine appropriate contact with chosen Higher Power
2. Acceptance of help / guidance
3. Lessening of impulsivity / self-will
4. Restoration of spiritual and ethical self
5. Acceptance, surrender and handing over

...and with community

1. Become role model for recovery within peer group
2. Become active member of chosen Fellowship/s
3. Make positive contribution to wider community activities
4. Find employment which makes social and financial contribution to wider society
5. Ability to manage independent living.

Completion of Second Stage Treatment

Appendix 3

Eating plan

Name of resident:

Breakfast:

Mid-morning:

Lunch:

Mid-afternoon:

Dinner:

Evening snack 9 p.m.

Drinks per day: Water when thirsty. Moderate hot drinks. No more than 1 fizzy drink per day.

....

1. All meals are to be a moderate or small plateful as specified and include portions of each dish on the menu.
2. Everything on your plate is to be eaten.
3. No second helpings.
4. No eating other than as specified on this eating plan.
5. No food of any description is to be kept or eaten in your bedroom.

This is an abstinence programme designed to help you with gaining freedom from your food addiction. Any under-eating, over-eating, vomiting or purging, or excessive exercise is contrary to this programme. Please talk about your preoccupation with any, or all, of these behaviours. If you are having difficulties maintaining this programme please discuss your concerns with your counsellor and your group.

This plan may only be amended after discussion with a counsellor, and will be reviewed with your focal counsellor on

....

<u>Contract</u>

1. I will invite feedback from my peers on how they seemed managing this abstinence programme and act on their replies.

2. I will check with my peers what is a 'moderate amount' and act in accordance with their feedback.

3. I will stay in the communal area for a minimum period of 20 minutes after each meal and share with my peers the thoughts and feelings I am having about food and eating.

Signed ....
Date   ....

Appendix 4

Step 4 Guide

The guide is divided into five sections plus a 6th which is specifically for residents of The Rehab. Section 6 is for residents' peers to give feedback on the positive changes they have seen the resident make since entering treatment. There is advice on how to complete each section. Each one contains specific headings or questions for you to consider.

The sections are:

1. Blocks to your recovery
2. Principles/values
3. Assets
4. Faith, hope and love
5. Attitudes/responsibilities
(6.) Peer feedback

You are advised to include in each answer as much detail as you can. You are writing this inventory for no one's benefit but your own. Be brave, take a risk, and put in your shameful secrets. The more honest effort you put in, the more benefit you will get out.

Section 1. Blocks to your recovery

In this section, you need to re-acquaint yourself with how your addiction has affected your personality and behaviour, how it has harmed or caused pain to you and other people whom you care about and who care about you.

For each of the headings in this section consider how you identify with this block. Write specific examples of how you have acted on it. In each example give as much detail as you can: say what happened, who was involved, what were the consequences, how you felt at the time, how you feel about it now, and what connection such behaviour has with your addiction.

1. Selfishness

This means putting your own comfort or advantage first. Do you spend a lot of time worrying about your own interests without regard for the interests of others? How have self-centredness, selfishness, and preoccupation with chemicals affected you?

2. Dishonesty

Not being honest comes in many forms: hiding, making excuses, thinking dishonestly, justifying, telling half-truths, being phoney, lying, cheating, conning, breaking promises, people-pleasing.

3. False pride

False pride places you above other people so you will not admit to any human weakness. It prevents you from looking realistically at your own behaviour and will not allow you to admit to any mistakes. False pride says your addiction is not as bad as other people's and you do not need help. Sometimes false pride glorifies your addiction and tells you are too bad to get well using this programme.

4. Resentments and mismanaged anger

Resentful people hold on to angry feelings, sometimes for years, and use their resentments to justify their irresponsible behaviour. Do you hold resentments because of someone else's behaviour? Do you allow anger to rule you? Do you deal with your anger in a destructive way?

5. Intolerance

This is unwillingness to put up with beliefs, practices, customs, or habits that are different from our own. Intolerance can result from resentments or fear. Are you able to accept imperfections in yourself or others? How were you intolerant of others in the past?

6. Impatience

This is unwillingness to bear delay, opposition, pain, worry. Describe some situations in which your impatience caused damage to you or others.

7. Envy/comparing

Envy is sadness or resentment at another person's good fortune. It springs from comparing yourself to others and wishing for what is not yours. How have you acted on envy in the past?

8. Procrastination

Putting off things that need to be done can lead to irresponsibility, anxiety, guilt, and anger, and can have serious damaging consequences. What have you put off and what happened as a result?

9. Self-pity

Self-pity is a feeling of hopelessness and helplessness: feeling like a victim of circumstances. Maybe you feel that others do not understand you, or that nothing will ever change. Self-pity is a danger signal and a high-risk relapse trigger. How has self-pity damaged you and others?

10. Feelings easily hurt

Are you over-sensitive, touchy, thin-skinned, immature? How have you reacted when your feelings were hurt? How has your over-sensitivity affected your relationships with others?

11. Fear

Our deepest fears are not about spiders or snakes. What are your deepest, secret fears? Do you fear that you are unlovable, or bound to fail? Do you live with a vague sense of dread? Are you afraid that your bad deeds are about to catch up with you, or that the real you is about to be exposed? How do you behave when you are afraid? How has your fear damaged your life or others' lives?

12. Irresponsibility

This is failing to act on the responsibilities you have towards yourself and others. When have you neglected to do what is rightfully your responsibility to do? How have you acted to make other people take responsibility for you?

13. Controlling behaviour

Trying to make life happen the way you think it ought to happen, because you know best. Trying to manipulate people, situations, and outcomes to get the result you want. How has this caused problems for you and others?

14. Perfectionism

Setting impossibly high standards and expectations of yourself and others. How do you feel about yourself when you fail to meet your unachievable perfect goals? How do you behave to others who fail to meet the unachievable high standards you set for them?

15. Self-hate

Do you hate yourself because of something you have done? Do you hate yourself because of something that has been done to you? How does hating yourself affect the quality of your life? How does your self- hate impact on others?

16. Sexuality

Have you acted in ways that offended your values and beliefs about sex? Has your past sexual behaviour hurt you? Has it hurt other people? Have you been hurt because of someone else's sexual behaviour? Do you carry shame about any sexual activity that you wish to be free from?

17. Guilt feelings

What do you feel guilty about? What actions do you feel guilty about? What thoughts do you feel guilty about? Do you carry guilty secrets? How big a part does guilt play in your life? How does guilt make you behave? How does your guilt impact on others?

18. Special reserve section

You may have secrets which you have never been able to share. This section allows you the time and space to put down in writing any secrets which still cause you pain.

Section 2. Principles/values

In active addiction you can become lost, lonely, and isolated. People and things that you value or enjoy get forgotten and excluded from your life. The preoccupation with chemicals and the obsession to use them becomes all consuming. This section asks you to consider how this has shown itself throughout your addiction.
1. Over whom or what has your using become more important or taken precedence?
2. How have you taken advantage of other people's time, love, support?
3. How have your beliefs, judgements, and opinions been distorted by your addiction?
4. What effect has your addiction had on your respect for yourself and for others?
5. How has addiction influenced your attitude to other people's rights and property?
6. How has your addiction influenced you in regard to being faithful or loyal to your partner, family, and friends?

This marks the end of the negative side of the inventory. From this point forward the focus will be on the positive. Attempts to minimise your assets by justifying are not allowed! 'I was honest on that occasion, but only because I had to be', is not acceptable. Nor is, 'I was kind and helpful to that person, but only because I would have felt guilty if I had not.' As you need to accept your blocks to recovery you need to accept your good qualities, no matter how uncomfortable that may make you feel.

<u>Section 3. Assets</u>

An inventory should provide a balanced view: credits as well as debits. In active addiction there is a tendency for more negative traits to be observed than positive traits. Everybody has strengths and qualities. This section is to explore your assets and to provide you with an awareness of what you have in your personality to counteract your negative traits, to build on and to reinforce new levels of self-respect. For each of the headings in this section consider how you identify with this asset and write specific examples of how you have acted on it since starting your recovery.

1. Loyalty
A sense of obligation to others, it is the opposite of self-centredness. It is not possible to be self-centred and loyal at the same time.

2. Use of time

How productive has your time in recovery been? How does this compare with your use of time before recovery?

3. Punctuality

This involves self-discipline, order, and consideration of others. If people are valuable then so is their time. How does your punctuality now compare with your punctuality when you were using?

4. Sincerity

Sincerity comes from the heart and carries conviction. It is the opposite of being false. How sincere are you, now that you are in recovery?

5. Caution in speech

This is sensitivity to others and thinking before you speak. How have you shown tact in recovery?

6. Care

Care is an attitude which involves action. Give examples of how you have shown care to others since you stopped using.

7. Patience

Patience involves tolerance and acceptance. Give examples of when you have shown patience and helped to make life more pleasant for others.

8. Honesty

Honesty involves being at one with what is. How do you find yourself being honest at this point in your recovery?

9. Acceptance

Many things and people that we encounter require us to practise acceptance. There is a great deal we cannot change. Are you now more able to accept the things you cannot change?

10. Courage

To have courage does not mean to be without fear, it means you do not let your fear hold you back. In recovery we are asked to do things that are difficult. These things make us uncomfortable and force us to grow. How have you used courage to help you face things in your recovery?

11. Gratitude

Gratitude is an attitude which influences behaviour. It is a wonderful antidote to self-pity. For what do you feel grateful now? How do you show your gratitude in action?

12. Generosity

A generous spirit will give willingly, without resentment, without strings. Have you done this?

13. Humour

Fun, laughter, and enjoyment are important in recovery. Do you have the ability to use humour appropriately to lighten the day for yourself and others?

14. Self-respect

Self-respect is crucial for your recovery; you need to believe you are worth getting well for. Self-respect is evident in the way you are, how you behave, and the choices you make. Compare the self-respect you feel now to how you felt about yourself when you were using.

Section 4. Faith, hope, and love

This section deals with the qualities of faith, hope, and love, three wonderful assets to have. What place do these three assets have in your life now that you are in recovery?

First think about what faith, hope, and love have meant to you in the past. Think about what happened to your faith, hope, and love while you were in active addiction. Then consider what each of them means to you now that you have done work on Steps 2 and 3 and started to rebuild relationships with yourself and others. Consider why each is important in your life and your recovery today, and how you plan to develop it in your future.

Faith

Faith means leaving your future to the care of something more powerful than yourself, believing it will work for your well-being.

Hope

Hope reflects attitude. It gives purpose to your daily life and can become a driving force for change. Compare the hope you have now with your hopelessness in the past.

Love
Have you learned how to hear other people, to see them, to know them? Do you care about them? Do you know how to respond to their needs, to give of yourself? Have you learnt how to share with them? Have you learnt how to feel good about yourself? How does this feel?

Section 5. Attitudes and responsibilities

Your attitudes relate to your thoughts and feelings. Your responsibilities relate to your plans, actions, and future goals, and your interactions with others.

Take time to consider your attitudes and responsibilities in each of the following areas of your life, then write a paragraph on each which illustrates and describes your thoughts, feelings, and plans.

1. To myself
2. To my family and friends
3. To my community
4. To a 12 Step fellowship
5. To the power greater than myself in which I put my trust.

Section 6. Peer feedback

Ask your peers to write down and give you their honest answers to these two questions:

1. What changes do you see in me since I came into treatment?
2. What do you see as my strengths/qualities?

This completes your Step 4 inventory. You are now ready to take all this information and move on to Step 5.

Appendix 5

Step 10 Daily Inventory

At the end of each day take stock of your recovery by asking yourself these questions:

1. Have I been aware of any of my blocks today?

2. Which of my assets have I acted on today?

3. Have I been 'restored to sanity' today, or has my old way of thinking been operating?

4. Have I acted out on feelings today, or have I managed them better than I used to?

5. Has my attitude been in accordance with my recovery values, or has my old attitude returned today?
6. Has my behaviour been in accordance with my recovery values, or have I acted in accordance with my old behaviour pattern today?

7. Am I aware of any relapse warning signs today?

8. Do I need to do anything about this? and, if so, what?

9. Do I need to apologise to anyone today?

10. Do I need to do anything differently tomorrow?

Appendix 6

Relapse Warning Signs

The Road to Relapse

- I'm getting pretty stressed
- and I'm having mood swings.
- I put on an act
- and look OK from the outside, but on the inside I am not right.
- I do not want to talk about this.
- I say to myself and other people that I am adamant I will never use alcohol or drugs again.
- I start acting on impulse instead of thinking about what I am doing.
- Because I make poor judgements my plans start to fail.
- I exaggerate my failures
- and ignore my successes,
- so I have feelings of guilt and worthlessness.
- My thinking becomes confused.
- I start to feel crazy.
- I am usually irritable and get angry with everyone
- so prefer to avoid people.
- I abandon my usual daily routine
- and my life is without structure.
- I eat fast food
- and sleep poorly.
- I become deeply dissatisfied with life in general
- and start to feel hopeless.
- I reject all offers of help
- and lie to those people who want to help me.
- I have thoughts of drugs and alcohol
- and think if this is what life in recovery is like I might as well be using.
- I think I can control my using this time so it will not get so bad.

- I pick up again
- and feel so ashamed, guilty, and weak that
- I lie about it
- and stop contact with my peers in recovery.
- I am now back where I started, only worse, because I know what recovery was like
- and I think I have lost it now.

The Steps We Took

The words of this book's title are said aloud every day by thousands of people meeting together to help each other recover from addiction's the addictions may be to alcohol or cocaine, gambling or food, violence or sex, but the path to recovery is the same.

The exciting thing about the Twelve Steps is that they teach us how to live. Once we know the design of living and the principles of living a successful life, we find that we not only get over the problems we see, but we avoid many other problems we would have had. To me, the miracle is that all this was boiled down into twelve simple Steps that anybody can apply.

This is a book of plain-spoken wisdom for people with addictions and people who love them. Joe McQ has been a student of the Twelve Steps for more than three decades. He, like tens of thousands of others, lives them every day, one day at a time. In The Steps We Took, Joe takes us through them, one Step at a time, and helps us understand how they work-and how they can change our lives.